BOOKS & CHARACTERS
FRENCH & ENGLISH

BY THE SAME AUTHOR

EMINENT VICTORIANS
QUEEN VICTORIA

Vue du levant de Fernex   Calquée sur un Tableau de Mr Huber

VOLTAIRE

BOOKS AND CHARACTERS

FRENCH & ENGLISH

BY

LYTTON STRACHEY

NEW YORK
HARCOURT, BRACE AND COMPANY
1922

PRINTED IN THE U. S. A. BY
THE QUINN & BODEN COMPANY
RAHWAY, N. J.

TO
JOHN MAYNARD KEYNES

The following papers are reprinted by kind permission of the Editors of the Independent Review, the New Quarterly, the Athenæum, and the Edinburgh Review.

The " Dialogue " is now printed for the first time, from a manuscript, apparently in the handwriting of Voltaire and belonging to his English period.

CONTENTS

ILLUSTRATIONS

RACINE

RACINE

WHEN Ingres painted his vast "Apotheosis of Homer," he represented, grouped round the central throne, all the great poets of the ancient and modern worlds, with a single exception—Shakespeare. After some persuasion, he relented so far as to introduce into his picture a *part* of that offensive personage; and English visitors at the Louvre can now see, to their disgust or their amusement, the truncated image of rather less than half of the author of *King Lear* just appearing at the extreme edge of the enormous canvas. French taste, let us hope, has changed since the days of Ingres; Shakespeare would doubtless now be advanced—though perhaps chiefly from a sense of duty—to the very steps of the central throne. But if an English painter were to choose a similar subject, how would he treat the master who stands acknowledged as the most characteristic representative of the literature of France? Would Racine find a place in the picture at all? Or, if he did, would more of him be visible than the last curl of his full-bottomed wig, whisking away into the outer darkness?

There is something inexplicable about the intensity of national tastes and the violence of national differences. If, as in the good old days, I could boldly believe a Frenchman to be an inferior creature, while he, as simply, wrote me down a savage, there would be an easy end of the matter. But alas! *nous avons changé tout cela*. Now we are each

3

of us obliged to recognise that the other has a full share
of intelligence, ability, and taste; that the accident of our
having been born on different sides of the Channel is no
ground for supposing either that I am a brute or that he
is a ninny. But, in that case, how does it happen that
while on one side of that " span of waters " Racine is despised and Shakespeare is worshipped, on the other, Shakespeare is tolerated and Racine is adored? The perplexing
question was recently emphasised and illustrated in a singular way. Mr. John Bailey, in a volume of essays entitled
The Claims of French Poetry, discussed the qualities
of Racine at some length, placed him, not without con-
tumely, among the second rank of writers, and drew the
conclusion that, though indeed the merits of French poetry
are many and great, it is not among the pages of Racine
that they are to be found. Within a few months of the
appearance of Mr. Bailey's book, the distinguished French
writer and brilliant critic, M. Lemaître, published a series
of lectures on Racine, in which the highest note of un-
qualified panegyric sounded uninterruptedly from beginning to end. The contrast is remarkable, and the conflicting criticisms seem to represent, on the whole, the views
of the cultivated classes in the two countries. And it is
worthy of note that neither of these critics pays any heed,
either explicitly or by implication, to the opinions of the
other. They are totally at variance, but they argue along
lines so different and so remote that they never come into
collision. Mr. Bailey, with the utmost sang-froid, sweeps
on one side the whole of the literary tradition of France.
It is as if a French critic were to assert that Shakespeare,

the Elizabethans, and the romantic poets of the nineteenth
century were all negligible, and that England's really valuable contribution to the poetry of the world was to be
found among the writings of Dryden and Pope. M.
Lemaître, on the other hand, seems sublimely unconscious
that any such views as Mr. Bailey's could possibly exist.
Nothing shows more clearly Racine's supreme dominion
over his countrymen than the fact that M. Lemaître never
questions it for a moment, and tacitly assumes on every
page of his book that his only duty is to illustrate and
amplify a greatness already recognised by all. Indeed, after
reading M. Lemaître's book, one begins to understand more
clearly why it is that English critics find it difficult to
appreciate to the full the literature of France. It is no
paradox to say that that country is as insular as our own.
When we find so eminent a critic as M. Lemaître observing
that Racine " a vraiment ' achievé ' et porté à son point
suprème de perfection *la tragédie,* cette étonnante forme
d'art, et qui est bien de chez nous: car on la trouve peu
chez les Anglais," is it surprising that we should hastily
jump to the conclusion that the canons and the principles
of a criticism of this kind will not repay, and perhaps do
not deserve, any careful consideration? Certainly they are
not calculated to spare the susceptibilities of Englishmen.
And, after all, this is only natural; a French critic addresses
a French audience; like a Rabbi in a synagogue, he has
no need to argue and no wish to convert. Perhaps, too,
whether he willed or no, he could do very little to the
purpose; for the difficulties which beset an Englishman in
his endeavours to appreciate a writer such as Racine are

precisely of the kind which a Frenchman is least able either
to dispel or even to understand. The object of this essay
is, first, to face these difficulties with the aid of Mr. Bailey's
paper, which sums up in an able and interesting way the
average English view of the matter; and, in the second
place, to communicate to the English reader a sense of the
true significance and the immense value of Racine's work.
Whether the attempt succeed or fail, some important general
questions of literary doctrine will have been discussed; and,
in addition, at least an effort will have been made to vin-
dicate a great reputation. For, to a lover of Racine, the
fact that English critics of Mr. Bailey's calibre can write
of him as they do, brings a feeling not only of entire disagreement, but of almost personal distress. Strange as it
may seem to those who have been accustomed to think of
that great artist merely as a type of the frigid pomposity
of an antiquated age, his music, to ears that are attuned
to hear it, comes fraught with a poignancy of loveliness
whose peculiar quality is shared by no other poetry in the
world. To have grown familiar with the voice of Racine,
to have realised once and for all its intensity, its beauty,
and its depth, is to have learnt a new happiness, to have discovered something exquisite and splendid, to have enlarged
the glorious boundaries of art. For such benefits as these
who would not be grateful? Who would not seek to make
them known to others, that they too may enjoy, and render
thanks?

M. Lemaître, starting out, like a native of the mountains, from a point which can only be reached by English
explorers after a long journey and a severe climb, devotes

by far the greater part of his book to a series of brilliant
psychological studies of Racine's characters. He leaves on
one side almost altogether the questions connected both with
Racine's dramatic construction, and with his style; and
these are the very questions by which English readers are
most perplexed, and which they are most anxious to discuss.
His style in particular—using the word in its widest sense—
forms the subject of the principal part of Mr. Bailey's
essay; it is upon this count that the real force of Mr. Bailey's
impeachment depends; and, indeed, it is obvious that no
poet can be admired or understood by those who quarrel
with the whole fabric of his writing and condemn the very
principles of his art. Before, however, discussing this, the
true crux of the question, it may be well to consider briefly
another matter which deserves attention, because the English
reader is apt to find in it a stumbling-block at the very
outset of his inquiry. Coming to Racine with Shakespeare
and the rest of the Elizabethans warm in his memory, it is
only to be expected that he should be struck with a chilling
sense of emptiness and unreality. After the colour, the moving multiplicity, the imaginative luxury of our early tragedies,
which seem to have been moulded out of the very stuff of life
and to have been built up with the varied and generous structure of Nature herself, the Frenchman's dramas, with their
rigid uniformity of setting, their endless duologues, their immense harangues, their spectral confidants, their strict ex-
clusion of all visible action, give one at first the same sort of
impression as a pretentious pseudo-classical summer-house
appearing suddenly at the end of a vista, after one has been
rambling through an open forest. " La scène est à Buth-

rote, ville d'Epire, dans une salle du palais de Pyrrhus "—
could anything be more discouraging than such an announce-
ment? Here is nothing for the imagination to feed on, nothing to raise expectation, no wondrous vision of "blasted
heaths," or the "seaboard of Bohemia"; here is only a
hypothetical drawing-room conjured out of the void for five
acts, simply in order that the persons of the drama may have
a place to meet in and make their speeches. The "three unities" and the rest of the "rules" are a burden which the
English reader finds himself quite unaccustomed to carry;
he grows impatient of them; and, if he is a critic, he points
out the futility and the unreasonableness of those antiquated
conventions. Even Mr. Bailey, who, curiously enough, believes that Racine "stumbled, as it were, half by accident
into great advantages" by using them, speaks of the
"discredit" into which "the once famous unities" have
now fallen, and declares that "the unities of time and
place are of no importance in themselves." So far as critics
are concerned this may be true; but critics are apt to forget
that plays can exist somewhere else than in books, and a
very small acquaintance with contemporary drama is enough
to show that, upon the stage at any rate, the unities, so far
from having fallen into discredit, are now in effect triumphant. For what is the principle which underlies and justi-
fies the unities of time and place? Surely it is not, as
Mr. Bailey would have us believe, that of the "unity of
action or interest," for it is clear that every good drama,
whatever its plan of construction, must possess a single dominating interest, and that it may happen—as in *Antony and
Cleopatra,* for instance—that the very essence of this interest

lies in the accumulation of an immense variety of local activities and the representation of long epochs of time. The
true justification for the unities of time and place is to be
found in the conception of drama as the history of a spiritual
crisis—the vision, thrown up, as it were, by a bull's-eye lantern, of the final catastrophic phases of a long series of
events. Very different were the views of the Elizabethan
tragedians, who aimed at representing not only the catastrophe, but the whole development of circumstances of
which it was the effect; they traced, with elaborate and
abounding detail, the rise, the growth, the decline, and the
ruin of great causes and great persons; and the result was a
series of masterpieces unparalleled in the literature of the
world. But, for good or evil, these methods have become
obsolete, and to-day our drama seems to be developing along
totally different lines. It is playing the part, more and more
consistently, of the bull's-eye lantern; it is concerned with
the crisis, and nothing but the crisis; and, in proportion as
its field is narrowed and its vision intensified, the unities of
time and place come more and more completely into play.
Thus, from the point of view of form, it is true to say that
it has been the drama of Racine rather than that of Shakespeare that has survived. Plays of the type of *Macbeth* have
been superseded by plays of the type of *Britannicus. Britannicus,* no less than *Macbeth,* is the tragedy of a criminal;
but it shows us, instead of the gradual history of the temptation and the fall, followed by the fatal march of consequences, nothing but the precise psychological moment in
which the first irrevocable step is taken, and the criminal is
made. The method of *Macbeth* has been, as it were, ab-

sorbed by that of the modern novel; the method of *Britannicus* still rules the stage. But Racine carried out his ideals more rigorously and more boldly than any of his successors. He fixed the whole of his attention upon the spiritual crisis; to him that alone was of importance; and the conventional classicism so disheartening to the English reader—the " unities," the harangues, the confidences, the absence of local colour, and the concealment of the action—was no more than the machinery for enhancing the effect of the inner tragedy, and for doing away with every side issue and every chance of distraction. His dramas must be read as one looks at an airy, delicate statue, supported by artificial props, whose only importance lies in the fact that without them the statue itself would break in pieces and fall to the ground. Approached in this light, even the " salle du palais de Pyrrhus " begins to have a meaning. We come to realise that, if it is nothing else, it is at least the meeting-ground of great passions, the invisible framework for one of those noble conflicts which " make one little room an everywhere." It will show us no views, no spectacles, it will give us no sense of atmosphere or of imaginative romance; but it will allow us to be present at the climax of a tragedy, to follow the closing struggle of high destinies, and to witness the final agony of human hearts.

It is remarkable that Mr. Bailey, while seeming to approve of the classicism of Racine's dramatic form, nevertheless finds fault with him for his lack of a quality with which, by its very nature, the classical form is incompatible. Racine's vision, he complains, does not " take in the whole of life "; we do not find in his plays " the whole pell-mell of

human existence "; and this is true, because the particular
effects which Racine wished to produce necessarily involved
this limitation of the range of his interests. His object was
to depict the tragic interaction of a small group of persons at
the culminating height of its intensity; and it is as irra-
tional to complain of his failure to introduce into his compositions " the whole pell-mell of human existence " as it
would be to find fault with a Mozart quartet for not containing the orchestration of Wagner. But it is a little difficult
to make certain of the precise nature of Mr. Bailey's criticism. When he speaks of Racine's vision not including " the
whole of life," when he declares that Racine cannot be reck-
oned as one of the " world-poets," he seems to be taking
somewhat different ground and discussing a more general
question. All truly great poets, he asserts, have " a wide
view of humanity," " a large view of life "—a profound
sense, in short, of the relations between man and the universe; and, since Racine is without this quality, his claim to
true poetic greatness must be denied. But, even upon the
supposition that this view of Racine's philosophical outlook
is the true one—and, in its most important sense, I believe
that it is not—does Mr. Bailey's conclusion really follow?
Is it possible to test a poet's greatness by the largeness of his
" view of life "? How wide, one would like to know, was
Milton's " view of humanity "? And, though Wordsworth's
sense of the position of man in the universe was far more
profound than Dante's, who will venture to assert that he
was the greater poet? The truth is that we have struck here
upon a principle which lies at the root, not only of Mr.
Bailey's criticism of Racine, but of an entire critical method

—the method which attempts to define the essential elements of poetry in general, and then proceeds to ask of any particular poem whether it possesses these elements, and to judge it accordingly. How often this method has been employed, and how often it has proved disastrously fallacious! For, after all, art is not a superior kind of chemistry, amenable to the rules of scientific induction. Its component parts cannot be classified and tested, and there is a spark within it which defies foreknowledge. When Matthew Arnold declared that the value of a new poem might be gauged by comparing it with the greatest passages in the acknowledged masterpieces of literature, he was falling into this very error; for who could tell that the poem in question was not itself a masterpiece, living by the light of an unknown beauty, and a law unto itself? It is the business of the poet to break rules and to baffle expectation; and all the masterpieces in the world cannot make a precedent. Thus Mr. Bailey's attempts to discover, by quotations from Shakespeare, Sophocles, and Goethe, the qualities without which no poet can be great, and his condemnation of Racine because he is without them, is a fallacy in criticism. There is only one way to judge a poet, as Wordsworth, with that paradoxical sobriety so characteristic of him, has pointed out—and that is, by loving him. But Mr. Bailey, with regard to Racine at any rate, has not followed the advice of Wordsworth. Let us look a little more closely into the nature of his attack.

"L'épithète rare," said the De Goncourts, "voilà la marque de l'écrivain." Mr. Bailey quotes the sentence with approval, observing that if, with Sainte-Beuve, we extend

the phrase to " le mot rare " we have at once one of those invaluable touchstones with which we may test the merit of
poetry. And doubtless most English readers would be inclined to agree with Mr Bailey, for it so happens that our
own literature is one in which rarity of style, pushed often to
the verge of extravagance, reigns supreme. Owing mainly,
no doubt, to the double origin of our language, with its
strange and violent contrasts between the highly-coloured
crudity of the Saxon words and the ambiguous splendour of
the Latin vocabulary, owing partly, perhaps, to a national
taste for the intensely imaginative, and partly, too, to the
vast and penetrating influence of those grand masters of
bizarrerie—the Hebrew Prophets—our poetry, our prose,
and our whole conception of the art of writing have fallen
under the dominion of the emphatic, the extraordinary, and
the bold. No one in his senses would regret this, for it has
given our literature all its most characteristic glories, and, of
course, in Shakespeare, with whom expression is stretched
to the bursting point, the national style finds at once its consummate example and its final justification. But the result
is that we have grown so unused to other kinds of poetical
beauty, that we have now come to believe, with Mr. Bailey,
that poetry apart from " le mot rare " is an impossibility.
The beauties of restraint, of clarity, of refinement, and of
precision we pass by unheeding; we can see nothing there
but coldness and uniformity; and we go back with eagerness
to the fling and the bravado that we love so well. It is as if
we had become so accustomed to looking at boxers, wrestlers,
and gladiators that the sight of an exquisite minuet produced
no effect on us; the ordered dance strikes us as a monotony,

for we are blind to the subtle delicacies of the dancers, which are fraught with such significance to the practised eye. But let us be patient, and let us look again.

> Ariane ma sœur, de quel amour blessée,
> Vous mourûtes aux bords où vous fûtes laissée.

Here, certainly, are no " mots rares "; here is nothing to catch the mind or dazzle the understanding; here is only the most ordinary vocabulary, plainly set forth. But is there not an enchantment? Is there not a vision? Is there not a flow of lovely sound whose beauty grows upon the ear, and dwells exquisitely within the memory? Racine's triumph is precisely this—that he brings about, by what are apparently the simplest means, effects which other poets must strain every nerve to produce. The narrowness of his vocabulary is in fact nothing but a proof of his amazing art. In the following passage, for instance, what a sense of dignity and melancholy and power is conveyed by the commonest words!

> Enfin j'ouvre les yeux, et je me fais justice:
> C'est faire à vos beautés un triste sacrifice
> Que de vous présenter, madame, avec ma foi,
> Tout l'âge et le malheur que je traîne avec moi.
> Jusqu'ici la fortune et la victoire mêmes
> Cachaient mes cheveux blancs sous trente diadêmes.
> Mais ce temps-là n'est plus: je regnais; et je fuis:
> Mes ans se sont accrus; mes honneurs sont detruits.

Is that wonderful " trente " an " épithète rare "? Never, surely, before or since, was a simple numeral put to such a use—to conjure up so triumphantly such mysterious grandeurs! But these are subtleties which pass unnoticed by

those who have been accustomed to the violent appeals of the
great romantic poets. As Sainte-Beuve says, in a fine comparison between Racine and Shakespeare, to come to the one
after the other is like passing to a portrait by Ingres from a
decoration by Rubens. At first, " comme on a l'œil rempli de
l'éclatante verité pittoresque du grand maître flamand, on ne
voit dans l'artiste français qu'un ton assez uniforme, une
teinte diffuse de pâle et douce lumière. Mais qu'on approche
de plus près et qu'on observe avec soin: mille nuances fines
vont éclore sous le regard; mille intentions savantes vont
sortir de ce tissu profond et serré; on ne peut plus en dé-
tacher ses yeux."

Similarly when Mr. Bailey, turning from the vocabulary
to more general questions of style, declares that there is no
" element of fine surprise " in Racine, no trace of the " daring metaphors and similes of Pindar and the Greek chor-
uses "—the reply is that he would find what he wants if he
only knew where to look for it. " Who will forget," he
says, " the comparison of the Atreidæ to the eagles wheeling
over their empty nest, of war to the money-changer whose
gold dust is that of human bodies, of Helen to the lion's
whelps? . . . Everyone knows these. Who will match them
among the formal elegances of Racine? " And it is true that
when Racine wished to create a great effect he did not adopt
the romantic method; he did not chase his ideas through the
four quarters of the universe to catch them at last upon the
verge of the inane; and anyone who hopes to come upon
" fine surprises " of this kind in his pages will be disappointed. His daring is of a different kind; it is not the daring of adventure but of intensity; his fine surprises are seized

out of the very heart of his subject, and seized in a single stroke. Thus many of his most astonishing phrases burn with an inward concentration of energy, which, difficult at first to realise to the full, comes in the end to impress itself ineffaceably upon the mind.

C'était pendant l'horreur d'une profonde nuit.

The sentence is like a cavern whose mouth a careless traveller might pass by, but which opens out, to the true explorer, into vista after vista of strange recesses rich with inexhaustible gold. But, sometimes, the phrase, compact as dynamite, explodes upon one with an immediate and terrific force—

C'est Vénus toute entière à sa proie attachée!

A few " formal elegances " of this kind are surely worth having.

But what is it that makes the English reader fail to recognise the beauty and the power of such passages as these? Besides Racine's lack of extravagance and bravura, besides his dislike of exaggerated emphasis and far-fetched or fantastic imagery, there is another characteristic of his style to which we are perhaps even more antipathetic—its suppression of detail. The great majority of poets—and especially of English poets—produce their most potent effects by the accumulation of details—details which in themselves fascinate us either by their beauty or their curiosity or their supreme appropriateness. But with details Racine will have nothing to do; he builds up his poetry out of words which are not only absolutely simple but extremely general, so

that our minds, failing to find in it the peculiar delights to
which we have been accustomed, fall into the error of reject-
ing it altogether as devoid of significance. And the error is
a grave one, for in truth nothing is more marvellous than the
magic with which Racine can conjure up out of a few expressions of the vaguest import a sense of complete and intimate reality. When Shakespeare wishes to describe a silent
night he does so with a single stroke of detail—" not a
mouse stirring "! And Virgil adds touch upon touch of exquisite minutiæ:

> Cum tacet omnis ager, pecudes, pictaeque volucres,
> Quaeque lacus late liquidos, quaeque aspera dumis
> Rura tenent, etc.

Racine's way is different, but is it less masterly?

> Mais tout dort, et l'armée, et les vents, et Neptune.

What a flat and feeble set of expressions! is the Englishman's first thought—with the conventional " Neptune," and
the vague " armée," and the commonplace " vents." And he
forgets to notice the total impression which these words produce—the atmosphere of darkness and emptiness and vast-
ness and ominous hush.

It is particularly in regard to Racine's treatment of nature
that this generalised style creates misunderstandings. " Is
he so much as aware," exclaims Mr. Bailey, " that the sun
rises and sets in a glory of colour, that the wind plays deliciously on human cheeks, that the human ear will never
have enough of the music of the sea? He might have written every page of his work without so much as looking out

of the window of his study." The accusation gains support
from the fact that Racine rarely describes the processes of
nature by means of pictorial detail; that, we know, was not
his plan. But he is constantly, with his subtle art, suggesting them. In this line, for instance, he calls up, without a
word of definite description, the vision of a sudden and brilliant sunrise:

> Déjà le jour plus grand nous frappe et nous éclaire.

And how varied and beautiful are his impressions of the sea!
He can give us the desolation of a calm:

> La rame inutile
> Fatigua vainement une mer immobile;

or the agitated movement of a great fleet of galleys:

> Voyez tout l'Hellespont blanchissant sous nos rames;

or he can fill his verses with the disorder and the fury of a
storm:

> Quoi! pour noyer les Grecs et leurs mille vaisseaux,
> Mer, tu n'ouvriras pas des abymes nouveaux!
> Quoi! lorsque les chassant du port qui les recèle,
> L'Aulide aura vomi leur flotte criminelle,
> Les vents, les mêmes vents, si longtemps accusés,
> Ne te couvriront pas de ses vaisseaux brisés!

And then, in a single line, he can evoke the radiant spectacle
of a triumphant flotilla riding the dancing waves:

> Prets à vous recevoir mes vaisseaux vous attendent;
> Et du pied de l'autel vous y pouvez monter,
> Souveraine des mers qui vous doivent porter.

The art of subtle suggestion could hardly go further than in
this line, where the alliterating v's, the mute e's, and the
placing of the long syllables combine so wonderfully to produce the required effect.

But it is not only suggestions of nature that readers like
Mr. Bailey are unable to find in Racine—they miss in him no
less suggestions of the mysterious and the infinite. No doubt
this is partly due to our English habit of associating these
qualities with expressions which are complex and unfamiliar.
When we come across the mysterious accent of fatality and
remote terror in a single perfectly simple phrase—

La fille de Minos et de Pasiphaé

we are apt not to hear that it is there. But there is another
reason—the craving, which has seized upon our poetry and
our criticism ever since the triumph of Wordsworth and
Coleridge at the beginning of the last century, for metaphysical stimulants. It would be easy to prolong the discussion of this matter far beyond the boundaries of " sublunary debate," but it is sufficient to point out that Mr.
Bailey's criticism of Racine affords an excellent example of
the fatal effects of this obsession. His pages are full of references to " infinity " and " the unseen " and " eternity "
and " a mystery brooding over a mystery " and " the key to
the secret life "; and it is only natural that he should find
in these watchwords one of those tests of poetic greatness of
which he is so fond. The fallaciousness of such views as
these becomes obvious when we remember the plain fact
that there is not a trace of this kind of mystery or of these
" feelings after the key to the secret of life," in *Paradise*

Lost, and that *Paradise Lost* is one of the greatest poems in the world. But Milton is sacrosanct in England; no theory, however mistaken, can shake that stupendous name, and the damage which may be wrought by a vicious system of criticism only becomes evident in its treatment of writers like Racine, whom it can attack with impunity and apparent success. There is no " mystery " in Racine—that is to say, there are no metaphysical speculations in him, no suggestions of the transcendental, no hints as to the ultimate nature of reality and the constitution of the world; and so away with him, a creature of mere rhetoric and ingenuities, to the outer limbo! But if, instead of asking what a writer is without, we try to discover simply what he is, will not our results be more worthy of our trouble? And in fact, if we once put out of our heads our longings for the mystery of metaphysical suggestion, the more we examine Racine, the more clearly we shall discern in him another kind of mystery, whose presence may eventually console us for the loss of the first—the mystery of the mind of man. This indeed is the framework of his poetry, and to speak of it adequately would demand a wider scope than that of an essay; for how much might be written of that strange and moving background, dark with the profundity of passion and glowing with the beauty of the sublime, wherefrom the great personages of his tragedies—Hermione and Mithridate, Roxane and Agrippine, Athalie and Phèdre—seem to emerge for a moment towards us, whereon they breathe and suffer, and among whose depths they vanish for ever from our sight! Look where we will we shall find among his pages the traces of an inward mystery and the obscure infinities of the heart.

Nous avons su toujours nous aimer et nous taire.

The line is a summary of the romance and the anguish of
two lives. That is all affection; and this all desire—

J'aimais jusqu'à ses pleurs que je faisais couler.

Or let us listen to the voice of Phèdre, when she learns that
Hippolyte and Aricie love one another:

> Les a-t-on vus souvent se parler, se chercher?
> Dans le fond des forêts alloient-ils se cacher?
> Hélas! ils se voyaient avec pleine licence;
> Le ciel de leurs soupirs approuvait l'innocence;
> Ils suivaient sans remords leur penchant amoureux;
> Tous les jours se levaient clairs et sereins pour eux.

This last line—written, let us remember, by a frigidly ingenious rhetorician, who had never looked out of his study-
window—does it not seem to mingle, in a trance of absolute
simplicity, the peerless beauty of a Claude with the misery
and ruin of a great soul?

It is, perhaps, as a psychologist that Racine has achieved
his most remarkable triumphs; and the fact that so subtle
and penetrating a critic as M. Lemaître has chosen to devote
the greater part of a volume to the discussion of his characters shows clearly enough that Racine's portrayal of human
nature has lost nothing of its freshness and vitality with the
passage of time. On the contrary, his admirers are now
tending more and more to lay stress upon the brilliance of his
portraits, the combined vigour and intimacy of his painting,
his amazing knowledge and his unerring fidelity to truth.
M. Lemaître, in fact, goes so far as to describe Racine as a
supreme realist, while other writers have found in him the

essence of the modern spirit. These are vague phrases, no doubt, but they imply a very definite point of view; and it is curious to compare with it our English conception of Racine as a stiff and pompous kind of dancing-master, utterly out of date and infinitely cold. And there is a similar disagreement over his style. Mr. Bailey is never tired of asserting that Racine's style is rhetorical, artificial, and monotonous; while M. Lemaître speaks of it as " nu et familier," and Sainte-Beuve says " il rase la prose, mais avec des ailes." The explanation of these contradictions is to be found in the fact that the two critics are considering different parts of the poet's work. When Racine is most himself, when he is seizing upon a state of mind and depicting it with all its twistings and vibrations, he writes with a directness which is indeed naked, and his sentences, refined to the utmost point of significance, flash out like swords, stroke upon stroke, swift, certain, irresistible. This is how Agrippine, in the fury of her tottering ambition, bursts out to Burrhus, the tutor of her son:

> Pretendez-vous longtemps me cacher l'empereur?
> Ne le verrai-je plus qu'à titre d'importune?
> Ai-je donc élevé si haut votre fortune
> Pour mettre une barrière entre mon fils et moi?
> Ne l'osez-vous laisser un moment sur sa foi?
> Entre Sénèque et vous disputez-vous la gloire
> A qui m'éffacera plus tôt de sa mémoire?
> Vous l'ai-je confié pour en faire un ingrat
> Pour être, sous son nom, les maîtres de l'état?
> Certes, plus je médite, et moins je me figure
> Que vous m'osiez compter pour votre créature;
> Vous, dont j'ai pu laisser vieillir l'ambition
> Dans les honneurs obscurs de quelque légion;

> Et moi, qui sur le trône ai suivi mes ancêtres,
> Moi, fille, femme, sœur, et mère de vos maîtres!

When we come upon a passage like this we know, so to speak, that the hunt is up and the whole field tearing after the quarry. But Racine, on other occasions, has another way of writing. He can be roundabout, artificial, and vague; he can involve a simple statement in a mist of high-sounding words and elaborate inversions.

> Jamais l'aimable sœur des cruels Pallantides
> Trempa-t-elle aux complots de ses frères perfides.

That is Racine's way of saying that Aricie did not join in her brothers' conspiracy. He will describe an incriminating letter as " De sa trahison ce gage trop sincère." It is obvious that this kind of expression has within it the germs of the " noble " style of the eighteenth century tragedians, one of whom, finding himself obliged to mention a dog, got out of the difficulty, by referring to—" De la fidélité le respectable appui." This is the side of Racine's writing that puzzles and disgusts Mr. Bailey. But there is a meaning in it, after all. Every art is based upon a selection, and the art of Racine selected the things of the spirit for the material of its work. The things of sense—physical objects and details, and all the necessary but insignificant facts that go to make up the machinery of existence—these must be kept out of the picture at all hazards. To have called a spade a spade would have ruined the whole effect; spades must never be mentioned, or, at the worst, they must be dimly referred to as agricultural implements, so that the entire attention may be fixed upon the central and dominating features of the com-

position—the spiritual states of the characters—which, laid
bare with uncompromising force and supreme precision, may
thus indelibly imprint themselves upon the mind. To condemn Racine on the score of his ambiguities and his pom-
posities is to complain of the hastily dashed-in column and
curtain in the background of a portrait, and not to mention
the face. Sometimes indeed his art seems to rise superior to
its own conditions, endowing even the dross and refuse of
what it works in with a wonderful significance. Thus when
the Sultana, Roxane, discovers her lover's treachery, her
mind flies immediately to thoughts of revenge and death,
and she exclaims—

> Ah! je respire enfin, et ma joie est extrême
> Que le traître une fois se soit trahi lui-même.
> Libre des soins cruels où j'allais m'engager,
> Ma tranquille fureur n'a plus qu'a se venger.
> Qu'il meure. Vengeons-nous. Courez. Qu'on le saisisse!
> Que la main des muets s'arme pour son supplice;
> Qu'ils viennent preparer ces nœuds infortunés
> Par qui de ses pareils les jours sont terminés.

To have called a bowstring a bowstring was out of the question; and Racine, with triumphant art, has managed to introduce the periphrasis in such a way that it exactly expresses
the state of mind of the Sultana. She begins with revenge
and rage, until she reaches the extremity of virulent resolu-
tion; and then her mind begins to waver, and she finally orders the execution of the man she loves, in a contorted agony
of speech.

But, as a rule, Racine's characters speak out most clearly
when they are most moved, so that their words, at the height

of passion, have an intensity of directness unknown in actual
life. In such moments, the phrases that leap to their lips
quiver and glow with the compressed significance of character and situation; the " Qui te l'a dit? " of Hermione, the
" Sortez " of Roxane, the " Je vais à Rome " of Mithridate,
the " Dieu des Juifs, tu l'emportes! " of Athalie—who can
forget these things, these wondrous microcosms of tragedy?
Very different is the Shakespearean method. There, as
passion rises, expression becomes more and more poetical
and vague. Image flows into image, thought into thought,
until at last the state of mind is revealed, inform and molten,
driving darkly through a vast storm of words. Such revelations, no doubt, come closer to reality than the poignant epigrams of Racine. In life, men's minds are not sharpened,
they are diffused, by emotion; and the utterance which best
represents them is fluctuating and agglomerated rather than
compact and defined. But Racine's aim was less to reflect
the actual current of the human spirit than to seize upon its
inmost being and to give expression to that. One might be
tempted to say that his art represents the sublimed essence
of reality, save that, after all, reality has no degrees. Who
can affirm that the wild ambiguities of our hearts and the
gross impediments of our physical existence are less real
than the most pointed of our feelings and " thoughts beyond
the reaches of our souls "?

It would be nearer the truth to rank Racine among the
idealists. The world of his creation is not a copy of our
own; it is a heightened and rarefied extension of it; moving,
in triumph and in beauty, through " an ampler ether, a
diviner air." It is a world where the hesitations and the

pettinesses and the squalors of this earth have been fired
out; a world where ugliness is a forgotten name, and lust itself has grown ethereal; where anguish has become a grace
and death a glory, and love the beginning and the end of all.
It is, too, the world of a poet, so that we reach it, not through
melody nor through vision, but through the poet's sweet
articulation—through verse. Upon English ears the rhymed
couplets of Racine sound strangely; and how many besides
Mr. Bailey have dubbed his alexandrines " monotonous "!
But to his lovers, to those who have found their way into the
secret places of his art, his lines are impregnated with a
peculiar beauty, and the last perfection of style. Over them,
the most insignificant of his verses can throw a deep enchantment, like the faintest wavings of a magician's wand.
" A-t-on vu de ma part le roi de Comagène? "—How is it
that words of such slight import should hold such thrilling
music? Oh! they are Racine's words. And, as to his
rhymes, they seem perhaps, to the true worshipper, the final
crown of his art. Mr. Bailey tells us that the couplet is only
fit for satire. Has he forgotten *Lamia?* And he asks, " How
is it that we read Pope's *Satires,* and Dryden's, and Johnson's with enthusiasm still, while we never touch *Irene,* and
rarely the *Conquest of Granada? "* Perhaps the answer is
that if we cannot get rid of our *a priori* theories, even the
fiery art of Dryden's drama may remain dead to us, and
that, if we touched *Irene* even once, we should find it was in
blank verse. But Dryden himself has spoken memorably
upon rhyme. Discussing the imputed unnaturalness of the
rhymed " repartee " he says: " Suppose we acknowledge it:
how comes this confederacy to be more displeasing to you

than in a dance which is well contrived? You see there the
united design of many persons to make up one figure; . . .
the confederacy is plain amongst them, for chance could
never produce anything so beautiful; and yet there is nothing in it that shocks your sight. . . . 'Tis an art which appears; but it appears only like the shadowings of painture,
which, being to cause the rounding of it, cannot be absent;
but while that is considered, they are lost: so while we attend to the other beauties of the matter, the care and labour
of the rhyme is carried from us, or at least drowned in its
own sweetness, as bees are sometimes buried in their honey."
In this exquisite passage Dryden seems to have come near,
though not quite to have hit, the central argument for rhyme
—its power of creating a beautiful atmosphere, in which
what is expressed may be caught away from the associations
of common life and harmoniously enshrined. For Racine,
with his prepossessions of sublimity and perfection, some
such barrier between his universe and reality was involved
in the very nature of his art. His rhyme is like the still clear
water of a lake, through which we can see, mysteriously
separated from us and changed and beautified, the forms of
his imagination, " quivering within the wave's intenser day."
And truly not seldom are they " so sweet, the sense faints
picturing them "!

> Oui, prince, je languis, je brûle pour Thésée . . .
> Il avait votre port, vos yeux, votre langage,
> Cette noble pudeur colorait son visage,
> Lorsque de notre Crète il traversa les flots,
> Digne sujet des vœux des filles de Minos.
> Que faisiez-vous alors? Pourquoi, sans Hippolyte,
> Des héros de la Grèce assembla-t-il l'élite?

Pourquoi, trop jeune encor, ne pûtes-vous alors
Entrer dans le vaisseau qui le mit sur nos bords?
Par vous aurait péri le monstre de la Crète,
Malgré tous les détours de sa vaste retraite:
Pour en développer l'embarras incertain
Ma sœur du fil fatal eût armé votre main.
Mais non: dans ce dessein je l'aurais devancée;
L'amour m'en eût d'abord inspiré la pensée;
C'est moi, prince, c'est moi dont l'utile secours
Vous eût du labyrinthe enseigné les detours.
Que de soins m'eût coûtés cette tête charmante!

It is difficult to " place " Racine among the poets. He has
affinities with many; but likenesses to few. To balance him
rigorously against any other—to ask whether he is better or
worse than Shelley or than Virgil—is to attempt impossi-
bilities; but there is one fact which is too often forgotten in
comparing his work with that of other poets—with Virgil's
for instance—Racine wrote for the stage. Virgil's poetry is
intended to be read, Racine's to be declaimed; and it is only
in the theatre that one can experience to the full the potency
of his art. In a sense we can know him in our library, just
as we can hear the music of Mozart with silent eyes. But,
when the strings begin, when the whole volume of that divine
harmony engulfs us, how differently then we understand and
feel! And so, at the theatre, before one of those high
tragedies, whose interpretation has taxed to the utmost ten
generations of the greatest actresses of France, we realise,
with the shock of a new emotion, what we had but half-felt
before. To hear the words of Phèdre spoken by the mouth
of Bernhardt, to watch, in the culminating horror of crime
and of remorse, of jealousy, of rage, of desire, and of despair,

all the dark forces of destiny crowd down upon that great spirit, when the heavens and the earth reject her, and Hell opens, and the terrific urn of Minos thunders and crashes to the ground—that indeed is to come close to immortality, to plunge shuddering through infinite abysses, and to look, if only for a moment, upon eternal light.

1908.

SIR THOMAS BROWNE

SIR THOMAS BROWNE

The life of Sir Thomas Browne does not afford much scope for the biographer. Everyone knows that Browne was a physician who lived at Norwich in the seventeenth century; and, so far as regards what one must call, for want of a better term, his " life," that is a sufficient summary of all there is to know. It is obvious that, with such scanty and unexciting materials, no biographer can say very much about what Sir Thomas Browne did; it is quite easy, however, to expatiate about what he wrote. He dug deeply into so many subjects, he touched lightly upon so many more, that his works offer innumerable openings for those half-conversational digressions and excursions of which perhaps the pleasantest kind of criticism is composed.

Mr. Gosse, in his volume on Sir Thomas Browne in the " English Men of Letters Series," has evidently taken this view of his subject. He has not attempted to treat it with any great profundity or elaboration; he has simply gone " about it and about." The result is a book so full of entertainment, of discrimination, of quiet humour, and of literary tact, that no reader could have the heart to bring up against it the obvious—though surely irrelevant—truth, that the general impression which it leaves upon the mind is in the nature of a composite presentment, in which the features of Sir Thomas have become somehow indissolubly blended with those of his biographer. It would be rash, indeed, to attempt to improve upon Mr. Gosse's example; after his luminous and suggestive chapters on Browne's life at Norwich, on the *Vulgar Errors,* and on the self-revelations in the *Religio Medici,* there seems to be no room for further comment. One can only admire in silence, and hand on the volume to one's neighbour.

There is, however, one side of Browne's work upon which it may be worth while to dwell at somewhat greater length. Mr. Gosse, who has so much to say on such a variety of topics, has unfortunately limited to a very small number of pages his considerations upon what is, after all, the most important thing about the author of *Urn Burial* and *The Garden of Cyrus*—his style. Mr. Gosse himself confesses that it is chiefly as a master of literary form that Browne deserves to be remembered. Why then does he tell us so little about his literary form, and so much about his family, and his religion, and his scientific opinions, and his porridge, and who fished up the *murex?*

Nor is it only owing to its inadequacy that Mr. Gosse's treatment of Browne as an artist in language is the least satisfactory part of his book: for it is difficult not to think that upon this crucial point Mr. Gosse has for once been deserted by his sympathy and his acumen. In spite of what appears to be a genuine delight in Browne's most splendid and characteristic passages, Mr. Gosse cannot help protesting somewhat acrimoniously against that very method of writing whose effects he is so ready to admire. In practice, he approves; in theory, he condemns. He ranks the *Hydriotaphia* among the gems of English literature; and the prose style of

which it is the most consummate expression he denounces as
fundamentally wrong. The contradiction is obvious; but
there can be little doubt that, though Browne has, as it were,
extorted a personal homage, Mr. Gosse's real sympathies lie
on the other side. His remarks upon Browne's effect upon
eighteenth-century prose show clearly enough the true bent
of his opinions; and they show, too, how completely mis-
leading a preconceived theory may be.

The study of Sir Thomas Browne, Mr. Gosse says, " encouraged Johnson, and with him a whole school of rhetorical
writers in the eighteenth century, to avoid circumlocution
by the invention of superfluous words, learned but pedantic,
in which darkness was concentrated without being dis-
pelled." Such is Mr. Gosse's account of the influence of
Browne and Johnson upon the later eighteenth-century
writers of prose. But to dismiss Johnson's influence as something altogether deplorable, is surely to misunderstand the
whole drift of the great revolution which he brought about
in English letters. The characteristics of the pre-Johnsonian
prose style—the style which Dryden first established and
Swift brought to perfection—are obvious enough. Its advantages are those of clarity and force; but its faults, which,
of course, are unimportant in the work of a great master,
become glaring in that of the second-rate practitioner. The
prose of Shaftesbury, for instance, or of Bishop Butler, suffers, in spite of its clarity and vigour, from grave defects.
It is very flat and very loose; it has no formal beauty, no
elegance, no balance, no trace of the deliberation of art.
Johnson, there can be no doubt, determined to remedy these
evils by giving a new mould to the texture of English prose;

and he went back for a model to Sir Thomas Browne. Now, as Mr. Gosse himself observes, Browne stands out in a remarkable way from among the great mass of his contemporaries and predecessors, by virtue of his highly developed artistic consciousness. He was, says Mr. Gosse, " never carried away. His effects are closely studied, they are the result of forethought and anxious contrivance "; and no one can doubt the truth or the significance of this dictum who compares, let us say, the last paragraphs of *The Garden of Cyrus* with any page in *The Anatomy of Melancholy*. The peculiarities of Browne's style—the studied pomp of its latinisms, its wealth of allusion, its tendency towards sonorous antithesis—culminated in his last, though not his best, work, the *Christian Morals,* which almost reads like an elaborate and magnificent parody of the Book of Proverbs. With the *Christian Morals* to guide him, Dr. Johnson set about the transformation of the prose of his time. He decorated, he pruned, he balanced; he hung garlands, he draped robes; and he ended by converting the Doric order of Swift into the Corinthian order of Gibbon. Is it quite just to describe this process as one by which " a whole school of rhetorical writers " was encouraged " to avoid circumlocution " by the invention " of superfluous words," when it was this very process that gave us the peculiar savour of polished ease which characterises nearly all the important prose of the last half of the eighteenth century—that of Johnson himself, of Hume, of Reynolds, of Horace Walpole—which can be traced even in Burke, and which fills the pages of Gibbon? It is, indeed, a curious reflection, but one which is amply justified by the facts, that the *Decline and Fall* could not have been precisely what it is, had Sir Thomas Browne never written the *Christian Morals*.

That Johnson and his disciples had no inkling of the inner spirit of the writer to whose outward form they owed so much, has been pointed out by Mr. Gosse, who adds that Browne's " genuine merits were rediscovered and asserted by Coleridge and Lamb." But we have already observed that Mr. Gosse's own assertion of these merits lies a little open to question. His view seems to be, in fact, the precise antithesis of Dr. Johnson's; he swallows the spirit of Browne's writing, and strains at the form. Browne, he says, was " seduced by a certain obscure romance in the terminology of late Latin writers," he used " adjectives of classical extraction, which are neither necessary nor natural," he forgot that it is better for a writer " to consult women and people who have not studied, than those who are too learnedly oppressed by a knowledge of Latin and Greek." He should not have said " oneiro-criticism," when he meant the interpretation of dreams, nor " omneity " instead of " oneness "; and he had " no excuse for writing about the " pensile " gardens of Babylon, when all that is required is expressed by " hanging." Attacks of this kind—attacks upon the elaboration and classicism of Browne's style—are difficult to reply to, because they must seem, to anyone who holds a contrary opinion, to betray such a total lack of sympathy with the subject as to make argument all but impossible. To the true Browne enthusiast, indeed, there is something almost shocking about the state of mind which would exchange " pensile " for " hanging," and " asperous " for " rough," and would do away with " digladiation " and

" quodlibetically " altogether. The truth is, that there is
a great gulf fixed between those who naturally dislike the
ornate, and those who naturally love it. There is no remedy; and to attempt to ignore this fact only emphasises
it the more. Anyone who is jarred by the expression
" prodigal blazes " had better immediately shut up Sir
Thomas Browne. The critic who admits the jar, but continues to appreciate, must present, to the true enthusiast, a
spectacle of curious self-contradiction.

If once the ornate style be allowed as a legitimate form of
art, no attack such as Mr. Gosse makes on Browne's latinisms can possibly be valid. For it is surely an error to judge
and to condemn the latinisms without reference to the whole
style of which they form a necessary part. Mr. Gosse, it is
true, inclines to treat them as if they were a mere excrescence
which could be cut off without difficulty, and might never
have existed if Browne's views upon the English language
had been a little different. Browne, he says, " had come to
the conclusion that classic words were the only legitimate
ones, the only ones which interpreted with elegance the
thoughts of a sensitive and cultivated man, and that the rest
were barbarous." We are to suppose, then, that if he had
happened to hold the opinion that Saxon words were the only
legitimate ones, the *Hydriotaphia* would have been as free
from words of classical derivation as the sermons of Latimer.
A very little reflection and inquiry will suffice to show how
completely mistaken this view really is. In the first place,
the theory that Browne considered all unclassical words
" barbarous " and unfit to interpret his thoughts, is clearly
untenable, owing to the obvious fact that his writings are

full of instances of the deliberate use of such words. So much is this the case, that Pater declares that a dissertation upon style might be written to illustrate Browne's use of the words " thin " and " dark." A striking phrase from the *Christian Morals* will suffice to show the deliberation with which Browne sometimes employed the latter word:—" the areopagy and dark tribunal of our hearts." If Browne had thought the Saxon epithet " barbarous," why should he have gone out of his way to use it, when " mysterious " or " secret " would have expressed his meaning? The truth is clear enough. Browne saw that " dark " was the one word which would give, better than any other, the precise impression of mystery and secrecy which he intended to produce; and so he used it. He did not choose his words according to rule, but according to the effect which he wished them to have. Thus, when he wished to suggest an extreme contrast between simplicity and pomp, we find him using Saxon words in direct antithesis to classical ones. In the last sentence of *Urn Burial*, we are told that the true believer, when he is to be buried, is " as content with six foot as the Moles of Adrianus." How could Browne have produced the remarkable sense of contrast which this short phrase conveys, if his vocabulary had been limited, in accordance with a linguistic theory, to words of a single stock?

There is, of course, no doubt that Browne's vocabulary is extraordinarily classical. Why is this? The reason is not far to seek. In his most characteristic moments he was almost entirely occupied with thoughts and emotions which can, owing to their very nature, only be expressed in Latinistic language. The state of mind which he wished to produce in his readers was nearly always a complicated one: they were to be impressed and elevated by a multiplicity of suggestions and a sense of mystery and awe. "Let thy thoughts," he says himself, "be of things which have not entered into the hearts of beasts: think of things long past, and long to come: acquaint thyself with the choragium of the stars, and consider the vast expanse beyond them. Let intellectual tubes give thee a glance of things which visive organs reach not. Have a glimpse of incomprehensibles; and thoughts of things, which thoughts but tenderly touch." Browne had, in fact, as Dr. Johnson puts it, "uncommon sentiments"; and how was he to express them unless by a language of pomp, of allusion, and of elaborate rhythm? Not only is the Saxon form of speech devoid of splendour and suggestiveness; its simplicity is still further emphasised by a spondaic rhythm which seems to produce (by some mysterious rhythmic law) an atmosphere of ordinary life, where, though the pathetic may be present, there is no place for the complex or the remote. To understand how unsuitable such conditions would be for the highly subtle and rarefied art of Sir Thomas Browne, it is only necessary to compare one of his periods with a typical passage of Saxon prose.

Then they brought a faggot, kindled with fire, and laid the same down at Doctor Ridley's feet. To whom Master Latimer spake in this manner: "Be of good comfort, Master Ridley, and play the man. We shall this day light such a candle, by God's grace, in England, as I trust shall never be put out."

Nothing could be better adapted to the meaning and sentiment of this passage than the limpid, even flow of its rhythm. But who could conceive of such a rhythm being ever applicable to the meaning and sentiment of these sentences from the *Hydriotaphia?*

To extend our memories by monuments, whose death we daily pray for, and whose duration we cannot hope without injury to our expectations in the advent of the last day, were a contradiction to our beliefs. We, whose generations are ordained in this setting part of time, are providentially taken off from such imaginations; and, being necessitated to eye the remaining particle of futurity, are naturally constituted unto thoughts of the next world, and cannot excusably decline the consideration of that duration, which maketh pyramids pillars of snow, and all that's past a moment.

Here the long, rolling, almost turgid clauses, with their enormous Latin substantives, seem to carry the reader forward through an immense succession of ages, until at last, with a sudden change of the rhythm, the whole of recorded time crumbles and vanishes before his eyes. The entire effect depends upon the employment of a rhythmical complexity and subtlety which is utterly alien to Saxon prose. It would be foolish to claim a superiority for either of the two styles; it would be still more foolish to suppose that the effects of one might be produced by means of the other.

Wealth of rhythmical elaboration was not the only benefit which a highly Latinised vocabulary conferred on Browne. Without it, he would never have been able to achieve those splendid strokes of stylistic *bravura*, which were evidently so dear to his nature, and occur so constantly in his finest passages. The precise quality cannot be easily described, but is impossible to mistake; and the pleasure which it produces seems to be curiously analogous to that given by a piece of magnificent brushwork in a Rubens or a Velasquez. Browne's " brushwork " is certainly unequalled in English literature, except by the very greatest masters of sophisticated art, such as Pope and Shakespeare; it is the inspiration of sheer technique. Such expressions as: " to subsist in bones and be but pyramidally extant "—" sad and sepulchral pitchers which have no joyful voices "—" predicament of chimæras "—" the irregularities of vain glory, and wild enormities of ancient magnanimity "—are examples of this consummate mastery of language, examples which, with a multitude of others, singly deserve whole hours of delicious gustation, whole days of absorbed and exquisite worship. It is pleasant to start out for a long walk with such a splendid phrase upon one's lips as: " According to the ordainer of order and mystical mathematicks of the City of Heaven," to go for miles and miles with the marvellous syllables still rich upon the inward ear, and to return home with them in triumph. It is then that one begins to understand how mistaken it was of Sir Thomas Browne not to have written in simple, short, straightforward Saxon English.

One other function performed by Browne's latinisms must be mentioned, because it is closely connected with the most essential and peculiar of the qualities which distinguish his method of writing. Certain classical words, partly owing to their allusiveness, partly owing to their sound, possess a remarkable flavour which is totally absent from those of Saxon derivation. Such a word, for instance, as " pyramidally," gives one at once an immediate sense of something mysterious, something extraordinary, and, at the same time, something almost grotesque. And this subtle blending of mystery and queerness characterises not only Browne's choice of words, but his choice of feelings and of thoughts. The grotesque side of his art, indeed, was apparently all that was visible to the critics of a few generations back, who admired him simply and solely for what they called his " quaintness "; while Mr. Gosse has flown to the opposite extreme, and will not allow Browne any sense of humour at all. The confusion no doubt arises merely from a difference in the point of view. Mr. Gosse, regarding Browne's most important and general effects, rightly fails to detect anything funny in them. The Early Victorians, however, missed the broad outlines, and were altogether taken up with the obvious *bizarrerie* of the details. When they found Browne asserting that " Cato seemed to dote upon Cabbage," or embroidering an entire paragraph upon the subject of " Pyrrhus his Toe," they could not help smiling; and surely they were quite right. Browne, like an impressionist painter, produced his pictures by means of a multitude of details which, if one looks at them in themselves, are discordant, and extraordinary, and even absurd.

There can be little doubt that this strongly-marked taste for curious details was one of the symptoms of the scientific bent of his mind. For Browne was scientific just up to the point where the examination of detail ends, and its co-ordination begins. He knew little or nothing of general laws; but his interest in isolated phenomena was intense. And the more singular the phenomena, the more he was attracted. He was always ready to begin some strange inquiry. He cannot help wondering: " Whether great-ear'd persons have short necks, long feet, and loose bellies? " " Marcus Antoninus Philosophus," he notes in his common-place book, " wanted not the advice of the best physicians; yet how warrantable his practice was, to take his repast in the night, and scarce anything but treacle in the day, may admit of great doubt." To inquire thus is, perhaps, to inquire too curiously; yet such inquiries are the stuff of which great scientific theories are made. Browne, however, used his love of details for another purpose: he co-ordinated them, not into a scientific theory, but into a work of art. His method was one which, to be successful, demanded a self-confidence, an imagination, and a technical power, possessed by only the very greatest artists. Everyone knows Pascal's overwhelming sentence:—" Le silence éternel de ces espaces infinis m'effraie." It is overwhelming, obviously and imme-diately; it, so to speak, knocks one down. Browne's ultimate object was to create some such tremendous effect as that, by no knock-down blow, but by a multitude of delicate, subtle, and suggestive touches, by an elaborate evocation of memo-ries and half-hidden things, by a mysterious combination of pompous images and odd unexpected trifles drawn to-gether from the ends of the earth and the four quarters of heaven. His success gives him a place beside Webster and Blake, on one of the very highest peaks of Parnassus. And, if not the highest of all, Browne's peak is—or so at least it seems from the plains below—more difficult of access than some which are no less exalted. The road skirts the preci-pice the whole way. If one fails in the style of Pascal, one is merely flat; if one fails in the style of Browne, one is ridiculous. He who plays with the void, who dallies with eternity, who leaps from star to star, is in danger at every moment of being swept into utter limbo, and tossed forever in the Paradise of Fools.

Browne produced his greatest work late in life; for there is nothing in the *Religio Medici* which reaches the same level of excellence as the last paragraphs of *The Garden of Cyrus* and the last chapter of *Urn Burial*. A long and calm experience of life seems, indeed, to be the background from which his most amazing sentences start out into being. His strangest phantasies are rich with the spoils of the real world. His art matured with himself; and who but the most expert of artists could have produced this perfect sentence in *The Garden of Cyrus,* so well-known, and yet so impossible not to quote?

Nor will the sweetest delight of gardens afford much comfort in sleep; wherein the dullness of that sense shakes hands with delectable odours; and though in the bed of Cleopatra, can hardly with any delight raise up the ghost of a rose.

This is Browne in his most exquisite mood. For his most characteristic, one must go to the concluding pages of *Urn Burial,* where, from the astonishing sentence beginning— " Meanwhile Epicurus lies deep in Dante's hell "—to the end of the book, the very quintessence of his work is to be found. The subject—mortality in its most generalised aspect—has brought out Browne's highest powers; and all the resources of his art—elaboration of rhythm, brilliance of phrase, wealth and variety of suggestion, pomp and splendour of imagination—are accumulated in every paragraph. To crown all, he has scattered through these few pages a multitude of proper names, most of them gorgeous in sound, and each of them carrying its own strange freight of reminiscences and allusions from the unknown depths of the past. As one reads, an extraordinary procession of persons seems to pass before one's eyes—Moses, Archimedes, Achilles, Job, Hector and Charles the Fifth, Cardan and Alaric, Gordianus, and Pilate, and Homer, and Cambyses, and the Canaanitish woman. Among them, one visionary figure flits with a mysterious pre-eminence, flickering over every page, like a familiar and ghostly flame. It is Methuselah; and, in Browne's scheme, the remote, almost infinite, and almost ridiculous patriarch is—who can doubt?—the only possible centre and symbol of all the rest. But it would be vain to dwell further upon this wonderful and famous chapter, except to note the extraordinary sublimity and serenity of its general tone. Browne never states in so many words what his own feelings towards the universe actually are. He speaks of everything but that; and yet, with triumphant art, he manages to convey into our minds an indelible impression of the vast and comprehensive grandeur of his soul.

It is interesting—or at least amusing—to consider what are the most appropriate places in which different authors should be read. Pope is doubtless at his best in the midst of a formal garden, Herrick in an orchard, and Shelley in a boat at sea. Sir Thomas Browne demands, perhaps, a more exotic atmosphere. One could read him floating down the Euphrates, or past the shores of Arabia; and it would be pleasant to open the *Vulgar Errors* in Constantinople, or to get by heart a chapter of the *Christian Morals* between the paws of a Sphinx. In England, the most fitting background for his strange ornament must surely be some habitation consecrated to learning, some University which still smells of antiquity and has learnt the habit of repose. The present writer, at any rate, can bear witness to the splendid echo of Browne's syllables amid learned and ancient walls; for he has known, he believes, few happier moments than those in which he has rolled the periods of the *Hydriotaphia* out to the darkness and the nightingales through the studious cloisters of Trinity.

But, after all, who can doubt that it is at Oxford that Browne himself would choose to linger? May we not guess that he breathed in there, in his boyhood, some part of that mysterious and charming spirit which pervades his words? For one traces something of him, often enough, in the old gardens, and down the hidden streets; one has heard his footstep beside the quiet waters of Magdalen; and his smile still hovers amid that strange company of faces which guard, with such a large passivity, the circumference of the Sheldonian.

1906.

SHAKESPEARE'S FINAL PERIOD

SHAKESPEARE'S FINAL PERIOD

THE whole of the modern criticism of Shakespeare has been fundamentally affected by one important fact. The chronological order of the plays, for so long the object of the vaguest speculation, of random guesses, or at best of isolated "points," has been now discovered and reduced to a coherent law. It is no longer possible to suppose that *The Tempest* was written before *Romeo and Juliet;* that *Henry VI.* was produced in succession to *Henry V.;* or that *Antony and Cleopatra* followed close upon the heels of *Julius Cæsar.* Such theories were sent to limbo for ever, when a study of those plays of whose date we have external evidence revealed the fact that, as Shakespeare's life advanced, a corresponding development took place in the metrical structure of his verse. The establishment of metrical tests, by which the approximate position and date of any play can be readily ascertained, at once followed; chaos gave way to order; and, for the first time, critics became able to judge, not only of the individual works, but of the whole succession of the works of Shakespeare.

Upon this firm foundation modern writers have been only too eager to build. It was apparent that the Plays, arranged in chronological order, showed something more than a mere development in the technique of verse—a development, that is to say, in the general treatment of characters and subjects, and in the sort of feelings which those characters and subjects were intended to arouse; and from this it was easy to draw conclusions as to the development of the mind of Shakespeare itself. Such conclusions have, in fact, been constantly drawn. But it must be noted that they all rest upon the tacit assumption, that the character of any given drama is, in fact, a true index to the state of mind of the dramatist composing it. The validity of this assumption has never been proved; it has never been shown, for instance, why we should suppose a writer of farces to be habitually merry; or whether we are really justified in concluding, from the fact that Shakespeare wrote nothing but tragedies for six years, that, during that period, more than at any other, he was deeply absorbed in the awful problems of human existence. It is not, however, the purpose of this essay to consider the question of what are the relations between the artist and his art; for it will assume the truth of the generally accepted view, that the character of the one can be inferred from that of the other. What it will attempt to discuss is whether, upon this hypothesis, the most important part of the ordinary doctrine of Shakespeare's mental development is justifiable.

What, then, is the ordinary doctrine? Dr. Furnivall states it as follows:

Shakespeare's course is thus shown to have run from the amorousness and fun of youth, through the strong patriotism of early manhood, to the wrestlings with the dark problems that beset the man of middle age, to the gloom which weighed on Shakespeare (as on so many men) in later life, when, though outwardly successful, the world seemed all against him, and his mind dwelt with sympathy on scenes of faithlessness of friends, treachery of relations and subjects, ingratitude of children, scorn

of his kind; till at last, in his Stratford home again, peace came
to him, Miranda and Perdita in their lovely freshness and charm
greeted him, and he was laid by his quiet Avon side.

And the same writer goes on to quote with approval Professor Dowden's

likening of Shakespeare to a ship, beaten and storm-tossed, but
yet entering harbour with sails full-set, to anchor in peace.

Such, in fact, is the general opinion of modern writers upon
Shakespeare; after a happy youth and a gloomy middle age
he reached at last—it is the universal opinion—a state of
quiet serenity in which he died. Professor Dowden's book
on *Shakespeare's Mind and Art* gives the most popular
expression to this view, a view which is also held by Mr. Ten
Brink, by Mr. Gollancz, and, to a great extent, by Dr.
Brandes. Professor Dowden, indeed, has gone so far as to
label this final period with the appellation of *On the
Heights,* in opposition to the preceding one, which, he says,
was passed *In the Depths.* Sir Sidney Lee, too, seems
to find, in the Plays at least, if not in Shakespeare's mind,
the orthodox succession of gaiety, of tragedy, and of the
serenity of meditative romance. Now it is clear that the
most important part of this version of Shakespeare's mental
history is the end of it. That he did eventually attain to a
state of calm content, that he did, in fact, die happy—it is
this that gives colour and interest to the whole theory. For
some reason or another, the end of a man's life seems naturally to afford the light by which the rest of it should be
read; last thoughts do appear in some strange way to be
really best and truest; and this is particularly the case when

they fit in nicely with the rest of the story, and are, perhaps, just what one likes to think oneself. If it be true that Shakespeare, to quote Professor Dowden, " did at last attain to the serene self-possession which he had sought with such persistent effort "; that, in the words of Dr. Furnivall, " forgiven and forgiving, full of the highest wisdom and peace, at one with family and friends and foes, in harmony with Avon's flow and Stratford's level meads, Shakespeare closed his life on earth "—we have obtained a piece of knowledge which is both interesting and pleasant. But if it be not true, if, on the contrary, it can be shown that something very different was actually the case, then will it not follow that we must not only reverse our judgment as to this particular point, but also readjust our view of the whole drift and bearing of Shakespeare's " inner life "?

The group of works which has given rise to this theory of ultimate serenity was probably entirely composed after Shakespeare's final retirement from London, and his establishment at New Place. It consists of three plays—*Cymbeline, The Winter's Tale,* and *The Tempest*—and three fragments—the Shakespearean parts of *Pericles, Henry VIII.,* and *The Two Noble Kinsmen.* All these plays and portions of plays form a distinct group; they resemble each other in a multitude of ways, and they differ in a multitude of ways from nearly all Shakespeare's previous work.

One other complete play, however, and one other fragment, do resemble in some degree these works of the final period; for, immediately preceding them in date, they show clear traces of the beginnings of the new method, and they are themselves curiously different from the plays they immediately succeed—that great series of tragedies which began with *Hamlet* in 1601 and ended in 1608 with *Antony and Cleopatra*. In the latter year, indeed, Shakespeare's entire method underwent an astonishing change. For six years he had been persistently occupied with a kind of writing which he had himself not only invented but brought to the highest point of excellence—the tragedy of character. Every one of his masterpieces has for its theme the action of tragic situation upon character; and, without those stupendous creations in character, his greatest tragedies would obviously have lost the precise thing that has made them what they are. Yet, after *Antony and Cleopatra* Shakespeare deliberately turned his back upon the dramatic methods of all his past career. There seems no reason why he should not have continued, year after year, to produce " Othellos," " Hamlets," and "Macbeths "; instead, he turned over a new leaf, and wrote *Coriolanus*.

Coriolanus is certainly a remarkable, and perhaps an intolerable play: remarkable, because it shows the sudden first appearance of the Shakespeare of the final period; intolerable, because it is impossible to forget how much better it might have been. The subject is thick with situations; the conflicts of patriotism and pride, the effects of sudden disgrace following upon the very height of fortune, the struggles between family affection on the one hand and every interest of revenge and egotism on the other— these would have made a tragic and tremendous setting for some character worthy to rank with Shakespeare's best. But' it pleased him to ignore completely all these opportunities;

and, in the play he has given us, the situations, mutilated and degraded, serve merely as miserable props for the gorgeous clothing of his rhetoric. For rhetoric, enormously magnificent and extraordinarily elaborate, is the beginning and the middle and the end of *Coriolanus*. The hero is not a human being at all; he is the statue of a demi-god cast in bronze, which roars its perfect periods, to use a phrase of Sir Walter Raleigh's, through a melodious megaphone. The vigour of the presentment is, it is true, amazing; but it is a presentment of decoration, not of life. So far and so quickly had Shakespeare already wandered from the subtleties of " Cleopatra." The transformation is indeed astonishing; one wonders, as one beholds it, what will happen next.

At about the same time, some of the scenes in *Timon of Athens* were in all probability composed: scenes which resemble *Coriolanus* in their lack of characterisation and abundance of rhetoric, but differ from it in the peculiar grossness of their tone. For sheer virulence of foul-mouthed abuse, some of the speeches in Timon are probably unsurpassed in any literature; an outraged drayman would speak so, if draymen were in the habit of talking poetry. From this whirlwind of furious ejaculation, this splendid storm of nastiness, Shakespeare, we are confidently told, passed in a moment to tranquillity and joy, to blue skies, to young ladies, and to general forgiveness.

From 1604 to 1610 [says Professor Dowden] a show of tragic figures, like the kings who passed before Macbeth, filled the vision of Shakespeare; until at last the desperate image of Timon rose before him; when, as though unable to endure or to conceive a more lamentable ruin of man, he turned for relief to the pastoral loves of Prince Florizel and Perdita; and as soon as the tone of his mind was restored, gave expression to its ultimate mood of grave serenity in *The Tempest*, and so ended.

This is a pretty picture, but is it true? It may, indeed, be admitted at once that " Prince Florizel and Perdita " are charming creatures, that Prospero is " grave," and that Hermione is more or less " serene "; but why is it that, in our consideration of the later plays, the whole of our attention must always be fixed upon these particular characters? Modern critics, in their eagerness to appraise everything that is beautiful and good at its proper value, seem to have entirely forgotten that there is another side to the medal; and they have omitted to point out that these plays contain a series of portraits of peculiar infamy, whose wickedness finds expression in language of extraordinary force. Coming fresh from their pages to the pages of *Cymbeline*, *The Winter's Tale*, and *The Tempest*, one is astonished and perplexed. How is it possible to fit into their scheme of roses and maidens that " Italian fiend " the " yellow Iachimo," or Cloten, that " thing too bad for bad report," or the " crafty devil," his mother, or Leontes, or Caliban, or Trinculo? To omit these figures of discord and evil from our consideration, to banish them comfortably to the background of the stage, while Autolycus and Miranda dance before the footlights, is surely a fallacy in proportion; for the presentment of the one group of persons is every whit as distinct and vigorous as that of the other. Nowhere, indeed, is Shakespeare's violence of expression more constantly displayed than in the " gentle utterances " of his last period; it is here that one finds Paulina, in a torrent of indignation

as far from " grave serenity " as it is from " pastoral love,"
exclaiming to Leontes:

> What studied torments, tyrant, hast for me?
> What wheels? racks? fires? what flaying? boiling
> In leads or oils? what old or newer torture
> Must I receive, whose every word deserves
> To taste of thy most worst? Thy tyranny,
> Together working with thy jealousies,
> Fancies too weak for boys, too green and idle
> For girls of nine, O! think what they have done,
> And then run mad indeed, stark mad; for all
> Thy by-gone fooleries were but spices of it.
> That thou betray'dst Polixenes, 'twas nothing;
> That did but show thee, of a fool, inconstant
> And damnable ingrateful; nor was't much
> Thou would'st have poison'd good Camillo's honour,
> To have him kill a king; poor trespasses,
> More monstrous standing by; whereof I reckon
> The casting forth to crows thy baby daughter
> To be or none or little; though a devil
> Would have shed water out of fire ere done't.
> Nor is't directly laid to thee, the death
> Of the young prince, whose honourable thoughts,
> Thoughts high for one so tender, cleft the heart
> That could conceive a gross and foolish sire
> Blemished his gracious dam.

Nowhere are the poet's metaphors more nakedly material;
nowhere does he verge more often upon a sort of brutality of
phrase, a cruel coarseness. Iachimo tells us how:

> The cloyed will,
> That satiate yet unsatisfied desire, that tub
> Both filled and running, ravening first the lamb,
> Longs after for the garbage.

and talks of:

> an eye
> Base and unlustrous as the smoky light
> That's fed with stinking tallow.

" The south fog rot him! " Cloten bursts out to Imogen,
cursing her husband in an access of hideous rage.

What traces do such passages as these show of " serene
self-possession," of " the highest wisdom and peace," or of
" meditative romance "? English critics, overcome by the
idea of Shakespeare's ultimate tranquillity, have generally
denied to him the authorship of the brothel scenes in *Pericles;* but these scenes are entirely of a piece with the gross-
nesses of *The Winter's Tale* and *Cymbeline*.

> Is there no way for men to be, but women
> Must be half-workers?

says Posthumus when he hears of Imogen's guilt.

> We are all bastards;
> And that most venerable man, which I
> Did call my father, was I know not where
> When I was stamped. Some coiner with his tools
> Made me a counterfeit; yet my mother seemed
> The Dian of that time; so doth my wife
> The nonpareil of this—O vengeance, vengeance!
> Me of my lawful pleasure she restrained
> And prayed me, oft, forbearance; did it with
> A prudency so rosy, the sweet view on't
> Might well have warmed old Saturn, that I thought her
> As chaste as unsunned snow—O, all the devils!—
> This yellow Iachimo, in an hour,—was't not?
> Or less,—at first: perchance he spoke not; but,
> Like a full-acorned boar, a German one,
> Cried, oh! and mounted: found no opposition

But what he looked for should oppose, and she
Should from encounter guard.

And Leontes, in a similar situation, expresses himself in
images no less to the point.

> There have been
> Or I am much deceived, cuckolds ere now,
> And many a man there is, even at this present,
> Now, while I speak this, holds his wife by the arm,
> That little thinks she has been sluiced in's absence
> And his pond fished by his next neighbour, by
> Sir Smile, his neighbour: nay, there's comfort in't.
> Whiles other men have gates, and those gates opened,
> As mine, against their will. Should all despair
> That have revolted wives, the tenth of mankind
> Would hang themselves. Physic for't there's none;
> It is a bawdy planet, that will strike
> Where 'tis predominant; and 'tis powerful, think it,
> From east, west, north and south: be it concluded,
> No barricado for a belly, know't;
> It will let in and out the enemy
> With bag and baggage: many thousand on's
> Have the disease, and feel't not.

It is really a little difficult, in the face of such passages, to
agree with Professor Dowden's dictum: " In these latest
plays the beautiful pathetic light is always present."

But how has it happened that the judgment of so many
critics has been so completely led astray? Charm and
gravity, and even serenity, are to be found in many other
plays of Shakespeare. Ophelia is charming, Brutus is grave,
Cordelia is serene; are we then to suppose that *Hamlet*,
and *Julius Cæsar*, and *King Lear* give expression to the
same mood of high tranquillity which is betrayed by

Cymbeline, The Tempest, and *The Winter's Tale?* "Certainly not," reply the orthodox writers, "for you must distinguish. The plays of the last period are not tragedies; they all end happily "—" in scenes," says Mr. Gollancz, " of forgiveness, reconciliation, and peace." Virtue, in fact, is not only virtuous, it is triumphant; what would you more?

But to this it may be retorted, that, in the case of one of Shakespeare's plays, even the final vision of virtue and beauty triumphant over ugliness and vice fails to dispel a total effect of horror and of gloom. For, in *Measure for Measure,* Isabella is no whit less pure and lovely than any Perdita or Miranda, and her success is as complete; yet who would venture to deny that the atmosphere of *Measure for Measure* was more nearly one of despair than of serenity? What is it, then, that makes the difference? Why should a happy ending seem in one case futile, and in another satisfactory? Why does it sometimes matter to us a great deal, and sometimes not at all, whether virtue is rewarded or not?

The reason, in this case, is not far to seek. *Measure for Measure* is, like nearly every play of Shakespeare's before *Coriolanus,* essentially realistic. The characters are real men and women; and what happens to them upon the stage has all the effect of what happens to real men and women in actual life. Their goodness appears to be real goodness, their wickedness real wickedness; and, if their sufferings are terrible enough, we regret the fact, even though in the end they triumph, just as we regret the real sufferings of our friends. But, in the plays of the final period, all this has changed; we are no longer in the real world, but in a world of enchantment, of mystery, of wonder, a world of shifting visions, a world of hopeless anachronisms, a world in which anything may happen next. The pretences of reality are indeed usually preserved, but only the pretences. Cymbeline is supposed to be the king of a real Britain, and the real Augustus is supposed to demand tribute of him; but these are the reasons which his queen, in solemn audience with the Roman ambassador, urges to induce her husband to declare for war:

> Remember, sir, my liege,
> The Kings your ancestors, together with
> The natural bravery of your isle, which stands
> As Neptune's park, ribbed and paled in
> With rocks unscaleable and roaring waters,
> With sands that will not bear your enemies' boats,
> But suck them up to the topmast. A kind of conquest
> Cæsar made here; but made not here his brag
> Of " Came, and saw, and overcame "; with shame—
> The first that ever touched him—he was carried
> From off our coast, twice beaten; and his shipping—
> Poor ignorant baubles!—on our terrible seas,
> Like egg-shells moved upon the surges, crack'd
> As easily 'gainst our rocks; for joy whereof
> The famed Cassibelan, who was once at point—
> O giglot fortune!—to master Cæsar's sword,
> Made Lud's town with rejoicing fires bright
> And Britons strut with courage.

It comes with something of a shock to remember that this medley of poetry, bombast, and myth will eventually reach the ears of no other person than the Octavius of *Antony and Cleopatra;* and the contrast is the more remarkable when one recalls the brilliant scene of negotiation and diplomacy in the latter play, which passes between Oc-

tavius, Maecenas and Agrippa on the one side, and Antony
and Enobarbus on the other, and results in the reconciliation of the rivals and the marriage of Antony and Octavia.

Thus strangely remote is the world of Shakespeare's latest
period; and it is peopled, this universe of his invention, with
beings equally unreal, with creatures either more or less
than human, with fortunate princes and wicked step-
mothers, with goblins and spirits, with lost princesses and
insufferable kings. And of course, in this sort of fairy land,
it is an essential condition that everything shall end well;
the prince and princess are bound to marry and live happily
ever afterwards, or the whole story is unnecessary and absurd; and the villains and the goblins must naturally repent
and be forgiven. But it is clear that such happy endings,
such conventional closes to fantastic tales, cannot be taken
as evidences of serene tranquillity on the part of their maker;
they merely show that he knew, as well as anyone else, how
such stories ought to end.

Yet there can be no doubt that it is this combination of
charming heroines and happy endings which has blinded the
eyes of modern critics to everything else. Iachimo, and
Leontes, and even Caliban, are to be left out of account, as
if, because in the end they repent or are forgiven, words
need not be wasted on such reconciled and harmonious fiends.
It is true they are grotesque; it is true that such personages
never could have lived; but who, one would like to know,
has ever met Miranda, or become acquainted with Prince
Florizel of Bohemia? In this land of faëry, is it right to
neglect the goblins? In this world of dreams, are we justified in ignoring the nightmares? Is it fair to say that Shake-

speare was in a " gentle, lofty spirit, a peaceful, tranquil mood," when he was creating the Queen in *Cymbeline,* or writing the first two acts of *The Winter's Tale?*

Attention has never been sufficiently drawn to one other characteristic of these plays, though it is touched upon both by Professor Dowden and Dr. Brandes—the singular carelessness with which great parts of them were obviously written. Could anything drag more wretchedly than the *dénouement* of *Cymbeline?* And with what perversity is the great pastoral scene in *The Winter's Tale* interspersed with long-winded intrigues, and disguises, and homilies? For these blemishes are unlike the blemishes which enrich rather than lessen the beauty of the earlier plays; they are not, like them, interesting or delightful in themselves; they are usually merely necessary to explain the action, and they are sometimes purely irrelevant. One is, it cannot be denied, often bored, and occasionally irritated, by Polixenes and Camillo and Sebastian and Gonzalo and Belarius; these personages have not even the life of ghosts; they are hardly more than speaking names, that give patient utterance to involution upon involution. What a contrast to the minor characters of Shakespeare's earlier works!

It is difficult to resist the conclusion that he was getting bored himself. Bored with people, bored with real life, bored with drama, bored, in fact, with everything except poetry and poetical dreams. He is no longer interested, one often feels, in what happens, or who says what, so long as he can find place for a faultless lyric, or a new, unimagined rhythmical effect, or a grand and mystic speech. In this mood he must have written his share in the *Two Noble*

Kinsmen, leaving the plot and characters to Fletcher to deal with as he pleased, and reserving to himself only the opportunities for pompous verse. In this mood he must have broken off half-way through the tedious history of *Henry VIII.;* and in this mood he must have completed, with all the resources of his rhetoric, the miserable archaic fragment of *Pericles.*

Is it not thus, then, that we should imagine him in the last years of his life? Half-enchanted by visions of beauty and loveliness, and half-bored to death; on the one side inspired by a soaring fancy to the singing of ethereal songs, and on the other urged by a general disgust to burst occasionally through his torpor into bitter and violent speech? If we are to learn anything of his mind from his last works, it is surely this.

And such is the conclusion which is particularly forced upon us by a consideration of the play which is in many ways most typical of Shakespeare's later work, and the one which critics most consistently point to as containing the very essence of his final benignity—*The Tempest.* There can be no doubt that the peculiar characteristics which distinguish *Cymbeline* and *The Winter's Tale* from the dramas of Shakespeare's prime, are present here in a still greater degree. In *The Tempest,* unreality has reached its apotheosis. Two of the principal characters are frankly not human beings at all; and the whole action passes, through a series of impossible occurrences, in a place which can only by courtesy be said to exist. The Enchanted Island, indeed, peopled, for a timeless moment, by this strange fantastic medley of persons and of things, has been cut adrift for ever from common sense, and floats, buoyed up by a sea, not of waters, but of poetry. Never did Shakespeare's magnificence of diction reach more marvellous heights than in some of the speeches of Prospero, or his lyric art a purer beauty than in the songs of Ariel; nor is it only in these ethereal regions that the triumph of his language asserts itself. It finds as splendid a vent in the curses of Caliban:

> All the infection that the sun sucks up
> From bogs, fens, flats, on Prosper fall, and make him
> By inch-meal a disease!

and in the similes of Trinculo:

Yond' same black cloud, yond' huge one, looks like a foul bombard that would shed his liquor.

The *dénouement* itself, brought about by a preposterous piece of machinery, and lost in a whirl of rhetoric, is hardly more than a peg for fine writing.

> O, it is monstrous, monstrous!
> Methought the billows spoke and told me of it;
> The winds did sing it to me; and the thunder,
> That deep and dreadful organ-pipe, pronounced
> The name of Prosper; it did bass my trespass.
> Therefore my son i' th' ooze is bedded, and
> I'll seek him deeper than e'er plummet sounded,
> And with him there lie mudded.

And this gorgeous phantasm of a repentance from the mouth of the pale phantom Alonzo is a fitting climax to the whole fantastic play.

A comparison naturally suggests itself, between what was

perhaps the last of Shakespeare's completed works, and that early drama which first gave undoubted proof that his imagination had taken wings. The points of resemblance between *The Tempest* and *A Mid-summer Night's Dream*, their common atmosphere of romance and magic, the beautiful absurdities of their intrigues, their studied contrasts of the grotesque with the delicate, the ethereal with the earthy, the charm of their lyrics, the *verve* of their vulgar comedy—these, of course, are obvious enough; but it is the points of difference which really make the comparison striking. One thing, at any rate, is certain about the wood near Athens—it is full of life. The persons that haunt it—though most of them are hardly more than children, and some of them are fairies, and all of them are too agreeable to be true—are nevertheless substantial creatures, whose loves and jokes and quarrels receive our thorough sympathy; and the air they breathe—the lords and the ladies, no less than the mechanics and the elves—is instinct with an exquisite good-humour, which makes us as happy as the night is long. To turn from Theseus and Titania and Bottom to the Enchanted Island, is to step out of a country lane into a conservatory. The roses and the dandelions have vanished before preposterous cactuses, and fascinating orchids too delicate for the open air; and, in the artificial atmosphere, the gaiety of youth has been replaced by the disillusionment of middle age. Prospero is the central figure of *The Tempest;* and it has often been wildly asserted that he is a portrait of the author—an embodiment of that spirit of wise benevolence which is supposed to have thrown a halo over Shakespeare's later life. But, on closer inspection, the portrait seems to be as imaginary as the original. To an irreverent eye, the ex-Duke of Milan would perhaps appear as an unpleasantly crusty personage, in whom a twelve years' monopoly of the conversation had developed an inordinate propensity for talking. These may have been the sentiments of Ariel, safe at the Bermoothes; but to state them is to risk at least ten years in the knotty entrails of an oak, and it is sufficient to point out, that if Prospero is wise, he is also self-opinionated and sour, that his gravity is often another name for pedantic severity, and that there is no character in the play to whom, during some part of it, he is not studiously disagreeable. But his Milanese country-men are not even disagreeable; they are simply dull. " This is the silliest stuff that e'er I heard," remarked Hippolyta of Bottom's amateur theatricals; and one is tempted to wonder what she would have said to the dreary puns and interminable conspiracies of Alonzo, and Gonzalo, and Sebastian, and Antonio, and Adrian, and Francisco, and other ship-wrecked noblemen. At all events, there can be little doubt that they would not have had the entrée at Athens.

The depth of the gulf between the two plays is, however, best measured by a comparison of Caliban and his masters with Bottom and his companions. The guileless group of English mechanics, whose sports are interrupted by the mis-chief of Puck, offers a strange contrast to the hideous trio of the " jester," the " drunken butler," and the " savage and deformed slave," whose designs are thwarted by the magic of Ariel. Bottom was the first of Shakespeare's masterpieces in characterisation, Caliban was the last: and what a world of bitterness and horror lies between them! The charming coxcomb it is easy to know and love; but the " freckled whelp hag-born " moves us mysteriously to pity and to terror, eluding us for ever in fearful allegories, and strange coils of disgusted laughter and phantasmagorical tears. The physical vigour of the presentment is often so remorseless as to shock us. " I left them," says Ariel, speaking of Caliban and his crew:

> I' the filthy-mantled pool beyond your cell,
> There dancing up to the chins, that the foul lake
> O'erstunk their feet.

But at other times the great half-human shapes seems to swell, like the " Pan " of Victor Hugo, into something un-imaginably vast.

> You taught me language, and my profit on't
> Is, I know how to curse.

Is this Caliban addressing Prospero, or Job addressing God? It may be either; but it is not serene, nor benign, nor pastoral, nor " On the Heights."

1906.

THE LIVES OF THE POETS

THE LIVES OF THE POETS[1]

No one needs an excuse for re-opening the *Lives of the Poets;*
the book is too delightful. It is not, of course, as delightful
as Boswell; but who re-opens Boswell? Boswell is in another category; because, as every one knows, when he has
once been opened he can never be shut. But, on its different
level, the *Lives* will always hold a firm and comfortable
place in our affections. After Boswell, it is the book which
brings us nearer than any other to the mind of Dr. Johnson.
That is its primary import. We do not go to it for information or for instruction, or that our tastes may be improved,
or that our sympathies may be widened; we go to it to
see what Dr. Johnson thought. Doubtless, during the
process, we are informed and instructed and improved in
various ways; but these benefits are incidental, like the
invigoration which comes from a mountain walk. It is not
for the sake of the exercise that we set out; but for the
sake of the view. The view from the mountain which is
Samuel Johnson is so familiar, and has been so constantly
analysed and admired, that further description would be
superfluous. It is sufficient for us to recognise that he is
a mountain, and to pay all the reverence that is due. In

[1] *Lives of the English Poets.* By Samuel Johnson, LL.D. Edited
by George Birkbeck Hill, D.C.L. Oxford: at the Clarendon Press,
1905.

one of Emerson's poems a mountain and a squirrel begin to discuss each other's merits; and the squirrel comes to the triumphant conclusion that he is very much the better of the two, since he can crack a nut, while the mountain can do no such thing. The parallel is close enough between this impudence and the attitude—implied, if not expressed —of too much modern criticism towards the sort of qualities —the easy, indolent power, the searching sense of actuality, the combined command of sanity and paradox, the immovable independence of thought—which went to the making of the *Lives of the Poets*. There is only, perhaps, one flaw in the analogy: that, in this particular instance, the mountain was able to crack nuts a great deal better than any squirrel that ever lived.

That the *Lives* continue to be read, admired, and edited, is in itself a high proof of the eminence of Johnson's intellect; because, as serious criticism, they can hardly appear to the modern reader to be very far removed from the futile. Johnson's æsthetic judgments are almost invariably subtle, or solid, or bold; they have always some good quality to recommend them—except one: they are never right. That is an unfortunate deficiency; but no one can doubt that Johnson has made up for it, and that his wit has saved all. He has managed to be wrong so cleverly, that nobody minds. When Gray, for instance, points the moral to his poem on Walpole's cat with a reminder to the fair that all that glisters is not gold, Johnson remarks that this is " of no relation to the purpose; if *what glistered* had been *gold,* the cat would not have gone into the water; and, if she had, would not less have been drowned." Could anything be more ingenious, or more neatly put, or more obviously true? But then, to use Johnson's own phrase, could anything be of less " relation to the purpose "? It is his wit—and we are speaking, of course, of wit in its widest sense—that has sanctified Johnson's perversities and errors, that has embalmed them for ever, and that has put his book, with all its mass of antiquated doctrine, beyond the reach of time.

For it is not only in particular details that Johnson's criticism fails to convince us; his entire point of view is patently out of date. Our judgments differ from his, not only because our tastes are different, but because our whole method of judging has changed. Thus, to the historian of letters, the *Lives* have a special interest, for they afford a standing example of a great dead tradition—a tradition whose characteristics throw more than one curious light upon the literary feelings and ways which have become habitual to ourselves. Perhaps the most striking difference between the critical methods of the eighteenth century and those of the present day, is the difference in sympathy. The most cursory glance at Johnson's book is enough to show that he judged authors as if they were criminals in the dock, answerable for every infraction of the rules and regulations laid down by the laws of art, which it was his business to administer without fear or favour. Johnson never inquired what poets were trying to do; he merely aimed at discovering whether what they had done complied with the canons of poetry. Such a system of criticism was clearly unexceptionable, upon one condition—that the critic was quite certain what the canons of poetry were; but the moment that

it became obvious that the only way of arriving at a conclusion upon the subject was by consulting the poets themselves, the whole situation completely changed. The judge
had to bow to the prisoner's ruling. In other words, the
critic discovered that his first duty was, not to criticise, but
to understand the object of his criticism. That is the essential distinction between the school of Johnson and the school
of Sainte-Beuve. No one can doubt the greater width and
profundity of the modern method; but it is not without
its drawbacks. An excessive sympathy with one's author
brings its own set of errors: the critic is so happy to explain
everything, to show how this was the product of the age,
how that was the product of environment, and how the
other was the inevitable result of inborn qualities and tastes
—that he sometimes forgets to mention whether the work
in question has any value. It is then that one cannot help
regretting the Johnsonian black cap.

But other defects, besides lack of sympathy, mar the *Lives
of the Poets*. One cannot help feeling that no matter how
anxious Johnson might have been to enter into the spirit
of some of the greatest of the masters with whom he was
concerned, he never could have succeeded. Whatever critical
method he might have adopted, he still would have been
unable to appreciate certain literary qualities, which, to our
minds at any rate, appear to be the most important of all.
His opinion of *Lycidas* is well known: he found that poem
" easy, vulgar, and therefore disgusting." Of the songs
in *Comus* he remarks: " they are harsh in their diction, and
not very musical in their numbers." He could see nothing
in the splendour and elevation of Gray, but " glittering ac-

cumulations of ungraceful ornaments." The passionate
intensity of Donne escaped him altogether; he could only
wonder how so ingenious a writer could be so absurd. Such
preposterous judgments can only be accounted for by inherent deficiencies of taste; Johnson had no ear, and he
had no imagination. These are, indeed, grievous disabilities
in a critic. What could have induced such a man, the impatient reader is sometimes tempted to ask, to set himself
up as a judge of poetry?

The answer to the question is to be found in the remarkable change which has come over our entire conception of
poetry, since the time when Johnson wrote. It has often
been stated that the essential characteristic of that great
Romantic Movement which began at the end of the
eighteenth century, was the re-introduction of Nature into
the domain of poetry. Incidentally, it is curious to observe
that nearly every literary revolution has been hailed by its
supporters as a return to Nature. No less than the school of
Coleridge and Wordsworth, the school of Denham, of
Dryden, and of Pope, proclaimed itself as the champion
of Nature; and there can be little doubt that Donne himself
—the father of all the conceits and elaborations of the
seventeenth century—wrote under the impulse of a Naturalistic reaction against the conventional classicism of the
Renaissance. Precisely the same contradictions took place
in France. Nature was the watchword of Malherbe and
of Boileau; and it was equally the watchword of Victor
Hugo. To judge by the successive proclamations of poets,
the development of literature offers a singular paradox.
The further it goes back, the more sophisticated it becomes;

and it grows more and more natural as it grows distant from the State of Nature. However this may be, it is at least certain that the Romantic revival peculiarly deserves to be called Naturalistic, because it succeeded in bringing into vogue the operations of the external world—" the Vegetable Universe," as Blake called it—as subject-matter for poetry. But it would have done very little, if it had done nothing more than this. Thomson, in the full meridian of the eighteenth century, wrote poems upon the subject of Nature; but it would be foolish to suppose that Wordsworth and Coleridge merely carried on a fashion which Thomson had begun. Nature, with them, was something more than a peg for descriptive and didactic verse; it was the manifestation of the vast and mysterious forces of the world. The publication of *The Ancient Mariner* is a landmark in the history of letters, not because of its descriptions of natural objects, but because it swept into the poet's vision a whole new universe of infinite and eternal things; it was the discovery of the Unknown. We are still under the spell of *The Ancient Mariner;* and poetry to us means, primarily, something which suggests, by means of words, mysteries and infinitudes. Thus, music and imagination seem to us the most essential qualities of poetry, because they are the most potent means by which such suggestions may be invoked. But the eighteenth century knew none of these things. To Lord Chesterfield and to Pope, to Prior and to Horace Walpole, there was nothing at all strange about the world; it was charming, it was disgusting, it was ridiculous, and it was just what one might have expected. In such a world, why should poetry, more than anything else, be mysterious? No! Let it be sensible; that was enough.

The new edition of the *Lives,* which Dr. Birkbeck Hill prepared for publication before his death, and which has been issued by the Clarendon Press, with a brief Memoir of the editor, would probably have astonished Dr. Johnson. But, though the elaborate erudition of the notes and appendices might have surprised him, it would not have put him to shame. One can imagine his growling scorn of the scientific conscientiousness of the present day. And indeed, the three tomes of Dr. Hill's edition, with all their solid wealth of information, their voluminous scholarship, their accumulation of vast research, are a little ponderous and a little ugly; the hand is soon wearied with the weight, and the eye is soon distracted by the varying types, and the compressed columns of the notes, and the paragraphic numerals in the margins. This is the price that must be paid for increased efficiency. The wise reader will divide his attention between the new business-like edition and one of the charming old ones, in four comfortable volumes, where the text is supreme upon the page, and the paragraphs follow one another at leisurely intervals. The type may be a little faded, and the paper a little yellow; but what of that? It is all quiet and easy; and, as one reads, the brilliant sentences seem to come to one, out of the Past, with the intimacy of a conversation.

1906.

MADAME DU DEFFAND

MADAME DU DEFFAND

MADAME DU DEFFAND [1]

WHEN Napoleon was starting for his campaign in Russia, he ordered the proof-sheets of a forthcoming book about which there had been some disagreement among the censors of the press, to be put into his carriage, so that he might decide for himself what suppressions it might be necessary to make. " Je m'ennuie en route; je lirai ces volumes, et j'écrirai de Mayence ce qu'il y aura à faire." The volumes thus chosen to beguile the imperial leisure between Paris and Mayence contained the famous correspondence of Madame du Deffand with Horace Walpole. By the Emperor's command a few excisions were made, and the book—reprinted from Miss Berry's original edition which had appeared two years earlier in England—was published almost at once. The sensation in Paris was immense; the excitement of the Russian campaign itself was half-forgotten; and for some time the blind old inhabitant of the Convent of Saint Joseph held her own as a subject of conversation with the burning of Moscow and the passage of the Berezina. We cannot wonder that this was so. In the Parisian

[1] *Lettres de la Marquise du Deffand à Horace Walpole* (1766-80). Premièr Edition complète, augmentée d'environ 500 Lettres inédites, publiées, d'après les originaux, avec une introduction, des notes, et une table des noms, par Mrs. Paget Toynbee. 3 vols. Methuen, 1912.

drawing-room of those days the letters of Madame du Deffand must have exercised a double fascination—on the one hand as a mine of gossip about numberless persons and events still familiar to many a living memory, and, on the other, as a detailed and brilliant record of a state of society which had already ceased to be actual and become historical. The letters were hardly more than thirty years old; but the world which they depicted in all its intensity and all its singularity—the world of the old régime—had vanished for ever into limbo. Between it and the eager readers of the First Empire a gulf was fixed—a narrow gulf, but a deep one, still hot and sulphurous with the volcanic fires of the Revolution. Since then a century has passed; the gulf has widened; and the vision which these curious letters show us to-day seems hardly less remote—from some points of view, indeed, even more—than that which is revealed to us in the Memoirs of Cellini or the correspondence of Cicero. Yet the vision is not simply one of a strange and dead antiquity: there is a personal and human element in the letters which gives them a more poignant interest, and brings them close to ourselves. The soul of man is not subject to the rumour of periods; and these pages, impregnated though they be with the abolished life of the eighteenth century, can never be out of date.

A fortunate chance enables us now, for the first time, to appreciate them in their completeness. The late Mrs. Paget Toynbee, while preparing her edition of Horace Walpole's letters, came upon the trace of the original manuscripts, which had long laid hidden in obscurity in a country house in Staffordshire. The publication of these manuscripts in full, accompanied by notes and indexes in which Mrs. Toynbee's well-known accuracy, industry and tact are everywhere conspicuous, is an event of no small importance to lovers of French literature. A great mass of new and deeply interesting material makes its appearance. The original edition produced by Miss Berry in 1810, from which all the subsequent editions were reprinted with varying degrees of inaccuracy, turns out to have contained nothing more than a comparatively small fraction of the whole correspondence; of the 838 letters published by Mrs. Toynbee, 485 are entirely new, and of the rest only 52 were printed by Miss Berry in their entirety. Miss Berry's edition was, in fact, simply a selection, and as a selection it deserves nothing but praise. It skims the cream of the correspondence; and it faithfully preserves the main outline of the story which the letters reveal. No doubt that was enough for the readers of that generation; indeed, even for the more exacting reader of to-day, there is something a little overwhelming in the closely packed 2,000 pages of Mrs. Toynbee's volumes. Enthusiasm alone will undertake to grapple with them, but enthusiasm will be rewarded. In place of the truthful summary of the earlier editions, we have now the truth itself—the truth in all its subtle gradations, all its long-drawn-out suspensions, all its intangible and irremediable obscurities: it is the difference between a clear-cut drawing in black-and-white and a finished painting in oils. Probably Miss Berry's edition will still be preferred by the ordinary reader who wishes to become acquainted with a celebrated figure in French literature; but Mrs. Toynbee's will always be indispensable for the historical student, and

invaluable for any one with the leisure, the patience, and
the taste for a detailed and elaborate examination of a
singular adventure of the heart.

The Marquise du Deffand was perhaps the most typical
representative of that phase of civilisation which came into
existence in Western Europe during the early years of the
eighteenth century, and reached its most concentrated and
characteristic form about the year 1750 in the drawing-
rooms of Paris. She was supremely a woman of her age;
but it is important to notice that her age was the first, and
not the second, half of the eighteenth century: it was the
age of the Regent Orleans, Fontenelle, and the young Voltaire; not that of Rousseau, the *Encyclopædia,* and the
Patriarch of Ferney. It is true that her letters to Walpole,
to which her fame is mainly due, were written between 1766
and 1780; but they are the letters of an old woman, and
they bear upon every page of them the traces of a mind
to which the whole movement of contemporary life was profoundly distasteful. The new forces to which the eighteenth
century gave birth in thought, in art, in sentiment, in action
—which for us form its peculiar interest and its peculiar
glory—were anathema to Madame du Deffand. In her letters to Walpole, whenever she compares the present with the
past her bitterness becomes extreme. " J'ai eu autrefois,"
she writes in 1778, " des plaisirs indicibles aux opéras de
Quinault et de Lulli, et au jeu de Thévenart et de la Lemaur.
Pour aujourd'hui, tout me paraît détestable: acteurs,
auteurs, musiciens, beaux esprits, philosophes, tout est de
mauvais goût, tout est affreux, affreux." That great movement towards intellectual and political emancipation which

centred in the *Encyclopædia* and the *Philosophes* was the object of her particular detestation. She saw Diderot once—and that was enough for both of them. She could never understand why it was that M. de Voltaire would persist in wasting his talent for writing over such a dreary subject as religion. Turgot, she confessed, was an honest man, but he was also a " sot animal." His dismissal from office—that fatal act, which made the French Revolution inevitable—delighted her: she concealed her feelings from Walpole, who admired him, but she was outspoken enough to the Duchesse de Choiseul. " Le renvoi du Turgot me plaît extrêmement," she wrote; " tout me paraît en bon train." And then she added, more prophetically than she knew, " Mais, assurément, nous n'en resterons pas là." No doubt her dislike of the Encyclopædists and all their works was in part a matter of personal pique—the result of her famous quarrel with Mademoiselle de Lespinasse, under whose opposing banner d'Alembert and all the intellectual leaders of Parisian society had unhesitatingly ranged themselves. But that quarrel was itself far more a symptom of a deeply rooted spiritual antipathy than a mere vulgar struggle for influence between two rival *salonnières*. There are indications that, even before it took place, the elder woman's friendship for d'Alembert was giving way under the strain of her scorn for his advanced views and her hatred of his proselytising cast of mind. " Il y a de certains articles," she complained to Voltaire in 1763—a year before the final estrangement—" qui sont devenus pour lui affaires de parti, et sur lesquels je ne lui trouve pas le sens commun." The truth is that d'Alembert and his friends were moving,

and Madame du Deffand was standing still. Mademoiselle
de Lespinasse simply precipitated and intensified an inevitable rupture. She was the younger generation knocking at
the door.

Madame du Deffand's generation had, indeed, very little
in common with that ardent, hopeful, speculative, sentimental group of friends who met together every evening
in the drawing-room of Mademoiselle de Lespinasse. Born
at the close of the seventeenth century, she had come into
the world in the brilliant days of the Regent, whose witty
and licentious reign had suddenly dissipated the atmosphere
of gloom and bigotry imposed upon society by the moribund
Court of Louis XIV. For a fortnight (so she confessed to
Walpole) she was actually the Regent's mistress; and a
fortnight, in those days, was a considerable time. Then
she became the intimate friend of Madame de Prie—the
singular woman who, for a moment, on the Regent's death,
during the government of M. le Duc, controlled the destinies of France, and who committed suicide when that
amusement was denied her. During her early middle age
Madame du Deffand was one of the principal figures in the
palace of Sceaux, where the Duchesse du Maine, the grand-
daughter of the great Condé and the daughter-in-law of
Louis XIV., kept up for many years an almost royal state
among the most distinguished men and women of the time.
It was at Sceaux, with its endless succession of entertain-
ments and conversations—supper-parties and water-parties,
concerts and masked balls, plays in the little theatre and
picnics under the great trees of the park—that Madame du
Deffand came to her maturity and established her position

as one of the leaders of the society in which she moved.
The nature of that society is plainly enough revealed in the
letters and the memoirs that have come down to us. The
days of formal pomp and vast representation had ended for
ever when the " Grand Monarque " was no longer to be seen
strutting, in periwig and red-heeled shoes, down the glittering gallery of Versailles; the intimacy and seclusion of modern life had not yet begun. It was an intermediate period,
and the comparatively small group formed by the élite
of the rich, refined, and intelligent classes led an existence
in which the elements of publicity and privacy were curiously combined. Never, certainly, before or since, have any
set of persons lived so absolutely and unreservedly with and
for their friends as these high ladies and gentlemen of the
middle years of the eighteenth century. The circle of one's
friends was, in those days, the framework of one's whole
being; within which was to be found all that life had to
offer, and outside of which no interest, however fruitful,
no passion, however profound, no art, however soaring, was
of the slightest account. Thus while in one sense the ideal
of such a society was an eminently selfish one, it is none
the less true that there have been very few societies indeed
in which the ordinary forms of personal selfishness have
played so small a part. The selfishness of the eighteenth
century was a communal selfishness. Each individual was
expected to practise, and did in fact practise to a consummate degree, those difficult arts which make the wheels of
human intercourse run smoothly—the arts of tact and temper, of frankness and sympathy, of delicate compliment and
exquisite self-abnegation—with the result that a condition

of living was produced which, in all its superficial and obvious qualities, was one of unparalleled amenity. Indeed, those persons who were privileged to enjoy it showed their appreciation of it in an unequivocal way—by the tenacity with which they clung to the scene of such delights and graces. They refused to grow old; they almost refused to die. Time himself seems to have joined their circle, to have been infected with their politeness, and to have absolved them, to the furthest possible point, from the operation of his laws. Voltaire, d'Argental, Moncrif, Hénault, Madame d'Egmont, Madame du Deffand herself—all were born within a few years of each other, and all lived to be well over eighty, with the full zest of their activities unimpaired. Pont-de-Veyle, it is true, died young—at the age of seventy-seven. Another contemporary, Richelieu, who was famous for his adventures while Louis XIV. was still on the throne, lived till within a year of the opening of the States-General. More typical still of this singular and fortunate generation was Fontenelle, who, one morning in his hundredth year, quietly observed that he felt a difficulty in existing, and forthwith, even more quietly, ceased to do so.

Yet, though the wheels of life rolled round with such an alluring smoothness, they did not roll of themselves; the skill and care of trained mechanicians were needed to keep them going; and the task was no light one. Even Fontenelle himself, fitted as he was for it by being blessed (as one of his friends observed) with two brains and no heart, realised to the full the hard conditions of social happiness. " Il y a peu de choses," he wrote, " aussi difficiles et aussi dangereuses que le commerce des hommes." The sentence, true

for all ages, was particularly true for his own. The graceful, easy motions of that gay company were those of dancers
balanced on skates, gliding, twirling, interlacing, over the
thinnest ice. Those drawing-rooms, those little circles, so
charming with the familiarity of their privacy, were themselves the rigorous abodes of the deadliest kind of public
opinion—the kind that lives and glitters in a score of penetrating eyes. They required in their votaries the absolute
submission that reigns in religious orders—the willing sacrifice of the entire life. The intimacy of personal passion,
the intensity of high endeavour—these things must be left
behind and utterly cast away by all who would enter that
narrow sanctuary. Friendship might be allowed there, and
flirtation disguised as love; but the overweening and devour-
ing influence of love itself should never be admitted to destroy the calm of daily intercourse and absorb into a single
channel attentions due to all. Politics were to be tolerated,
so long as they remained a game; so soon as they grew
serious and envisaged the public good, they became insufferable. As for literature and art, though they might be excellent as subjects for recreation and good talk, what could
be more preposterous than to treat such trifles as if they
had a value of their own? Only one thing; and that was
to indulge, in the day-dreams of religion or philosophy, the
inward ardours of the soul. Indeed, the scepticism of that
generation was the most uncompromising that the world
has known; for it did not even trouble to deny: it simply
ignored. It presented a blank wall of perfect indifference
alike to the mysteries of the universe and to the solutions
of them. Madame du Deffand gave early proof that she

shared to the full this propensity of her age. While still
a young girl in a convent school, she had shrugged her
shoulders when the nuns began to instruct her in the articles
of their faith. The matter was considered serious, and the
great Massillon, then at the height of his fame as a preacher
and a healer of souls, was sent for to deal with the youthful
heretic. She was not impressed by his arguments. In his
person the generous fervour and the massive piety of an
age that could still believe felt the icy and disintegrating
touch of a new and strange indifference. " Mais qu'elle est
jolie! " he murmured as he came away. The Abbess ran
forward to ask what holy books he recommended. " Give
her a threepenny *Catechism*," was Massillon's reply. He
had seen that the case was hopeless.

An innate scepticism, a profound levity, an antipathy to
enthusiasm that wavered between laughter and disgust, combined with an unswerving devotion to the exacting and
arduous ideals of social intercourse—such were the characteristics of the brilliant group of men and women who had
spent their youth at the Court of the Regent, and dallied
out their middle age down the long avenues of Sceaux.
About the middle of the century the Duchesse du Maine
died, and Madame du Deffand established herself in Paris
at the Convent of Saint Joseph in a set of rooms which
still showed traces—in the emblazoned arms over the great
mantelpiece—of the occupation of Madame de Montespan.
A few years later a physical affliction overtook her: at the
age of fifty-seven she became totally blind; and this misfortune placed her, almost without a transition, among the
ranks of the old. For the rest of her life she hardly moved

from her drawing-room, which speedily became the most celebrated in Europe. The thirty years of her reign there fall into two distinct and almost equal parts. The first, during which d'Alembert was pre-eminent, came to an end with the violent expulsion of Mademoiselle de Lespinasse. During the second, which lasted for the rest of her life, her salon, purged of the Encyclopædists, took on a more decidedly worldly tone; and the influence of Horace Walpole was supreme.

It is this final period of Madame du Deffand's life that is reflected so minutely in the famous correspondence which the labours of Mrs. Toynbee have now presented to us for the first time in its entirety. Her letters to Walpole form in effect a continuous journal covering the space of fifteen years (1766-1780). They allow us, on the one hand, to trace through all its developments the progress of an extraordinary passion, and on the other to examine, as it were under the microscope of perhaps the bitterest perspicacity on record, the last phase of a doomed society. For the circle which came together in her drawing-room during those years had the hand of death upon it. The future lay elsewhere; it was simply the past that survived there— in the rich trappings of fashion and wit and elaborate gaiety —but still irrevocably the past. The radiant creatures of Sceaux had fallen into the yellow leaf. We see them in these letters, a collection of elderly persons trying hard to amuse themselves, and not succeeding very well. Pont-de-Veyle, the youthful septuagenarian, did perhaps succeed; for he never noticed what a bore he was becoming with his perpetual cough, and continued to go the rounds with inde-

fatigable animation, until one day his cough was heard no
more. Hénault—once notorious for his dinner-parties, and
for having written an historical treatise—which, it is true,
was worthless, but he had written it—Hénault was beginning to dodder, and Voltaire, grinning in Ferney, had already
dubbed him " notre délabré Président."   Various dowagers
were engaged upon various vanities.   The Marquise de
Boufflers was gambling herself to ruin; the Comtesse de
Boufflers was wringing out the last drops of her reputation
as the mistress of a Royal Prince; the Maréchale de Mirepoix
was involved in shady politics; the Maréchale de Luxembourg was obliterating a highly dubious past by a scrupulous
attention to " bon ton," of which, at last, she became the
arbitress: " Quel ton!   Quel effroyable ton! " she is said
to have exclaimed after a shuddering glance at the Bible;
" ah, Madame, quel dommage que le Saint Esprit eût aussi
peu de goût! "   Then there was the floating company of
foreign diplomats, some of whom were invariably to be
found at Madame du Deffand's: Caraccioli, for instance, the
Neapolitan Ambassador—" je perds les trois quarts de ce
qu'il dit," she wrote, " mais comme il en dit beaucoup, on
peut supporter cette perte "; and Bernstorff, the Danish
envoy, who became the fashion, was lauded to the skies for
his wit and fine manners, until, says the malicious lady,
" à travers tous ces éloges, je m'avisai de l'appeler Puffendorf," and Puffendorf the poor man remained for evermore.
Besides the diplomats, nearly every foreign traveller of
distinction found his way to the renowned *salon;* Englishmen were particularly frequent visitors; and among the
familiar figures of whom we catch more than one glimpse

in the letters to Walpole are Burke, Fox and Gibbon. Sometimes influential parents in England obtained leave for their
young sons to be admitted into the centre of Parisian refinement. The English cub, fresh from Eton, was introduced
by his tutor into the red and yellow drawing-room, where
the great circle of a dozen or more elderly important persons, glittering in jewels and orders, pompous in powder
and rouge, ranged in rigid order round the fireplace, followed with the precision of a perfect orchestra the leading
word or smile or nod of an ancient Sybil, who seemed to
survey the company with her eyes shut, from a vast chair
by the wall. It is easy to imagine the scene, in all its terrify-
ing politeness. Madame du Deffand could not tolerate young
people; she declared that she did not know what to say to
them; and they, no doubt, were in precisely the same difficulty. To an English youth, unfamiliar with the language
and shy as only English youths can be, a conversation with
that redoubtable old lady must have been a grim ordeal
indeed. One can almost hear the stumbling, pointless observations, almost see the imploring looks cast, from among
the infinitely attentive company, towards the tutor, and
the pink ears growing still more pink.

But such awkward moments were rare. As a rule the
days flowed on in easy monotony—or rather, not the days,
but the nights. For Madame du Deffand rarely rose till
five o'clock in the evening; at six she began her reception;
and at nine or half-past the central moment of the twenty-
four hours arrived—the moment of supper. Upon this event
the whole of her existence hinged. Supper, she used to
say, was one of the four ends of man, and what the other

three were she could never remember. She lived up to her dictum. She had an income of £1400 a year, and of this she spent more than half—£720—on food. These figures should be largely increased to give them their modern values; but, economise as she might, she found that she could only just manage to rub along. Her parties varied considerably in size; sometimes only four or five persons sat down to supper—sometimes twenty or thirty. No doubt they were elaborate meals. In a moment of economy we find the hospitable lady making pious resolutions: she would no longer give " des repas "—only ordinary suppers for six people at the most, at which there should be served nothing more than two entrées, one roast, two sweets, and—mysterious addition—" la pièce du milieu." This was certainly moderate for those days (Monsieur de Jonsac rarely provided fewer than fourteen entrées), but such resolutions did not last long. A week later she would suddenly begin to issue invitations wildly, and, day after day, her tables would be loaded with provisions for thirty guests. But she did not always have supper at home. From time to time she sallied forth in her vast coach and rattled through the streets of Paris to one of her still extant dowagers—a Maréchale, or a Duchesse—or the more and more " délabré Président." There the same company awaited her as that which met in her own house; it was simply a change of decorations; often enough for weeks together she had supper every night with the same half-dozen persons. The entertainment, apart from the supper itself, hardly varied. Occasionally there was a little music, more often there were cards and gambling. Madame du Deffand disliked gam-

bling, but she loathed going to bed, and, if it came to a
choice between the two, she did not hesitate: once, at the
age of seventy-three, she sat up till seven o'clock in the
morning playing vingt-et-un with Charles Fox. But distrac-
tions of that kind were merely incidental to the grand
business of the night—the conversation. In the circle that,
after an eight hours' sitting, broke up reluctantly at two
or three every morning to meet again that same evening
at six, talk continually flowed. For those strange creatures
it seemed to form the very substance of life itself. It was
the underlying essence, the circumambient ether, in which
alone the pulsations of existence had their being; it was the
one eternal reality; men might come and men might go,
but talk went on for ever. It is difficult, especially for
those born under the Saturnine influence of an English sky,
quite to realise the nature of such conversation. Brilliant,
charming, easy-flowing, gay and rapid it must have been;
never profound, never intimate, never thrilling; but also
never emphatic, never affected, never languishing, and never
dull. Madame du Deffand herself had a most vigorous flow
of language. " Ecoutez!   Ecoutez! " Walpole used constantly to exclaim, trying to get in his points; but in vain;
the sparkling cataract swept on unheeding. And indeed
to listen was the wiser part—to drink in deliciously the animation of those quick, illimitable, exquisitely articulated
syllables, to surrender one's whole soul to the pure and
penetrating precision of those phrases, to follow without a
breath the happy swiftness of that fine-spun thread of
thought. Then at moments her wit crystallised; the cataract
threw off a shower of radiant jewels, which one caught as

one might. Some of these have come down to us. Her remark on Montesquieu's great book—" C'est de l'esprit sur les lois "—is an almost final criticism. Her famous " mot de Saint Denis," so dear to the heart of Voltaire, deserves to be once more recorded. A garrulous and credulous Cardinal was describing the martyrdom of Saint Denis the Areopagite: when his head was cut off, he took it up and carried it in his hands. That, said the Cardinal, was well known; what was not well known was the extraordinary fact that he walked with his head under his arm all the way from Montmartre to the Church of Saint Denis—a distance of six miles. " Ah, Monseigneur! " said Madame du Deffand, " dans une telle situation, il n'y a que le premier pas qui coûte." At two o'clock the brilliance began to flag; the guests began to go; the dreadful moment was approaching. If Madame de Gramont happened to be there, there was still some hope, for Madame de Gramont abhorred going to bed almost as much as Madame du Deffand. Or there was just a chance that the Duc de Choiseul might come in at the last moment, and stay on for a couple of hours. But at length it was impossible to hesitate any longer; the chariot was at the door. She swept off, but it was still early; it was only half-past three; and the coachman was ordered to drive about the Boulevards for an hour before going home.

It was, after all, only natural that she should put off going to bed, for she rarely slept for more than two or three hours. The greater part of that empty time, during which conversation was impossible, she devoted to her books. But she hardly ever found anything to read that she really enjoyed. Of the two thousand volumes she possessed—all bound alike, and stamped on the back with her device of a cat—she had only read four or five hundred; the rest were impossible. She perpetually complained to Walpole of the extreme dearth of reading matter. In nothing, indeed, is the contrast more marked between that age and ours than in the quantity of books available for the ordinary reader. How the eighteenth century would envy us our innumerable novels, our biographies, our books of travel, all our easy approaches to knowledge and entertainment, our translations, our cheap reprints! In those days, even for a reader of catholic tastes, there was really very little to read. And, of course, Madame du Deffand's tastes were far from catholic—they were fastidious to the last degree. She considered that Racine alone of writers had reached perfection, and that only once—in *Athalie*. Corneille carried her away for moments, but on the whole he was barbarous. She highly admired " quelques certaines de vers de M. de Voltaire." She thought Richardson and Fielding excellent, and she was enraptured by the style—but only by the style —of *Gil Blas*. And that was all. Everything else appeared to her either affected or pedantic or insipid. Walpole recommended to her a History of Malta; she tried it, but she soon gave it up—it mentioned the Crusades. She began Gibbon, but she found him superficial. She tried Buffon, but he was " d'une monotonie insupportable; il sait bien ce qu'il sait, mais il ne s'occupe que des bêtes; il faut l'être un peu soi-même pour se dévouer à une telle occupation." She got hold of the memoirs of Saint-Simon in manuscript, and these amused her enormously; but she was so disgusted by the style that she was very nearly sick. At last, in despair, she embarked on a prose translation of Shakespeare. The result was unexpected; she was positively pleased. *Coriolanus,* it is true, " me semble, sauf votre respect, épouvantable, et n'a pas le sens commun "; and " pour La Tempête, je ne suis pas touchée de ce genre." But she was impressed by *Othello;* she was interested by *Macbeth;* and she admired *Julius Cæsar,* in spite of its bad taste. At *King Lear,* indeed, she had to draw the line. " Ah, mon Dieu! Quelle pièce! Réellement la trouvez-vous belle? Elle me noircit l'âme à un point que je ne puis exprimer; c'est un amas de toutes les horreurs infernales." Her reader was an old soldier from the Invalides, who came round every morning early, and took up his position by her bedside. She lay back among the cushions, listening, for long hours. Was there ever a more incongruous company, a queerer trysting-place, for Goneril and Desdemona, Ariel and Lady Macbeth?

Often, even before the arrival of the old pensioner, she was at work dictating a letter, usually to Horace Walpole, occasionally to Madame de Choiseul or Voltaire. Her letters to Voltaire are enchanting; his replies are no less so; and it is much to be regretted that the whole correspondence has never been collected together in chronological order, and published as a separate book. The slim volume would be, of its kind, quite perfect. There was no love lost between the two old friends; they could not understand each other; Voltaire, alone of his generation, had thrown himself into the very vanguard of thought; to Madame du Deffand progress had no meaning, and thought itself was hardly more

than an unpleasant necessity. She distrusted him profoundly, and he returned the compliment. Yet neither could
do without the other: through her, he kept in touch with
one of the most influential circles in Paris; and even she
could not be insensible to the glory of corresponding with
such a man. Besides, in spite of all their differences, they
admired each other genuinely, and they were held together
by the habit of a long familiarity. The result was a marvellous display of epistolary art. If they had liked each
other any better, they never would have troubled to write so
well. They were on their best behaviour—exquisitely cour-
teous and yet punctiliously at ease, like dancers in a minuet.
His cajoleries are infinite; his deft sentences, mingling flattery with reflection, have almost the quality of a caress.
She replies in the tone of a worshipper, glancing lightly
at a hundred subjects, purring out her " Monsieur de Voltaire," and seeking his advice on literature and life. He
rejoins in that wonderful strain of epicurean stoicism of
which he alone possessed the secret: and so the letters go
on. Sometimes one just catches the glimpse of a claw be-
neath the soft pad, a grimace under the smile of elegance;
and one remembers with a shock that, after all, one is reading the correspondence of a monkey and a cat.

Madame du Deffand's style reflects, perhaps even more
completely than that of Voltaire himself, the common-sense
of the eighteenth century. Its precision is absolute. It is
like a line drawn in one stroke by a master, with the prompt
exactitude of an unerring subtlety. There is no breadth in
it—no sense of colour and the concrete mass of things.
One cannot wonder, as one reads her, that she hardly re-

gretted her blindness. What did she lose by it? Certainly not

> The sweet approach of even or morn,
> Or sight of vernal bloom, or Summer's rose;

for what did she care for such particulars when her eyes were at their clearest? Her perception was intellectual; and to the penetrating glances of her mental vision the objects of the sensual world were mere irrelevance. The kind of writing produced by such a quality of mind may seem thin and barren to those accustomed to the wealth and variety of the Romantic school. Yet it will repay attention. The vocabulary is very small; but every word is the right one; this old lady of high society, who had never given a thought to her style, who wrote—and spelt— by the light of nature, was a past mistress of that most difficult of literary accomplishments—" l'art de dire en un mot tout ce qu'un mot peut dire." The object of all art is to make suggestions. The romantic artist attains that end by using a multitude of different stimuli, by calling up image after image, recollection after recollection, until the reader's mind is filled and held by a vivid and palpable evocation; the classic works by the contrary method of a fine economy, and, ignoring everything but what is essential, trusts, by means of the exact propriety of his presentation, to produce the required effect. Madame du Deffand carries the classical ideal to its furthest point. She never strikes more than once, and she always hits the nail on the head. Such is her skill that she sometimes seems to beat the Romantics even on their own ground: her reticences make a deeper impression than all the dottings of their i's. The following passage from a letter to Walpole is characteristic:

Nous eûmes une musique charmante, une dame qui joue de la harpe à merveille; elle me fit tant de plaisir que j'eus du regret que vous ne l'entendissiez pas; c'est un instrument admirable. Nous eûmes aussi un clavecin, mais quoiqu'il fût touché avec une grande perfection, ce n'est rien en comparaison de la harpe. Je fus fort triste toute la soirée; j'avais appris en partant que Mme. de Luxembourg, qui était allée samedi à Montmorency pour y passer quinze jours, s'était trouvée si mal qu'on avait fait venir Tronchin, et qu'on l'avait ramenée le dimanche à huit heures du soir, qu'on lui croyait de l'eau dans la poitrine. L'ancienneté de la connaissance; une habitude qui a l'air de l'amitié; voir disparaître ceux avec qui l'on vit; un retour sur soi-mêmc; sentir que l'on ne tient à rien, que tout fuit, que tout échappe, qu'on reste seule dans l'univers, et que malgré cela on craint de le quitter, voilà ce qui m'occupa pendant la musique.

Here are no coloured words, no fine phrases—only the most flat and ordinary expressions—" un instrument admirable " —" une grande perfection "—" fort triste." Nothing is described; and yet how much is suggested! The whole scene is conjured up—one does not know how; one's imagination is switched on to the right rails, as it were, by a look, by a gesture, and then left to run of itself. In the simple, faultless rhythm of that closing sentence, the trembling melancholy of the old harp seems to be lingering still.

While the letters to Voltaire show us nothing but the brilliant exterior of Madame du Deffand's mind, those to Walpole reveal the whole state of her soul. The revelation is not a pretty one. Bitterness, discontent, pessimism, cynicism, boredom, regret, despair—these are the feelings that dominate every page. To a superficial observer Madame du Deffand's lot must have seemed peculiarly enviable;

she was well off, she enjoyed the highest consideration, she possessed intellectual talents of the rarest kind which she had every opportunity of displaying, and she was surrounded by a multitude of friends. What more could any one desire? The harsh old woman would have smiled grimly at such a question. " A little appetite," she might have answered. She was like a dyspeptic at a feast; the finer the dishes that were set before her, the greater her distaste; that spiritual gusto which lends a savour to the meanest act of living, and without which all life seems profitless, had gone from her for ever. Yet—and this intensified her wretchedness—though the banquet was loathsome to her, she had not the strength to tear herself away from the table. Once, in a moment of desperation, she had thoughts of retiring to a convent, but she soon realised that such an action was out of the question. Fate had put her into the midst of the world, and there she must remain. " Je ne suis point assez heureuse," she said, " de me passer des choses dont je ne me soucie pas." She was extremely lonely. As fastidious in friendship as in literature, she passed her life among a crowd of persons whom she disliked and despised. " Je ne vois que des sots et des fripons," she said; and she did not know which were the most disgusting. She took a kind of deadly pleasure in analysing " les nuances des sottises " among the people with whom she lived. The varieties were many, from the foolishness of her companion, Mademoiselle Sanadon, who would do nothing but imitate her—" elle fait des définitions," she wails—to that of the lady who hoped to prove her friendship by unending presents of grapes and pears—" comme je n'y tâte pas, cela diminue mes scrupules du peu de goût que j'ai pour elle." Then there were those who were not quite fools but something very near it. " Tous les Matignon sont des sots," said somebody one day to the Regent, " excepté le Marquis de Matignon." " Cela est vrai," the Regent replied, " il n'est pas sot, mais on voit bien qu'il est le fils d'un sot." Madame du Deffand was an expert at tracing such affinities. For instance, there was Necker. It was clear that Necker was not a fool, and yet—what was it? Something was the matter—yes, she had it: he made you feel a fool yourself—" l'on est plus bête avec lui que l'on ne l'est tout seul." As she said of herself: " elle est toujours tentée d'arracher les masques qu'elle rencontre." Those blind, piercing eyes of hers spied out unerringly the weakness or the ill-nature or the absurdity that lurked behind the gravest or the most fascinating exterior; then her fingers began to itch, and she could resist no longer—she gave way to her besetting temptation. It is impossible not to sympathise with Rousseau's remark about her—" J'aimai mieux encore m'exposer au fléau de sa haine qu'à celui de son amitié." There, sitting in her great Diogenes-tub of an armchair—her " tonneau " as she called it—talking, smiling, scattering her bons mots, she went on through the night, in the remorseless secrecy of her heart, tearing off the masks from the faces that surrounded her. Sometimes the world in which she lived displayed itself before her horrified inward vision like some intolerable and meaningless piece of clock-work mechanism:

J'admirais hier au soir la nombreuse compagnie qui était chez moi; hommes et femmes me paraissaient des machines à ressorts, qui allaient, venaient, parlaient, riaient, sans penser, sans réfléchir, sans sentir; chacun jouait son rôle par habitude: Madame la Duchesse d'Aiguillon crevait de rire, Mme. de Forcalquier dédaignait tout, Mme. de la Vallière jabotait sur tout. Les hommes ne jouaient pas de meilleurs rôles, et moi j'étais abîmée dans les reflexions les plus noires; je pensai que j'avais passé ma vie dans les illusions; que je m'étais creusée tous les abîmes dans lesquels j'étais tombée.

At other times she could see around her nothing but a mass of mutual hatreds, into which she was plunged herself no less than her neighbours:

Je ramenai la Maréchale de Mirepoix chez elle; j'y descendis, je causai une heure avec elle; je n'en fus pas mécontente. Elle hait la petite Idole, elle hait la Maréchale de Luxembourg; enfin, sa haine pour tous les gens qui me déplaisent me fit lui pardonner l'indifférence et peut-être la haine qu'elle a pour moi. Convenez que voilà une jolie société, un charmant commerce.

Once or twice for several months together she thought that she had found in the Duchesse de Choiseul a true friend and a perfect companion. But there was one fatal flaw even in Madame de Choiseul: she *was* perfect!—" Elle est parfaite; et c'est un plus grand défaut qu'on ne pense et qu'on ne saurait imaginer." At last one day the inevitable happened —she went to see Madame de Choiseul, and she was bored. " Je rentrai chez moi à une heure, pénétrée, persuadée qu'on ne peut être content de personne."

One person, however, there was who pleased her; and it was the final irony of her fate that this very fact should have been the last drop that caused the cup of her unhappiness to overflow. Horace Walpole had come upon her at a psychological moment. Her quarrel with Mademoiselle de Lespinasse and the Encyclopædists had just occurred; she was within a few years of seventy; and it must have seemed to her that, after such a break, at such an age, there was little left for her to do but to die quietly. Then the gay, talented, fascinating Englishman appeared, and she suddenly found that, so far from her life being over, she was embarked for good and all upon her greatest adventure. What she experienced at that moment was something like a religious conversion. Her past fell away from her a dead thing; she was overwhelmed by an ineffable vision; she, who had wandered for so many years in the ways of worldly indifference, was uplifted all at once on to a strange summit, and pierced with the intensest pangs of an unknown devotion. Henceforward her life was dedicated; but, unlike the happier saints of a holier persuasion, she was to find no peace on earth. It was, indeed, hardly to be expected that Walpole, a blasé bachelor of fifty, should have reciprocated so singular a passion; yet he might at least have treated it with gentleness and respect. The total impression of him which these letters produce is very damaging. It is true that he was in a difficult position; and it is also true that, since only the merest fragments of his side of the correspondence have been preserved, our knowledge of the precise details of his conduct is incomplete; nevertheless, it is clear that, on the whole, throughout the long and painful episode, the principal motive which actuated him was an inexcusable egoism. He was obsessed by a fear of ridicule. He knew that letters were regularly opened at the French Post Office, and he lived in terror lest some spiteful story of his absurd relationship with a blind old woman of seventy should be con-

cocted and set afloat among his friends, or his enemies, in
England which would make him the laughing-stock of society for the rest of his days. He was no less terrified by
the intensity of the sentiment of which he had become the
object. Thoroughly superficial and thoroughly selfish, im-
mersed in his London life of dilettantism and gossip, the
weekly letters from France with their burden of a desperate
affection appalled him and bored him by turns. He did not
know what to do; and his perplexity was increased by the
fact that he really liked Madame du Deffand—so far as he
could like any one—and also by the fact that his vanity
was highly flattered by her letters. Many courses were
open to him, but the one he took was probably the most
cruel that he could have taken: he insisted with an absolute
rigidity on their correspondence being conducted in the tone
of the most ordinary friendship—on those terms alone, he
said, would he consent to continue it. And of course such
terms were impossible to Madame du Deffand. She accepted
them—what else could she do?—but every line she wrote
was a denial of them. Then, periodically, there was an
explosion. Walpole stormed, threatened, declared he would
write no more; and on her side there were abject apologies,
and solemn promises of amendment. Naturally, it was all
in vain. A few months later he would be attacked by a
fit of the gout, her solicitude would be too exaggerated, and
the same fury was repeated, and the same submission. One
wonders what the charm could have been that held that
proud old spirit in such a miserable captivity. Was it his
very coldness that subdued her? If he had cared for her
a little more, perhaps she would have cared for him a good

deal less. But it is clear that what really bound her to him was the fact that they so rarely met. If he had lived in Paris, if he had been a member of her little clique, subject to the unceasing searchlight of her nightly scrutiny, who can doubt that, sooner or later, Walpole too would have felt " le fléau de son amitié "? His mask too would have been torn to tatters like the rest. But, as it was, his absence saved him; her imagination clothed him with an almost mythic excellence; his brilliant letters added to the impression; and then, at intervals of about two years, he appeared in Paris for six weeks—just long enough to rivet her chains, and not long enough to loosen them. And so it was that she fell before him with that absolute and unquestioning devotion of which only the most dominating and fastidious natures are capable. Once or twice, indeed, she did attempt a revolt, but only succeeded in plunging herself into a deeper subjection. After one of his most violent and cruel outbursts, she refused to communicate with him further, and for three or four weeks she kept her word; then she crept back and pleaded for forgiveness. Walpole graciously granted it. It is with some satisfaction that one finds him, a few weeks later, laid up with a peculiarly painful attack of the gout.

About half-way through the correspondence there is an acute crisis, after which the tone of the letters undergoes a marked change. After seven years of struggle, Madame du Deffand's indomitable spirit was broken; henceforward she would hope for nothing; she would gratefully accept the few crumbs that might be thrown her; and for the rest she resigned herself to her fate. Gradually sinking into

extreme old age, her self-repression and her bitterness grew
ever more and more complete. She was always bored; and
her later letters are a series of variations on the perpetual
theme of " ennui." " C'est une maladie de l'âme," she says,
" dont nous afflige la nature en nous donnant l'existence;
c'est le ver solitaire qui absorbe tout." And again, " l'ennui
est l'avant-goût du néant, mais le néant lui est préférable."
Her existence had become a hateful waste—a garden, she
said, from which all the flowers had been uprooted and
which had been sown with salt. "Ah! Je le répète sans
cesse, il n'y a qu'un malheur, celui d'être né." The grass-
hopper had become a burden; and yet death seemed as
little desirable as life. " Comment est-il possible," she asks,
" qu'on craigne la fin d'une vie aussi triste? " When Death
did come at last, he came very gently. She felt his approaches, and dictated a letter to Walpole, bidding him, in
her strange fashion, an infinitely restrained farewell: "Diver-
tissez-vous, mon ami, le plus que vous pourrez; ne vous
affligez point de mon état, nous étions presque perdus l'un
pour l'autre; nous ne nous devions jamais revoir; vous me
regretterez, parce qu'on est bien aise de se savoir aimé."
That was her last word to him. Walpole might have reached
her before she finally lost consciousness, but, though he
realised her condition and knew well enough what his presence would have been to her, he did not trouble to move.
She died as she had lived—her room crowded with ac-
quaintances and the sound of a conversation in her ears.
When one reflects upon her extraordinary tragedy, when one
attempts to gauge the significance of her character and of
her life, it is difficult to know whether to pity most, to ad-

mire, or to fear. Certainly there is something at once pitiable
and magnificent in such an unflinching perception of the
futilities of living, such an uncompromising refusal to be
content with anything save the one thing that it is impossible
to have. But there is something alarming too; was she perhaps right after all?

1913.

VOLTAIRE AND ENGLAND

VOLTAIRE AND ENGLAND [1]

THE visit of Voltaire to England marks a turning-point in the history of civilisation. It was the first step in a long process of interaction—big with momentous consequences—between the French and English cultures. For centuries the combined forces of mutual ignorance and political hostility had kept the two nations apart: Voltaire planted a small seed of friendship which, in spite of a thousand hostile influences, grew and flourished mightily. The seed, no doubt, fell on good ground, and no doubt, if Voltaire had never left his native country, some chance wind would have carried it over the narrow seas, so that history in the main would have been unaltered. But actually his was the hand which did the work.

It is unfortunate that our knowledge of so important a period in Voltaire's life should be extremely incomplete. Carlyle, who gave a hasty glance at it in his life of Frederick, declared that he could find nothing but " mere inanity and darkness visible "; and since Carlyle's day the progress has been small. A short chapter in Desnoiresterres' long Biography and an essay by Churton Collins did something to co-ordinate the few known facts. Another step was taken a few years ago with the publication of M. Lanson's elaborate and exhaustive edition of the *Lettres Philosophiques*, the work in

[1] *Correspondance de Voltaire* (1726-1729). By Lucien Foulet. Paris: Hachette, 1913.

which Voltaire gave to the world the distilled essence of his English experiences. And now M. Lucien Foulet has brought together all the extant letters concerning the period, which he has collated with scrupulous exactitude and to which he has added a series of valuable appendices upon various obscure and disputed points. M. Lanson's great attainments are well known, and to say that M. Foulet's work may fitly rank as a supplementary volume to the edition of the *Lettres Philosophiques* is simply to say that he is a worthy follower of that noble tradition of profound research and perfect lucidity which has made French scholarship one of the glories of European culture.

Upon the events in particular which led up to Voltaire's departure for England, M. Foulet has been able to throw considerable light. The story, as revealed by the letters of contemporary observers and the official documents of the police, is an instructive and curious one. In the early days of January 1726 Voltaire, who was thirty-one years of age, occupied a position which, so far as could be seen upon the surface, could hardly have been more fortunate. He was recognised everywhere as the rising poet of the day; he was a successful dramatist; he was a friend of Madame de Prie, who was all-powerful at Court, and his talents had been rewarded by a pension from the royal purse. His brilliance, his gaiety, his extraordinary capacity for being agreeable had made him the pet of the narrow and aristocratic circle which dominated France. Dropping his middle-class antecedents as completely as he had dropped his middle-class name, young Arouet, the notary's offspring, floated at his ease through the palaces of dukes and princes, with whose

sons he drank and jested, and for whose wives—it was *de
rigueur* in those days—he expressed all the ardours of a passionate and polite devotion. Such was his roseate situation
when, all at once, the catastrophe came. One night at the
Opéra the Chevalier de Rohan-Chabot, of the famous and
powerful family of the Rohans, a man of forty-three, quar-
relsome, blustering, whose reputation for courage left something to be desired, began to taunt the poet upon his birth—
" Monsieur Arouet, Monsieur Voltaire—what *is* your
name? " To which the retort came quickly—" Whatever
my name may be, I know how to preserve the honour of it."
The Chevalier muttered something and went off, but the incident was not ended. Voltaire had let his high spirits and
his sharp tongue carry him too far, and he was to pay the
penalty. It was not an age in which it was safe to be too
witty with lords. " Now mind, Dancourt," said one of those
grands seigneurs to the leading actor of the day, " if you're
more amusing than I am at dinner to-night, *je te donnerai
cent coups de bâtons.*" It was dangerous enough to show
one's wits at all in the company of such privileged persons,
but to do so at their expense—! A few days later Voltaire
and the Chevalier met again, at the Comédie, in Adrienne
Lecouvreur's dressing-room. Rohan repeated his sneering
question, and " the Chevalier has had his answer " was Voltaire's reply. Furious, Rohan lifted his stick, but at that
moment Adrienne very properly fainted, and the company
dispersed. A few days more and Rohan had perfected the
arrangements for his revenge. Voltaire, dining at the Duc
de Sully's, where, we are told, he was on the footing of a son
of the house, received a message that he was wanted outside

in the street. He went out, was seized by a gang of lackeys, and beaten before the eyes of Rohan, who directed operations from a cab. " Epargnez la tête," he shouted, " elle est encore bonne pour faire rire le public "; upon which, according to one account, there were exclamations from the crowd which had gathered round of " Ah! le bon seigneur! " The sequel is known to everyone: how Voltaire rushed back, dishevelled and agonised, into Sully's dining-room, how he poured out his story in an agitated flood of words, and how that high-born company, with whom he had been living up to that moment on terms of the closest intimacy, now only displayed the signs of a frigid indifference. The caste-feeling had suddenly asserted itself. Poets, no doubt, were all very well in their way, but really, if they began squabbling with noblemen, what could they expect? And then the callous and stupid convention of that still half-barbarous age—the convention which made misfortune the proper object of ridicule—came into play no less powerfully. One might take a poet seriously, perhaps—until he was whipped; then, of course, one could only laugh at him. For the next few days, wherever Voltaire went he was received with icy looks, covert smiles, or exaggerated politeness. The Prince de Conti, who, a month or two before, had written an ode in which he placed the author of *Œdipe* side by side with the authors of *Le Cid* and *Phèdre*, now remarked, with a shrug of the shoulders, that " ces coups de batons étaient bien reçus et mal donnés." " Nous serions bien malheureux," said another well-bred personage, as he took a pinch of snuff, " si les poètes n'avaient pas des épaules." Such friends as remained faithful were helpless. Even Madame de Prie could do nothing.

" Le pauvre Voltaire me fait grande pitié," she said; " dans le fond il a raison." But the influence of the Rohan family was too much for her, and she could only advise him to disappear for a little into the country, lest worse should befall. Disappear he did, remaining for the next two months concealed in the outskirts of Paris, where he practised swordsmanship against his next meeting with his enemy. The situation was cynically topsy-turvy. As M. Foulet points out, Rohan had legally rendered himself liable, under the edict against duelling, to a long term of imprisonment, if not to the penalty of death. Yet the law did not move, and Voltaire was left to take the only course open in those days to a man of honour in such circumstances—to avenge the insult by a challenge and a fight. But now the law, which had winked at Rohan, began to act against Voltaire. The police were instructed to arrest him so soon as he should show any sign of an intention to break the peace. One day he suddenly appeared at Versailles, evidently on the lookout for Rohan, and then as suddenly vanished. A few weeks later, the police reported that he was in Paris, lodging with a fencing-master, and making no concealment of his desire to " insulter incessament et avec éclat M. le chevalier de Rohan." This decided the authorities, and accordingly on the night of the 17th of April, as we learn from the *Police Gazette*, " le sieur Arrouët de Voltaire, fameux poète," was arrested, and conducted " par ordre du Roi " to the Bastille.

A letter, written by Voltaire to his friend Madame de Bernières while he was still in hiding, reveals the effect which these events had produced upon his mind. It is the first letter in the series of his collected correspondence which is not all Epicurean elegance and caressing wit. The wit, the elegance, the finely turned phrase, the shifting smile—these things are still visible there no doubt, but they are informed and overmastered by a new, an almost ominous spirit: Voltaire, for the first time in his life, is serious.

J'ai été à l'extrémité; je n'attends que ma convalescence pour abandonner à jamais ce pays-ci. Souvenez-vous de l'amitié tendre que vous avez eue pour moi; au nom de cette amitié informez-moi par un mot de votre main de ce qui se passe, ou parlez à l'homme que je vous envoi, en qui vous pouvez prendre une entière confiance. Présentez mes respects à Madame du Deffand; dites à Thieriot que je veux absolument qu'il m'aime, ou quand je serai mort, ou quand je serai heureux; jusque-là, je lui pardonne son indifférence. Dites à M. le chevalier des Alleurs que je n'oublierai jamais la générosité de ses procédés pour moi. Comptez que tout détrompé que je suis de la vanité des amitiés humaines, la vôtre me sera à jamais précieuse. Je ne souhaite de revenir à Paris que pour vous voir, vous embrasser encore une fois, et vous faire voir ma constance dans mon amitié et dans mes malheurs.

"Présentez mes respects a Madame du Deffand!" Strange indeed are the whirligigs of Time! Madame de Bernières was then living in none other than that famous house at the corner of the Rue de Beaune and the Quai des Théatins (now Quai Voltaire) where, more than half a century later, the writer of those lines was to come, bowed down under the weight of an enormous celebrity, to look for the last time upon Paris and the world; where, too, Madame du Deffand herself, decrepit, blind, and bitter with the disillusionments of a strange lifetime, was to listen once more to the mellifluous enchantments of that extraordinary intelligence, which—so it seemed to her as she sat entranced—could never, never grow old.[1]

Voltaire was not kept long in the Bastille. For some time he had entertained a vague intention of visiting England, and he now begged for permission to leave the country. The authorities, whose one object was to prevent an unpleasant *fracas*, were ready enough to substitute exile for imprisonment; and thus, after a fortnight's detention, the " fameux poète " was released on condition that he should depart forthwith, and remain, until further permission, at a distance of at least fifty leagues from Versailles.

It is from this point onwards that our information grows scanty and confused. We know that Voltaire was in Calais early in May, and it is generally agreed that he crossed over to England shortly afterwards. His subsequent movements are uncertain. We find him established at Wandsworth in the middle of October, but it is probable that in the interval he had made a secret journey to Paris with the object—in which he did not succeed—of challenging the Chevalier de Rohan to a duel. Where he lived during these months is unknown, but apparently it was not in London. The date of his final departure from England is equally in doubt; M. Foulet adduces some reasons for supposing that he returned secretly to France in November 1728, and in that case the total length of the English visit was just two and a half years. Churton Collins, however, prolongs it until March,

---

[1] " Il est aussi animé qu'il ait jamais été. Il a quatre-vingt-quatre ans, et en vérité je le crois immortel; il jouit de tous ses sens, aucun même n'est affaibli; c'est un être bien singulier, et en vérité fort supérieur." Madame du Deffand to Horace Walpole, 12 Avril 1778.

1729. A similar obscurity hangs over all the details of Voltaire's stay. Not only are his own extant letters during this period unusually few, but allusions to him in contemporary English correspondences are almost entirely absent. We have to depend upon scattered hints, uncertain inferences, and conflicting rumours. We know that he stayed for some time at Wandsworth with a certain Everard Falkener in circumstances which he described to Thieriot in a letter in English—an English quaintly flavoured with the gay impetuosity of another race. " At my coming to London," he wrote, " I found my damned Jew was broken." (He had depended upon some bills of exchange drawn upon a Jewish broker.)

I was without a penny, sick to dye of a violent ague, stranger, alone, helpless, in the midst of a city wherein I was known to nobody; my Lord and Lady Bolingbroke were into the country; I could not make bold to see our ambassadour in so wretched a condition. I had never undergone such distress; but I am born to run through all the misfortunes of life. In these circumstances my star, that among all its direful influences pours allways on me some kind refreshment, sent to me an English gentleman unknown to me, who forced me to receive some money that I wanted. Another London citisen that I had seen but once at Paris, carried me to his own country house, wherein I lead an obscure and charming life since that time, without going to London, and quite given over to the pleasures of indolence and friendshipp. The true and generous affection of this man who soothes the bitterness of my life brings me to love you more and more. All the instances of friendshipp indear my friend Tiriot to me. I have seen often mylord and mylady Bolinbroke; I have found their affection still the same, even increased in proportion to my unhappiness; they offered me all, their money, their house; but I have refused all, because they are lords, and

I have accepted all from Mr. Faulknear because he is a single gentleman.

We know that the friendship thus begun continued for many years, but as to who or what Everard Falkener was— besides the fact that he was a " single gentleman "—we have only just information enough to make us wish for more.

" I am here," he wrote after Voltaire had gone, " just as you left me, neither merrier nor sadder, nor richer nor poorer, enjoying perfect health, having everything that makes life agreeable, without love, without avarice, without ambition, and without envy; and as long as all this lasts I shall take the liberty to call myself a very happy man." This stoical Englishman was a merchant who eventually so far overcame his distaste both for ambition and for love, as to become first Ambassador at Constantinople and then Postmaster-General—has anyone, before or since, ever held such a singular succession of offices?—and to wind up by marrying, as we are intriguingly told, at the age of sixty-three, " the illegitimate daughter of General Churchill."

We have another glimpse of Voltaire at Wandsworth in a curious document brought to light by M. Lanson. Edward Higginson, an assistant master at a Quaker's school there, remembered how the excitable Frenchman used to argue with him for hours in Latin on the subject of " water-baptism," until at last Higginson produced a text from St. Paul which seemed conclusive.

Some time after, Voltaire being at the Earl Temple's seat in Fulham, with Pope and others such, in their conversation fell on the subject of water-baptism. Voltaire assumed the part of a quaker, and at length came to mention that assertion of Paul. They questioned there being any such assertion in all his writings; on which was a large wager laid, as near as I remember of £500: and Voltaire, not retaining where it was, had one of the Earl's horses, and came over the ferry from Fulham to Putney. . . . When I came he desired me to give him in writing the place where Paul said, *he was not sent to baptize;* which I presently did. Then courteously taking his leave, he mounted and rode back—

and, we must suppose, won his wager.

He seemed so taken with me (adds Higginson) as to offer to buy out the remainder of my time. I told him I expected my master would be very exorbitant in his demand. He said, let his demand be what it might, he would give it on condition I would yield to be his companion, keeping the same company, and I should always, in every respect, fare as he fared, wearing my clothes like his and of equal value: telling me then plainly, he was a Deist; adding, so were most of the noblemen in France and in England; deriding the account given by the four Evangelists concerning the birth of Christ, and his miracles, etc., so far that I desired him to desist: for I could not bear to hear my Saviour so reviled and spoken against. Whereupon he seemed under a disappointment, and left me with some reluctance.

In London itself we catch fleeting visions of the eager gesticulating figure, hurrying out from his lodgings in Billiter Square—" Belitery Square " he calls it—or at the sign of the " White Whigg " in Maiden Lane, Covent Garden, to go off to the funeral of Sir Isaac Newton in Westminster Abbey, or to pay a call on Congreve, or to attend a Quakers' Meeting. One would like to know in which street it was that he found himself surrounded by an insulting crowd, whose jeers at the " French dog " he turned to enthusiasm by jumping upon a milestone, and delivering a harangue beginning—

" Brave Englishmen! Am I not sufficiently unhappy in not having been born among you? " Then there are one or two stories of him in the great country houses—at Bubb Dodington's, where he met Dr. Young and disputed with him upon the episode of Sin and Death in *Paradise Lost* with such vigour that at last Young burst out with the couplet:

> You are so witty, profligate, and thin,
> At once we think you Milton, Death, and Sin;

and at Blenheim, where the old Duchess of Marlborough hoped to lure him into helping her with her decocted memoirs, until she found that he had scruples, when in a fury she snatched the papers out of his hands. " I thought," she cried, " the man had sense; but I find him at bottom either a fool or a philosopher."

It is peculiarly tantalising that our knowledge should be almost at its scantiest in the very direction in which we should like to know most, and in which there was most reason to hope that our curiosity might have been gratified. Of Voltaire's relations with the circle of Pope, Swift, and Bolingbroke only the most meagre details have reached us. His correspondence with Bolingbroke, whom he had known in France and whose presence in London was one of his principal inducements in coming to England—a correspondence which must have been considerable—has completely disappeared. Nor, in the numerous published letters which passed about between the members of that distinguished group, is there any reference to Voltaire's name. Now and then some chance remark raises our expectations, only to make our disappointment more acute. Many years later, for instance, in 1765, a certain Major Broome paid a visit to Ferney, and made the following entry in his diary:

> Dined with Mons. Voltaire, who behaved very politely. He is very old, was dressed in a robe-de-chambre of blue sattan and gold spots in it, with a sort of blue sattan cap and tassle of gold. He spoke all the time in English. . . . His house is not very fine, but genteel, and stands upon a mount close to the mountains. He is tall and very thin, has a very piercing eye, and a look singularly vivacious. He told me of his acquaintance with Pope, Swift (with whom he lived for three months at Lord Peterborough's) and Gay, who first showed him the *Beggar's Opera* before it was acted. He says he admires Swift, and loved Gay vastly. He said that Swift had a great deal of the ridiculum acre.

And then Major Broome goes on to describe the " handsome new church " at Ferney, and the " very neat waterworks " at Geneva. But what a vision has he opened out for us, and, in that very moment, shut away for ever from our gaze in that brief parenthesis—" with whom he lived for three months at Lord Peterborough's "! What would we not give now for no more than one or two of the bright imperishable drops from that noble river of talk which flowed then with such a careless abundance!—that prodigal stream, swirling away, so swiftly and so happily, into the empty spaces of forgetfulness and the long night of Time!

So complete, indeed, is the lack of precise and well-authenticated information upon this, by far the most obviously interesting side of Voltaire's life in England, that some writers have been led to adopt a very different theory from that which is usually accepted, and to suppose that his relations with Pope's circle were in reality either of a purely superficial, or even of an actually disreputable, kind. Voltaire himself, no doubt, was anxious to appear as the intimate friend of the great writers of England; but what reason is there to believe that he was not embroidering upon the facts, and that his true position was not that of a mere literary hanger-on, eager simply for money and *réclame,* with, perhaps, no particular scruples as to his means of getting hold of those desirable ends? The objection to this theory is that there is even less evidence to support it than there is to support Voltaire's own story. There are a few rumours and anecdotes; but that is all. Voltaire was probably the best-hated man in the eighteenth century, and it is only natural that, out of the enormous mass of mud that was thrown at him, some handfuls should have been particularly aimed at his life in England. Accordingly, we learn that somebody was told by somebody else—" avec des détails que je ne rapporterai point "—that " M. de Voltaire se conduisit très-irrégulièrement en Angleterre: qu'il s'y est fait beaucoup d'ennemis, par des procédés qui n'accordaient pas avec les principes d'une morale exacte." And we are told that he left England " under a cloud "; that before he went he was " cudgelled " by an infuriated publisher; that he swindled Lord Peterborough out of large sums of money, and that the outraged nobleman drew his sword upon the miscreant, who only escaped with his life by a midnight flight. A more circumstantial story has been given currency by Dr. Johnson. Voltaire, it appears, was a spy in the pay of Walpole, and was in the habit of betraying Bolingbroke's political secrets to the Government. The tale first appears in a third-rate life of Pope by Owen Ruffhead, who had it from Warburton, who had it from Pope himself. Oddly enough Churton Collins apparently believed it, partly upon the evidence afforded by the " fulsome flattery " and " exaggerated compliments " to be found in Voltaire's correspondence, which, he says, reveal a man in whom " falsehood and hypocrisy are of the very essence of his composition. There is nothing, however base, to which he will not stoop: there is no law in the code of social honour which he is not capable of violating." Such an extreme and sweeping conclusion, following from such shadowy premises, seems to show that some of the mud thrown in the eighteenth century was still sticking in the twentieth. M. Foulet, however, has examined Ruffhead's charge in a very different spirit, with conscientious minuteness, and has concluded that it is utterly without foundation.

It is, indeed, certain that Voltaire's acquaintanceship was not limited to the extremely bitter Opposition circle which centred about the disappointed and restless figure of Bolingbroke. He had come to London with letters of introduction from Horace Walpole, the English Ambassador at Paris, to various eminent persons in the Government. " Mr. Voltaire, a poet and a very ingenious one," was recommended by Walpole to the favour and protection of the Duke of Newcastle, while Dodington was asked to support the subscription to " an excellent poem, called ' Henry IV.,' which, on account of some bold strokes in it against persecution and the priests, cannot be printed here." These letters had their effect, and Voltaire rapidly made friends at Court. When he brought out his London edition of the *Henriade,* there was hardly a great name in England which was not on the subscription list. He was allowed to dedicate the poem to Queen

Caroline, and he received a royal gift of £240. Now it is also certain that just before this time Bolingbroke and Swift were suspicious of a " certain pragmatical spy of quality, well known to act in that capacity by those into whose company he insinuates himself," who, they believed, was betraying their plans to the Government. But to conclude that this detected spy was Voltaire, whose favour at Court was known to be the reward of treachery to his friends, is, apart from the inherent improbability of the supposition, rendered almost impossible, owing to the fact that Bolingbroke and Swift were themselves subscribers to the *Henriade*—Bolingbroke took no fewer than twenty copies—and that Swift was not only instrumental in obtaining a large number of Irish subscriptions, but actually wrote a preface to the Dublin edition of another of Voltaire's works. What inducement could Bolingbroke have had for such liberality towards a man who had betrayed him? Who can conceive of the redoubtable Dean of St. Patrick's, then at the very summit of his fame, dispensing such splendid favours to a wretch whom he knew to be engaged in the shabbiest of all traffics at the expense of himself and his friends?

Voltaire's literary activities were as insatiable while he was in England as during every other period of his career. Besides the edition of the *Henriade,* which was considerably altered and enlarged—one of the changes was the silent removal of the name of Sully from its pages—he brought out a volume of two essays, written in English, upon the French Civil Wars and upon Epic Poetry, he began an adaptation of *Julius Cæsar* for the French stage, he wrote the opening acts of his tragedy of *Brutus,* and he collected a quantity of material for his *History of Charles XII*. In addition to all this, he was busily engaged with the preparations for his *Lettres Philosophiques*. The *Henriade* met with a great success. Every copy of the magnificent quarto edition was sold before publication; three octavo editions were exhausted in as many weeks; and Voltaire made a profit of at least ten thousand francs. M. Foulet thinks that he left England shortly after this highly successful transaction, and that he established himself secretly in some town in Normandy, probably Rouen, where he devoted himself to the completion of the various works which he had in hand. Be this as it may, he was certainly in France early in April 1729; a few days later he applied for permission to return to Paris; this was granted on the 9th of April, and the remarkable incident which had begun at the Opéra more than three years before came to a close.

It was not until five years later that the *Lettres Philosophiques* appeared. This epoch-making book was the lens by means of which Voltaire gathered together the scattered rays of his English impressions into a focus of brilliant and burning intensity. It so happened that the nation into whose midst he had plunged, and whose characteristics he had scrutinised with so avid a curiosity, had just reached one of the culminating moments in its history. The great achievement of the Revolution and the splendid triumphs of Marlborough had brought to England freedom, power, wealth, and that sense of high exhilaration which springs from victory and self-confidence. Her destiny was in the hands of an aristocracy which was not only capable and enlightened, like most successful aristocracies, but which possessed the peculiar attribute of being deep-rooted in popular traditions and popular sympathies and of drawing its life-blood from the popular will. The agitations of the reign of Anne were over; the stagnation of the reign of Walpole had not yet begun. There was a great outburst of intellectual activity and æsthetic energy. The amazing discoveries of Newton seemed to open out boundless possibilities of speculation; and in the meantime the great nobles were building palaces and reviving the magnificence of the Augustan Age, while men of letters filled the offices of state. Never, perhaps, before or since, has England been so thoroughly English; never have the national qualities of solidity and sense, independence of judgment and idiosyncrasy of temperament, received a more forcible and complete expression. It was the England of Walpole and Carteret, of Butler and Berkeley, of Swift and Pope. The two works which, out of the whole range of English literature, contain in a supreme degree those elements of power, breadth, and common sense, which lie at the root of the national genius—*Gulliver's Travels* and the *Dunciad*—both appeared during Voltaire's visit. Nor was it only in the high places of the nation's consciousness that these signs were manifest; they were visible everywhere, to every stroller through the London streets—in the Royal Exchange, where all the world came crowding to pour its gold into English purses, in the Meeting Houses of the Quakers, where the Holy Spirit rushed forth untrammelled to clothe itself in the sober garb of English idiom, and in the taverns of Cheapside, where the brawny fellow-countrymen of Newton and Shakespeare sat, in an impenetrable silence, over their English beef and English beer.

It was only natural that such a society should act as a powerful stimulus upon the vivid temperament of Voltaire, who had come to it with the bitter knowledge fresh in his mind of the medieval futility, the narrow-minded cynicism of his own country. Yet the book which was the result is in many ways a surprising one. It is almost as remarkable for what it does not say as for what it does. In the first place, Voltaire makes no attempt to give his readers an account of the outward surface, the social and spectacular aspects of English life. It is impossible not to regret this, especially since we know, from a delightful fragment which was not published until after his death, describing his first impressions on arriving in London, in how brilliant and inimitable a fashion he would have accomplished the task. A full-length portrait of Hanoverian England from the personal point of view, by Voltaire, would have been a priceless possession for posterity; but it was never to be painted. The first sketch, revealing in its perfection the hand of the master, was lightly drawn, and then thrown aside for ever. And in reality it is better so. Voltaire decided to aim at something higher and more important, something more original and more profound. He determined to write a book which should be, not the sparkling record of an ingenious traveller, but a work of propaganda and a declaration of faith. That new mood, which had come upon him first in Sully's dining-room and is revealed to us in the quivering phrases of the note to Madame de Bernières, was to grow, in the congenial air of England, into the dominating passion of his life. Henceforth, whatever quips and follies, whatever flouts and mockeries might play upon the surface, he was to be in deadly

earnest at heart.   He was to live and die a fighter in the
ranks of progress, a champion in the mighty struggle which
was now beginning against the powers of darkness in France.
The first great blow in that struggle had been struck ten
years earlier by Montesquieu in his *Lettres Persanes;* the
second was struck by Voltaire in the *Lettres Philosophiques.*
The intellectual freedom, the vigorous precision, the elegant
urbanity which characterise the earlier work appear in a yet
more perfect form in the later one.   Voltaire's book, as its
title indicates, is in effect a series of generalised reflections
upon a multitude of important topics, connected together by
a common point of view.   A description of the institutions
and manners of England is only an incidental part of the
scheme: it is the fulcrum by means of which the lever of
Voltaire's philosophy is brought into operation.   The book
is an extremely short one—it fills less than two hundred
small octavo pages; and its tone and style have just that
light and airy gaiety which befits the ostensible form of it—
a set of private letters to a friend.   With an extraordinary
width of comprehension, an extraordinary pliability of intelligence, Voltaire touches upon a hundred subjects of the
most varied interest and importance—from the theory of
gravitation to the satires of Lord Rochester, from the effects
of inoculation to the immortality of the soul—and every
touch tells.   It is the spirit of Humanism carried to its furthest, its quintessential point; indeed, at first sight, one is
tempted to think that this quality of rarefied universality
has been exaggerated into a defect.   The matters treated of
are so many and so vast, they are disposed of and dismissed
so swiftly, so easily, so unemphatically, that one begins to

wonder whether, after all, anything of real significance can have been expressed. But, in reality, what, in those few small pages, has been expressed is simply the whole philosophy of Voltaire. He offers one an exquisite dish of whipped cream; one swallows down the unsubstantial trifle, and asks impatiently if that is all? At any rate, it is enough. Into that frothy sweetness his subtle hand has insinuated a single drop of some strange liquor—is it a poison or is it an elixir of life?—whose penetrating influence will spread and spread until the remotest fibres of the system have felt its power. Contemporary French readers, when they had shut the book, found somehow that they were looking out upon a new world; that a process of disintegration had begun among their most intimate beliefs and feelings; that the whole rigid frame-work of society—of life itself—the hard, dark, narrow, antiquated structure of their existence—had suddenly, in the twinkling of an eye, become a faded, shadowy thing.

It might have been expected that, among the reforms which such a work would advocate, a prominent place would certainly have been given to those of a political nature. In England a political revolution had been crowned with triumph, and all that was best in English life was founded upon the political institutions which had been then established. The moral was obvious: one had only to compare the state of England under a free government with the state of France, disgraced, bankrupt, and incompetent, under autocratic rule. But the moral is never drawn by Voltaire. His references to political questions are slight and vague; he gives a sketch of English history, which reaches Magna Charta, suddenly mentions Henry VII., and then stops; he has not a

word to say upon the responsibility of Ministers, the independence of the judicature, or even the freedom of the press.
He approves of the English financial system, whose control
by the Commons he mentions, but he fails to indicate the importance of the fact. As to the underlying principles of the
constitution, the account which he gives of them conveys
hardly more to the reader than the famous lines in the
Henriade:

> Aux murs de Westminster on voit paraître ensemble
> Trois pouvoirs étonnés du nœud qui les rassemble.

Apparently Voltaire was aware of these deficiencies, for in
the English edition of the book he caused the following curious excuses to be inserted in the preface:

Some of his *English* Readers may perhaps be dissatisfied at
his not expatiating farther on their Constitution and their Laws,
which most of them revere almost to Idolatry; but, this Reserved-
ness is an effect of *M. de Voltaire's* Judgment. He contented
himself with giving his opinion of them in general Reflexions,
the Cast of which is entirely new, and which prove that he had
made this Part of the *British* Polity his particular Study. Besides, how was it possible for a Foreigner to pierce thro' their
Politicks, that gloomy Labyrinth, in which such of the *English*
themselves as are best acquainted with it, confess daily that they
are bewilder'd and lost?

Nothing could be more characteristic of the attitude, not only
of Voltaire himself, but of the whole host of his followers in
the later eighteenth century, towards the actual problems of
politics. They turned away in disgust from the " gloomy
Labyrinth " of practical fact to take refuge in those charming
" general Reflections " so dear to their hearts, " the Cast of

which was entirely new "—and the conclusion of which was also entirely new, for it was the French Revolution.

It was, indeed, typical of Voltaire and of his age that the *Lettres Philosophiques* should have been condemned by the authorities, not for any political heterodoxy, but for a few remarks which seemed to call in question the immortality of the soul. His attack upon the *ancien régime* was, in the main, a theoretical attack; doubtless its immediate effectiveness was thereby diminished but its ultimate force was increased. And the *ancien régime* itself was not slow to realise the danger: to touch the ark of metaphysical orthodoxy was in its eyes the unforgiveable sin. Voltaire knew well enough that he must be careful.

Il n'y a qu'une lettre touchant M. Loke [he wrote to a friend]. La seule matière philosophique que j'y traite est la petite bagatelle de l'immortalité de l'âme; mais la chose a trop de conséquence pour la traiter sérieusement. Il a fallu l'égorger pour ne pas heurter de front nos seigneurs les théologiens, gens qui voient si clairement la spiritualité de l'âme qu'ils feraient brûler, s'ils pouvaient, les corps de ceux qui en doutent.

Nor was it only " M. Loke " whom he felt himself obliged to touch so gingerly; the remarkable movement towards Deism, which was then beginning in England, Voltaire only dared to allude to in a hardly perceivable hint. He just mentions, almost in a parenthesis, the names of Shaftesbury, Collins, and Toland, and then quickly passes on. In this connexion, it may be noticed that the influence upon Voltaire of the writers of this group has often been exaggerated. To say, as Lord Morley says, that " it was the English onslaught which sowed in him the seed of the idea . . . of a systematic and reasoned attack " upon Christian theology, is to misjudge the situation. In the first place it is certain both that Voltaire's opinions upon those matters were fixed, and that his proselytising habits had begun, long before he came to England. There is curious evidence of this in an anonymous letter, preserved among the archives of the Bastille, and addressed to the head of the police at the time of Voltaire's imprisonment.

Vous venez de mettre à la Bastille [says the writer, who, it is supposed, was an ecclesiastic] un homme que je souhaitais y voir il y a plus de 15 années.

The writer goes on to speak of the

métier que faisait l'homme en question, prêchant le déisme tout à découvert aux toilettes de nos jeunes seigneurs. . . . L'Ancien Testament, selon lui, n'est qu'un tissu de contes et de fables, les apôtres étaient de bonnes gens idiots, simples, et crédules, et les pères de l'Eglise, Saint Bernard surtout, auquel il en veut le plus, n'étaient que des charlatans et des suborneurs.

" Je voudrais être homme d'authorité," he adds, " pour un jour seulement, afin d'enfermer ce poète entre quatre murailles pour toute sa vie." That Voltaire at this early date should have already given rise to such pious ecclesiastical wishes shows clearly enough that he had little to learn from the deists of England. And, in the second place, the deists of England had very little to teach a disciple of Bayle, Fontenelle, and Montesquieu. They were, almost without exception, a group of second-rate and insignificant writers whose " onslaught " upon current beliefs was only to a faint extent " systematic and reasoned." The feeble and fluctuating rationalism of Toland and Wollaston, the crude and confused rationalism of Collins, the half-crazy rationalism of Woolston may each and all, no doubt, have furnished Voltaire with arguments and suggestions, but they cannot have seriously influenced his thought. Bolingbroke was a more important figure, and he was in close personal relation with Voltaire; but his controversial writings were clumsy and superficial to an extraordinary degree. As Voltaire himself said, " in his works there are many leaves and little fruit; distorted expressions and periods intolerably long." Tindal and Middleton were more vigorous; but their work did not appear until a later period. The masterly and far-reaching speculations of Hume belong, of course, to a totally different class.

Apart from politics and metaphysics, there were two directions in which the *Lettres Philosophiques* did pioneer work of a highly important kind: they introduced both Newton and Shakespeare to the French public. The four letters on Newton show Voltaire at his best—succinct, lucid, persuasive, and bold. The few paragraphs on Shakespeare, on the other hand, show him at his worst. Their principal merit is that they mention his existence—a fact hitherto unknown in France; otherwise they merely afford a striking example of the singular contradiction in Voltaire's nature which made him a revolutionary in intellect and kept him a high Tory in taste. Never was such speculative audacity combined with such æsthetic timidity; it is as if he had reserved all his superstition for matters of art. From his account of Shakespeare, it is clear that he had never dared to open his eyes and frankly look at what he should see before him.

All was " barbare, dépourvu de bienséances, d'ordre, de vraisemblance "; in the hurly-burly he was dimly aware of a figured and elevated style, and of some few " lueurs étonnantes "; but to the true significance of Shakespeare's genius he remained utterly blind.

Characteristically enough, Voltaire, at the last moment, did his best to reinforce his tentative metaphysical observations on " M. Loke " by slipping into his book, as it were accidentally, an additional letter, quite disconnected from the rest of the work, containing reflexions upon some of the *Pensées* of Pascal. He no doubt hoped that these reflexions, into which he had distilled some of his most insidious venom, might, under cover of the rest, pass unobserved. But all his subterfuges were useless. It was in vain that he pulled wires and intrigued with high personages; in vain that he made his way to the aged Minister, Cardinal Fleury, and attempted, by reading him some choice extracts on the Quakers, to obtain permission for the publication of his book. The old Cardinal could not help smiling, though Voltaire had felt that it would be safer to skip the best parts—" the poor man! " he said afterwards, " he didn't realise what he had missed "—but the permission never came. Voltaire was obliged to have recourse to an illicit publication; and then the authorities acted with full force. The *Lettres Philosophiques* were officially condemned; the book was declared to be scandalous and " contraire à la religion, aux bonnes mœurs, et au respect dû aux puissances," and it was ordered to be publicly burned by the executioner. The result was precisely what might have been expected: the prohibitions and fulminations, so far from putting a stop to the sale of such exciting matter, sent it up by leaps and bounds. England suddenly became the fashion; the theories of M. Loke and Sir Newton began to be discussed; even the plays of " ce fou de Shakespeare " began to be read. And, at the same time, the whispered message of tolerance, of free inquiry, of enlightened curiosity, was carried over the land. The success of Voltaire's work was complete.

He himself, however, had been obliged to seek refuge from the wrath of the government in the remote seclusion of Madame du Châtelet's country house at Cirey. In this retirement he pursued his studies of Newton, and a few years later produced an exact and brilliant summary of the work of the great English philosopher. Once more the authorities intervened, and condemned Voltaire's book. The Newtonian system destroyed that of Descartes, and Descartes still spoke in France with the voice of orthodoxy; therefore, of course, the voice of Newton must not be heard. But, somehow or other, the voice of Newton *was* heard. The men of science were converted to the new doctrine; and thus it is not too much to say that the wonderful advances in the study of mathematics which took place in France during the later years of the eighteenth century were the result of the illuminating zeal of Voltaire.

With his work on Newton, Voltaire's direct connexion with English influences came to an end. For the rest of his life, indeed, he never lost his interest in England; he was never tired of reading English books, of being polite to English travellers, and of doing his best, in the intervals of more serious labours, to destroy the reputation of that deplorable English buffoon, whom, unfortunately, he himself had been so foolish as first to introduce to the attention of his country-men. But it is curious to notice how, as time went on, the force of Voltaire's nature inevitably carried him further and further away from the central standpoints of the English mind. The stimulus which he had received in England only served to urge him into a path which no Englishman has ever trod. The movement of English thought in the eighteenth century found its perfect expression in the profound, scepti-cal, and yet essentially conservative, genius of Hume. How different was the attitude of Voltaire! With what a reckless audacity, what a fierce uncompromising passion he charged and fought and charged again! He had no time for the nice discriminations of an elaborate philosophy, and no desire for the careful balance of the judicial mind; his creed was sim-ple and explicit, and it also possessed the supreme merit of brevity: " Écrasez l'infâme! " was enough for him.

1914.

A DIALOGUE

DIOGENES

Confess, oh *Moses!* Your Miracles were but conjuring-tricks, your Prophecies lucky Hazards, and your Laws a *Gallimaufry* of Commonplaces and Absurdities.

MR. LOKE

Confess that you were more skill'd in flattering the Vulgar than in ascertaining the Truth, and that your Reputation in the World would never have been so high, had your Lot fallen among a Nation of Philosophers.

DIOGENES

Confess that when you taught the *Jews* to spoil the *Egyptians* you were a sad rogue.

MR. LOKE

Confess that it was a Fable to give Horses to Pharaoh and an uncloven hoof to the Hare.

DIOGENES

Confess that you did never see the *Back Parts* of the Lord.

MR. LOKE

Confess that your style had too much Singularity and too little Taste to be that of the Holy Ghost.

MOSES

All this may be true, my good Friends; but what are the Conclusions you would draw from your Raillery? Do you suppose

that I am ignorant of all that a Wise Man might urge against
my Conduct, my Tales, and my Language? But alas! my path
was chalk'd out for me not by Choice but by Necessity. I had
not the Happiness of living in *England* or a *Tub*. I was the
Leader of an ignorant and superstitious People, who would never
have heeded the sober Counsels of Good Sense and Toleration,
and who would have laughed at the Refinements of a nice Philosophy. It was necessary to flatter their Vanity by telling
them that they were the favour'd Children of God, to satisfy
their Passions by allowing them to be treacherous and cruel to
their Enemies, and to tickle their Ears by Stories and Farces by
turns ridiculous and horrible, fit either for a Nursery or *Bedlam*.
By such Contrivances I was able to attain my Ends and to
establish the Welfare of my Countrymen. Do you blame me?
It is not the business of a Ruler to be truthful, but to be politick;
he must fly even from Virtue herself, if she sit in a different
Quarter from Expediency. It is his Duty to *sacrifice* the Best,
which is impossible, to a *little Good*, which is close at hand. I
was willing to lay down a Multitude of foolish Laws, so that,
under their Cloak, I might slip in a few Wise ones; and, had I
not shown myself to be both Cruel and Superstitious, the *Jews*
would never have escaped from the Bondage of the *Egyptians*.

DIOGENES

Perhaps that would not have been an overwhelming Disaster.
But, in truth, you are right. There is no viler Profession than
the Government of Nations. He who dreams that he can lead
a great Crowd of Fools without a great Store of Knavery is a
Fool himself.

MR. LOKE

Are not you too hasty? Does not History show that there
have been great Rulers who were good Men? Solon, Henry of
Navarre, and Milord Somers were certainly not Fools, and yet
I am unwilling to believe that they were Knaves either.

MOSES

No, not Knaves; but Dissemblers. In their different degrees, they all juggled; but 'twas not because Jugglery pleas'd 'em; 'twas because Men cannot be governed without it.

Mr. Loke

I would be happy to try the Experiment. If Men were told the Truth, might they not believe it? If the Opportunity of Virtue and Wisdom is never to be offer'd 'em, how can we be sure that they would not be willing to take it? Let Rulers be *bold* and *honest*, and it is possible that the Folly of their Peoples will disappear.

Diogenes

A pretty phantastick Vision! But History is against you.

Moses

And Prophecy.

Diogenes

And Common Observation. Look at the World at this moment, and what do we see? It is as it has always been, and always will be. So long as it endures, the World will continue to be rul'd by Cajolery, by Injustice, and by Imposture.

Mr. Loke

If that be so, I must take leave to lament the *Destiny* of the Human Race.

VOLTAIRE'S TRAGEDIES

VOLTAIRE'S TRAGEDIES

THE historian of Literature is little more than a historian of exploded reputations. What has he to do with Shakespeare, with Dante, with Sophocles? Has he entered into the springs of the sea? Or has he walked in the search of the depth? The great fixed luminaries of the firmament of Letters dazzle his optic glass; and he can hardly hope to do more than record their presence, and admire their splendours with the eyes of an ordinary mortal. His business is with the succeeding ages of men, not with all time; but Hyperion might have been written on the morrow of Salamis, and the Odes of Pindar dedicated to George the Fourth. The literary historian must rove in other hunting grounds. He is the geologist of literature, whose study lies among the buried strata of forgotten generations, among the fossil remnants of the past. The great men with whom he must deal are the great men who are no longer great—mammoths and ichthyosauri kindly preserved to us, among the siftings of so many epochs, by the impartial benignity of Time. It is for him to unravel the jokes of Erasmus, and to be at home among the platitudes of Cicero. It is for him to sit up all night with the spectral heroes of Byron; it is for him to exchange innumerable alexandrines with the faded heroines of Voltaire.

The great potentate of the eighteenth century has suffered cruelly indeed at the hands of posterity. Everyone, it is true, has heard of him; but who has read him? It is by his name that ye shall know him, and not by his works. With the exception of his letters, of *Candide,* of *Akakia,* and of a few other of his shorter pieces, the vast mass of his productions has been already consigned to oblivion. How many persons now living have travelled through *La Henriade* or *La Pucelle?* How many have so much as glanced at the imposing volumes of *L'Esprit des Mœurs? Zadig* and *Zaïre, Mérope* and *Charles XII.* still linger, perhaps, in the schoolroom; but what has become of *Oreste,* and of *Mahomet,* and of *Alzire? Où sont les neiges d'antan?*

Though Voltaire's reputation now rests mainly on his achievements as a precursor of the Revolution, to the eighteenth century he was as much a poet as a reformer. The whole of Europe beheld at Ferney the oracle, not only of philosophy, but of good taste; for thirty years every scribbler, every rising genius, and every crowned head submitted his verses to the censure of Voltaire; Voltaire's plays were performed before crowded houses; his epic was pronounced superior to Homer's, Virgil's, and Milton's; his epigrams were transcribed by every letter-writer, and got by heart by every wit. Nothing, perhaps, shows more clearly the gulf which divides us from our ancestors of the eighteenth century, than a comparison between our thoughts and their thoughts, between our feelings and their feelings, with regard to one and the same thing—a tragedy by Voltaire. For us, as we take down the dustiest volume in our bookshelf, as we open it vaguely at some intolerable tirade, as we make an effort to labour through the procession of pompous commonplaces which meets our eyes, as we abandon the task in despair, and hastily return the book to its forgotten corner—

to us it is well-nigh impossible to imagine the scene of charming brilliance which, five generations since, the same words
must have conjured up. The splendid gaiety, the refined excitement, the pathos, the wit, the passion—all these things
have vanished as completely from our perceptions as the
candles, the powder, the looking-glasses, and the brocades,
among which they moved and had their being. It may be
instructive, or at least entertaining, to examine one of these
forgotten master-pieces a little more closely; and we may
do so with the less hesitation, since we shall only be following in the footsteps of Voltaire himself. His examination of
Hamlet affords a precedent which is particularly applicable,
owing to the fact that the same interval of time divided him
from Shakespeare as that which divides ourselves from him.
One point of difference, indeed, does exist between the rela-
tive positions of the two authors. Voltaire, in his study of
Shakespeare, was dealing with a living, and a growing force;
our interest in the dramas of Voltaire is solely an antiquarian
interest. At the present moment,[1] a literal translation of
King Lear is drawing full houses at the Théâtre Antoine.
As a rule it is rash to prophesy; but, if that rule has any
exceptions, this is certainly one of them—a hundred years
hence a literal translation of *Zaïre* will not be holding the
English boards.

It is not our purpose to appreciate the best, or to expose
the worst, of Voltaire's tragedies. Our object is to review
some specimen of what would have been recognised by his
contemporaries as representative of the average flight of his
genius. Such a specimen is to be found in *Alzire, ou Les*

[1] April, 1905.

Américains, first produced with great success in 1736, when
Voltaire was forty-two years of age and his fame as a
dramatist already well established.

Act I.—The scene is laid in Lima, the capital of Peru,
some years after the Spanish conquest of America. When
the play opens, Don Gusman, a Spanish grandee, has just
succeeded his father, Don Alvarez, in the Governorship of
Peru. The rule of Don Alvarez had been beneficent and
just; he had spent his life in endeavouring to soften the
cruelty of his countrymen; and his only remaining wish was
to see his son carry on the work which he had begun. Unfortunately, however, Don Gusman's temperament was the
very opposite of his father's; he was tyrannical, harsh, head-
strong, and bigoted.

> L'Américain farouche est un monstre sauvage
> Qui mord en frémissant le frein de l'esclavage . . .
> Tout pouvoir, en un mot, périt par l'indulgence,
> Et la sévérité produit l'obéissance.

Such were the cruel maxims of his government—maxims
which he was only too ready to put into practice. It was in
vain that Don Alvarez reminded his son that the true Christian returns good for evil, and that, as he epigrammatically
put it, " Le vrai Dieu, mon fils, est un Dieu qui pardonne."
To enforce his argument, the good old man told the story of
how his own life had been spared by a virtuous American,
who, as he said, " au lieu de me frapper, embrassa mes
genoux." But Don Gusman remained unmoved by such narratives, though he admitted that there was one consideration
which impelled him to adopt a more lenient policy. He was

in love with Alzire, Alzire the young and beautiful daughter
of Montèze, who had ruled in Lima before the coming of the
Spaniards. " Je l'aime, je l'avoue," said Gusman to his
father, " et plus que je ne veux." With these words, the
dominating situation of the play becomes plain to the spectator. The wicked Spanish Governor is in love with the virtuous American princess. From such a state of affairs, what
interesting and romantic developments may not follow?
Alzire, we are not surprised to learn, still fondly cherished
the memory of a Peruvian prince, who had been slain in an
attempt to rescue his country from the tyranny of Don Gusman. Yet, for the sake of Montèze, her ambitious and
scheming father, she consented to give her hand to the Governor. She consented; but, even as she did so, she was still
faithful to Zamore. " Sa foi me fut promise," she declared
to Don Gusman, " il eut pour moi des charmes."

> Il m'aima: son trépas me coûte encore des larmes:
> Vous, loin d'oser ici condamner ma douleur,
> Jugez de ma constance, et connaissez mon cœur.

The ruthless Don did not allow these pathetic considerations to stand in the way of his wishes, and gave orders that
the wedding ceremony should be immediately performed.
But, at the very moment of his apparent triumph, the way
was being prepared for the overthrow of all his hopes.

Act II.—It was only natural to expect that a heroine
affianced to a villain should turn out to be in love with a
hero. The hero adored by Alzire had, it is true, perished;
but then what could be more natural than his resurrection?
The noble Zamore was not dead; he had escaped with his

life from the torture-chamber of Don Gusman, had returned
to avenge himself, had been immediately apprehended, and
was lying imprisoned in the lowest dungeon of the castle,
while his beloved princess was celebrating her nuptials with
his deadly foe.

In this distressing situation, he was visited by the venerable Alvarez, who had persuaded his son to grant him
an order for the prisoner's release. In the gloom of the
dungeon, it was at first difficult to distinguish the features
of Zamore; but the old man at last discovered that he was
addressing the very American who, so many years ago, instead of hitting him, had embraced his knees. He was
overwhelmed by this extraordinary coincidence. " Approach. O heaven! O Providence! It is he, behold the
object of my gratitude. . . . My benefactor! My son! "
But let us not pry further into so affecting a passage; it
is sufficient to state that Don Alvarez, after promising his
protection to Zamore, hurried off to relate this remarkable
occurrence to his son, the Governor.

Act III.—Meanwhile, Alzire had been married. But she
still could not forget her Peruvian lover. While she was
lamenting her fate, and imploring the forgiveness of the
shade of Zamore, she was informed that a released prisoner
begged a private interview. " Admit him." He was admitted. " Heaven! Such were his features, his gait, his
voice: Zamore! " She falls into the arms of her confidante.
" Je succombe; à peine je respire."

ZAMORE: Reconnais ton amant.
ALZIRE: Zamore aux pieds d'Alzire!
      Est-ce une illusion?

It was no illusion; and the unfortunate princess was obliged to confess to her lover that she was already married to Don Gusman. Zamore was at first unable to grasp the horrible truth, and, while he was still struggling with his conflicting emotions, the door was flung open, and Don Gusman, accompanied by his father, entered the room.

A double recognition followed. Zamore was no less horrified to behold in Don Gusman the son of the venerable Alvarez, than Don Gusman was infuriated at discovering that the prisoner to whose release he had consented was no other than Zamore. When the first shock of surprise was over, the Peruvian hero violently insulted his enemy, and upbraided him with the tortures he had inflicted. The Governor replied by ordering the instant execution of the prince. It was in vain that Don Alvarez reminded his son of Zamore's magnanimity; it was in vain that Alzire herself offered to sacrifice her life for that of her lover. Zamore was dragged from the apartment; and Alzire and Don Alvarez were left alone to bewail the fate of the Peruvian hero. Yet some faint hopes still lingered in the old man's breast. " Gusman fut inhumain," he admitted, " je le sais, j'en frémis;

> Mais il est ton époux, il t'aime, il est mon fils:
> Son âme à la pitié se peut ouvrir encore.

" Hélas! " (replied Alzire), " que n'êtes-vous le père de Zamore! "

Act IV.—Even Don Gusman's heart was, in fact, unable to steel itself entirely against the prayers and tears of his father and his wife; and he consented to allow a brief

demands vengeance from my agitated soul, I can still hear the
voice of thy benefactions. And thou, who wast my daughter,
thou whom in our misery I yet call by a name which makes our
tears to flow, ah! how far is it from thy father's wishes to add
to the agony which he already feels the horrible pleasure of
vengeance. I must lose, by an unheard-of catastrophe, at once
my liberator, my daughter, and my son. The Council has sen-
tenced you to death.

Upon one condition, however, and upon one alone, the
lives of the culprits were to be spared—that of Zamore's
conversion to Christianity. What need is there to say that
the noble Peruvians did not hesitate for a moment? " Death,
rather than dishonour! " exclaimed Zamore, while Alzire
added some elegant couplets upon the moral degradation
entailed by hypocritical conversion. Don Alvarez was in
complete despair, and was just beginning to make another
speech, when Don Gusman, with the pallor of death upon his
features, was carried into the room. The implacable Governor was about to utter his last words. Alzire was resigned; Alvarez was plunged in misery; Zamore was indomitable to the last. But lo! when the Governor spoke,
it was seen at once that an extraordinary change had come
over his mind. He was no longer proud, he was no longer
cruel, he was no longer unforgiving; he was kind, humble,
and polite; in short, he had repented. Everybody was par-
doned, and everybody recognised the truth of Christianity.
And their faith was particularly strengthened when Don
Gusman, invoking a final blessing upon Alzire and Zamore,
expired in the arms of Don Alvarez. For thus were the
guilty punished, and the virtuous rewarded. The noble
Zamore, who had murdered his enemy in cold blood, and

the gentle Alzire who, after bribing a sentry, had allowed her lover to do away with her husband, lived happily ever afterwards. That they were able to do so was owing entirely to the efforts of the wicked Don Gusman; and the wicked Don Gusman very properly descended to the grave.

Such is the tragedy of *Alzire,* which, it may be well to repeat, was in its day one of the most applauded of its author's productions. It was upon the strength of works of this kind that his contemporaries recognised Voltaire's right to be ranked in a sort of dramatic triumvirate, side by side with his great predecessors, Corneille and Racine. With Racine, especially, Voltaire was constantly coupled; and it is clear that he himself firmly believed that the author of *Alzire* was a worthy successor of the author of *Athalie.* At first sight, indeed, the resemblance between the two dramatists is obvious enough; but a closer inspection reveals an ocean of differences too vast to be spanned by any superficial likeness.

A careless reader is apt to dismiss the tragedies of Racine as mere *tours de force;* and, in one sense, the careless reader is right. For, as mere displays of technical skill, those works are certainly unsurpassed in the whole range of literature. But the notion of " a mere *tour de force* " carries with it something more than the idea of technical perfection; for it denotes, not simply a work which is technically perfect, but a work which is technically perfect and nothing more. The problem before a writer of *Chants Royales* is to overcome certain technical difficulties of rhyme and rhythm; he performs his *tour de force,* the difficulties are overcome, and his task is accomplished. But Racine's problem was very

blemishes are, doubtless, the outcome of simple carelessness; for Voltaire was too busy a man to give over-much
time to his plays. " This tragedy was the work of six days,"
he wrote to d'Alembert, enclosing *Olympie*. " You should
not have rested on the seventh," was d'Alembert's reply.
But, on the whole, Voltaire's verses succeed in keeping up
to a high level of medocrity; they are the verses, in fact,
of a very clever man. It is when his cleverness is out of
its depth, that he most palpably fails. A human being by
Voltaire bears the same relation to a real human being that
stage scenery bears to a real landscape; it can only be looked
at from in front. The curtain rises, and his villains and his
heroes, his good old men and his exquisite princesses, display for a moment their one thin surface to the spectator;
the curtain falls, and they are all put back into their box.
The glance which the reader has taken into the little case
labelled *Alzire* has perhaps given him a sufficient notion of
these queer discarded marionettes.

Voltaire's dramatic efforts were hampered by one further
unfortunate incapacity; he was almost completely devoid of
the dramatic sense. It is only possible to write good plays
without the power of character-drawing, upon one condition
—that of possessing the power of creating dramatic situations. The *Oedipus Tyrannus* of Sophocles, for instance, is
not a tragedy of character; and its vast crescendo of horror
is produced by a dramatic treatment of situation, not of
persons. One of the principal elements in this stupendous
example of the manipulation of a great dramatic theme has
been pointed out by Voltaire himself. The guilt of Oedipus,
he says, becomes known to the audience very early in the

play; and, when the *dénouement* at last arrives, it comes as a shock, not to the audience, but to the King. There can be no doubt that Voltaire has put his finger upon the very centre of those underlying causes which make the *Oedipus* perhaps the most awful of tragedies. To know the hideous truth, to watch its gradual dawn upon one after another of the characters, to see Oedipus at last alone in ignorance, to recognise clearly that he too must know, to witness his struggles, his distraction, his growing terror, and, at the inevitable moment, the appalling revelation—few things can be more terrible than this. But Voltaire's comment upon the masterstroke by which such an effect has been obtained illustrates, in a remarkable way, his own sense of the dramatic. " Nouvelle preuve," he remarks, " que Sophocle n'avait pas perfectionné son art."

More detailed evidence of Voltaire's utter lack of dramatic insight is to be found, of course, in his criticisms of Shakespeare. Throughout these, what is particularly striking is the manner in which Voltaire seems able to get into such intimate contact with his great predecessor, and yet to remain as absolutely unaffected by him as Shakespeare himself was by Voltaire. It is unnecessary to dwell further upon so hackneyed a subject; but one instance may be given of the lengths to which this dramatic insensibility of Voltaire's was able to go—his adaptation of *Julius Cæsar* for the French stage. A comparison of the two pieces should be made by any one who wishes to realise fully, not only the degradation of the copy, but the excellence of the original. Particular attention should be paid to the transmutation of Antony's funeral oration into French alexandrines.

mour. The Classical tradition has to answer for many sins; perhaps its most infamous achievement was that it prevented Molière from being a great tragedian. But there can be no doubt that its most astonishing one was to have taken— if only for some scattered moments—the sense of the ridiculous from Voltaire.

1905.

VOLTAIRE AND FREDERICK
THE GREAT

FREDERICK THE GREAT

VOLTAIRE AND FREDERICK
THE GREAT

At the present time,[1] when it is so difficult to think of anything but of what is and what will be, it may yet be worth while to cast occasionally a glance backward at what was. Such glances may at least prove to have the humble merit of being entertaining: they may even be instructive as well. Certainly it would be a mistake to forget that Frederick the Great once lived in Germany. Nor is it altogether useless to remember that a curious old gentleman, extremely thin, extremely active, and heavily bewigged, once decided that, on the whole, it would be as well for him *not* to live in France. For, just as modern Germany dates from the accession of Frederick to the throne of Prussia, so modern France dates from the establishment of Voltaire on the banks of the Lake of Geneva. The intersection of those two momentous lives forms one of the most curious and one of the most celebrated incidents in history. To English readers it is probably best known through the few brilliant paragraphs devoted to it by Macaulay; though Carlyle's masterly and far more elaborate narrative is familiar to every lover of *The History of Friedrich II.* Since Carlyle wrote, however, fifty years have passed. New points of view have arisen, and a certain amount of new material—including the valuable edition of the correspondence between Voltaire and Fred-

[1] October, 1915.

erick published from the original documents in the Archives at Berlin—has become available. It seems, therefore, in spite of the familiarity of the main outlines of the story, that another rapid review of it will not be out of place.

Voltaire was forty-two years of age, and already one of the most famous men of the day, when, in August 1736, he received a letter from the Crown Prince of Prussia. This letter was the first in a correspondence which was to last, with a few remarkable intervals, for a space of over forty years. It was written by a young man of twenty-four, of whose personal qualities very little was known, and whose importance seemed to lie simply in the fact that he was heir-apparent to one of the secondary European monarchies. Voltaire, however, was not the man to turn up his nose at royalty, in whatever form it might present itself; and it was moreover clear that the young Prince had picked up at least a smattering of French culture, that he was genuinely anxious to become acquainted with the tendencies of modern thought, and, above all, that his admiration for the author of the *Henriade* and *Zaïre* was unbounded.

La douceur et le support [wrote Frederick] que vous marquez pour tous ceux qui se vouent aux arts et aux sciences, me font espérer que vous ne m'exclurez pas du nombre de ceux que vous trouvez dignes de vos instructions. Je nomme ainsi votre commerce de lettres, qui ne peut être que profitable à tout être pensant. J'ose même avancer, sans déroger, au mérite d'autrui, que dans l'univers entier il n'y aurait pas d'exception à faire de ceux dont vous ne pourriez être le maître.

The great man was accordingly delighted; he replied with all that graceful affability of which he was a master, de-

clared that his correspondent was " un prince philosophe qui
rendra les hommes heureux," and showed that he meant business by plunging at once into a discussion of the metaphysical doctrines of " le sieur Wolf," whom Frederick had com-
mended as " le plus célèbre philosophe de nos jours." For
the next four years the correspondence continued on the lines
thus laid down. It was a correspondence between a master
and a pupil: Frederick, his passions divided between German
philosophy and French poetry, poured out with equal copi-
ousness disquisitions upon Free Will and *la raison suffisante*,
odes *sur la Flatterie*, and epistles *sur l'Humanité*, while Voltaire kept the ball rolling with no less enormous philosophical
replies, together with minute criticisms of His Royal High-
ness's mistakes in French metre and French orthography.
Thus, though the interest of these early letters must have
been intense to the young Prince, they have far too little
personal flavour to be anything but extremely tedious to the
reader of to-day. Only very occasionally is it possible to
detect, amid the long and careful periods, some faint signs
of feeling or of character. Voltaire's *empressement* seems to
take on, once or twice, the colours of something like a real
enthusiasm; and one notices that, after two years, Frederick's letters begin no longer with " Monsieur " but with
" Mon cher ami," which glides at last insensibly into " Mon
cher Voltaire "; though the careful poet continues with his
" Monseigneur " throughout. Then, on one occasion, Frederick makes a little avowal, which reads oddly in the light
of future events.

Souffrez [he says] que je vous fasse mon caractère, afin que
vous ne vous y mépreniez plus. . . . J'ai peu de mérite et peu de

savoir; mais j'ai beaucoup de bonne volonté, et un fonds in-
épuisable d'estime et d'amitié pour les personnes d'une vertu
distinguée et avec cela je suis capable de toute la constance que
la vraie amitié exige. J'ai assez de jugement pour vous rendre
toute la justice que vous méritez; mais je n'en ai pas assez pour
m'empêcher de faire de mauvais vers.

But this is exceptional; as a rule, elaborate compliments take
the place of personal confessions; and, while Voltaire is never
tired of comparing Frederick to Apollo, Alcibiades, and the
youthful Marcus Aurelius, of proclaiming the re-birth of
" les talents de Virgile et les vertus d'Auguste," or of declaring that " Socrate ne m'est rien, c'est Frédéric que
j'aime," the Crown Prince is on his side ready with an equal
flow of protestations, which sometimes rise to singular
heights. " Ne croyez pas," he says, " que je pousse mon
scepticisme à outrance . . . Je crois, par exemple, qu'il
n'y a qu'un Dieu et qu'un Voltaire dans le monde; je crois
encore que ce Dieu avait besoin dans ce siècle d'un Voltaire
pour le rendre aimable." Decidedly the Prince's compliments were too emphatic, and the poet's too ingenious; as
Voltaire himself said afterwards, " les épithètes ne nous
coûtaient rien "; yet neither was without a little residue of
sincerity. Frederick's admiration bordered upon the sentimental; and Voltaire had begun to allow himself to hope that
some day, in a provincial German court, there might be
found a crowned head devoting his life to philosophy, good
sense, and the love of letters. Both were to receive a curious
awakening.

In 1740 Frederick became King of Prussia, and a new
epoch in the relations between the two men began. The

next ten years were, on both sides, years of growing disillusionment. Voltaire very soon discovered that his phrase
about " un prince philosophe qui rendra les hommes
heureux " was indeed a phrase and nothing more. His *prince
philosophe* started out on a career of conquest, plunged all
Europe into war, and turned Prussia into a great military
power. Frederick, it appeared, was at once a far more important and a far more dangerous phenomenon than Voltaire
had suspected. And, on the other hand, the matured mind
of the King was not slow to perceive that the enthusiasm of
the Prince needed a good deal of qualification. This change
of view was, indeed, remarkably rapid. Nothing is more
striking than the alteration of the tone in Frederick's correspondence during the few months which followed his accession: the voice of the raw and inexperienced youth is
heard no more, and its place is taken—at once and for ever
—by the self-contained caustic utterance of an embittered
man of the world. In this transformation it was only natural
that the wondrous figure of Voltaire should lose some of its
glitter—especially since Frederick now began to have the
opportunity of inspecting that figure in the flesh with his
own sharp eyes. The friends met three or four times, and
it is noticeable that after each meeting there is a distinct
coolness on the part of Frederick. He writes with a sudden
brusqueness to accuse Voltaire of showing about his manuscripts, which, he says, had only been sent him on the condition of *un secret inviolable*. He writes to Jordan com-
plaining of Voltaire's avarice in very stringent terms. " Ton
avare boira la lie de son insatiable désir de s'enrichir . . .
Son apparition de six jours me coûtera par journée cinq cent

cinquante écus. C'est bien payer un fou; jamais bouffon de grand seigneur n'eut de pareils gages." He declares that " la cervelle du poète est aussi légère que le style de ses ouvrages," and remarks sarcastically that he is indeed a man *extraordinaire en tout*.

Yet, while his opinion of Voltaire's character was rapidly growing more and more severe, his admiration of his talents remained undiminished. For, though he had dropped metaphysics when he came to the throne, Frederick could never drop his passion for French poetry; he recognised in Voltaire the unapproachable master of that absorbing art; and for years he had made up his mind that, some day or other, he would *posséder*—for so he put it—the author of the *Henriade*, would keep him at Berlin as the brightest ornament of his court, and, above all, would have him always ready at hand to put the final polish on his own verses. In the autumn of 1743 it seemed for a moment that his wish would be gratified. Voltaire spent a visit of several weeks in Berlin; he was dazzled by the graciousness of his reception and the splendour of his surroundings; and he began to listen to the honeyed overtures of the Prussian Majesty. The great obstacle to Frederick's desire was Voltaire's relationship with Madame du Châtelet. He had lived with her for more than ten years; he was attached to her by all the ties of friendship and gratitude; he had constantly declared that he would never leave her—no, not for all the seductions of princes. She would, it is true, have been willing to accompany Voltaire to Berlin; but such a solution would by no means have suited Frederick. He was not fond of ladies—even of ladies like Madame du Châtelet—learned enough to translate Newton and to discuss by the hour the niceties of the Leibnitzian philosophy; and he had determined to *posséder* Voltaire either completely or not at all.   Voltaire, in spite of repeated temptations, had remained faithful; but now, for the first time, poor Madame du Châtelet began to be seriously alarmed.   His letters from Berlin grew fewer and fewer, and more and more ambiguous; she knew nothing of his plans; " il est ivre absolument " she burst out in her distress to d'Argental, one of his oldest friends.   By every post she dreaded to learn at last that he had deserted her for ever. But suddenly Voltaire returned.   The spell of Berlin had been broken, and he was at her feet once more.

What had happened was highly characteristic both of the Poet and of the King.   Each had tried to play a trick on the other, and each had found the other out.   The French Government had been anxious to obtain an insight into the diplomatic intentions of Frederick, in an unofficial way; Voltaire had offered his services, and it had been agreed that he should write to Frederick declaring that he was obliged to leave France for a time owing to the hostility of a member of the Government, the Bishop of Mirepoix, and asking for Frederick's hospitality.   Frederick had not been taken in: though he had not disentangled the whole plot, he had perceived clearly enough that Voltaire's visit was in reality that of an agent of the French Government; he also thought he saw an opportunity of securing the desire of his heart.   Voltaire, to give verisimilitude to his story, had, in his letter to Frederick, loaded the Bishop of Mirepoix with ridicule and abuse; and Frederick now secretly sent this letter to Mirepoix himself.   His calculation was that

Mirepoix would be so outraged that he would make it impossible for Voltaire ever to return to France; and in that case—well, Voltaire would have no other course open to him but to stay where he was, in Berlin, and Madame du Châtelet would have to make the best of it. Of course, Frederick's plan failed, and Voltaire was duly informed by Mirepoix of what had happened. He was naturally very angry. He had been almost induced to stay in Berlin of his own accord, and now he found that his host had been attempting, by means of treachery and intrigue, to force him to stay there whether he liked it or not. It was a long time before he forgave Frederick. But the King was most anxious to patch up the quarrel; he still could not abandon the hope of ultimately securing Voltaire; and besides, he was now possessed by another and a more immediate desire—to be allowed a glimpse of that famous and scandalous work which Voltaire kept locked in the innermost drawer of his cabinet and revealed to none but the most favoured of his intimates —*La Pucelle*.

Accordingly the royal letters became more frequent and more flattering than ever; the royal hand cajoled and implored. " Ne me faites point injustice sur mon caractère; d'ailleurs il vous est permis de badiner sur mon sujet comme il vous plaira." " *La Pucelle! La Pucelle! La Pucelle!* et encore *La Pucelle!* " he exclaims. " Pour l'amour de Dieu, ou plus encore pour l'amour de vous-même, envoyez-la-moi." And at last Voltaire was softened. He sent off a few fragments of his *Pucelle*—just enough to whet Frederick's appetite—and he declared himself reconciled. " Je vous ai aimé tendrement," he wrote in March 1749; " j'ai été fâché contre vous, je vous ai pardonné, et actuellement je vous aime à la folie." Within a year of this date his situation had undergone a complete change. Madame du Châtelet was dead; and his position at Versailles, in spite of the friendship of Madame de Pompadour, had become almost as impossible as he had pretended it to have been in 1743. Frederick eagerly repeated his invitation; and this time Voltaire did not refuse. He was careful to make a very good bargain; obliged Frederick to pay for his journey; and arrived at Berlin in July 1750. He was given rooms in the royal palaces both at Berlin and Potsdam; he was made a Court Chamberlain, and received the Order of Merit, together with a pension of £800 a year. These arrangements caused considerable amusement in Paris; and for some days hawkers, carrying prints of Voltaire dressed in furs, and crying " Voltaire le prussien! Six sols le fameux prussien! " were to be seen walking up and down the Quays.

The curious drama that followed, with its farcical περιπέτεια and its tragi-comic *dénouement,* can hardly be understood without a brief consideration of the feelings and intentions of the two chief actors in it. The position of Frederick is comparatively plain. He had now completely thrown aside the last lingering remnants of any esteem which he may once have entertained for the character of Voltaire. He frankly thought him a scoundrel. In September 1749, less than a year before Voltaire's arrival, and at the very period of Frederick's most urgent invitations, we find him using the following language in a letter to Algarotti: " Voltaire vient de faire un tour qui est indigne." (He had been showing to all his friends a garbled copy of one of Frederick's letters.)

Il mériterait d'être fleurdelisé au Parnasse. C'est bien dommage qu'une âme aussi lâche soit unie à un aussi beau génie. Il a les gentillesses et les malices d'un singe. Je vous conterai ce que c'est, lorsque je vous reverrai; cependant je ne ferai semblant de rien, car j'en ai besoin pour l'étude de l'élocution française. On peut apprendre de bonnes choses d'un scélérat. Je veux savoir son français; que m'importe sa morale? Cet homme a trouvé le moyen de réunir tous les contraires. On admire son esprit, en même temps qu'on méprise son caractère.

There is no ambiguity about this. Voltaire was a scoundrel; but he was a scoundrel of genius. He would make the best possible teacher of *l'élocution française;* therefore it was necessary that he should come and live in Berlin. But as for anything more—as for any real interchange of sympathies, any genuine feeling of friendliness, of respect, or even of regard—all that was utterly out of the question. The avowal is cynical, no doubt; but it is at any rate straightforward, and above all it is peculiarly devoid of any trace of self-deception. In the face of these trenchant sentences, the view of Frederick's attitude which is suggested so assiduously by Carlyle—that he was the victim of an elevated misapprehension, that he was always hoping for the best, and that, when the explosion came he was very much surprised and profoundly disappointed—becomes obviously untenable. If any man ever acted with his eyes wide open, it was Frederick when he invited Voltaire to Berlin.

Yet, though that much is clear, the letter to Algarotti

betrays, in more than one direction, a very singular state of mind. A warm devotion to *l'élocution française* is easy enough to understand; but Frederick's devotion was much more than warm; it was so absorbing and so intense that it left him no rest until, by hook or by crook, by supplication, or by trickery, or by paying down hard cash, he had obtained the close and constant proximity of—what?—of a man whom he himself described as a " singe " and a " scélérat," a man of base soul and despicable character. And Frederick appears to see nothing surprising in this. He takes it quite as a matter of course that he should be, not merely willing, but delighted to run all the risks involved by Voltaire's undoubted roguery, so long as he can be sure of benefiting from Voltaire's no less undoubted mastery of French versification. This is certainly strange; but the explanation of it lies in the extraordinary vogue—a vogue, indeed, so extraordinary that it is very difficult for the modern reader to realise it—enjoyed throughout Europe by French culture and literature during the middle years of the eighteenth century. Frederick was merely an extreme instance of a universal fact. Like all Germans of any education, he habitually wrote and spoke in French; like every lady and gentleman from Naples to Edinburgh, his life was regulated by the social conventions of France; like every amateur of letters from Madrid to St. Petersburg, his whole conception of literary taste, his whole standard of literary values, was French. To him, as to the vast majority of his contemporaries, the very essence of civilisation was concentrated in French literature, and especially in French poetry; and French poetry meant to him, as to his contemporaries, that particular kind of French poetry which had come into fashion at the court of Louis XIV. For this curious creed was as narrow as it was all-pervading. The *Grand Siècle* was the Church Infallible; and it was heresy to doubt the Gospel of Boileau.

Frederick's library, still preserved at Potsdam, shows us what literature meant in those days to a cultivated man: it is composed entirely of the French Classics, of the works of Voltaire, and of the masterpieces of antiquity translated into eighteenth-century French. But Frederick was not content with mere appreciation; he too would create; he would write Alexandrines on the model of Racine, and madrigals after the manner of Chaulieu; he would press in person into the sacred sanctuary, and burn incense with his own hands upon the inmost shrine. It was true that he was a foreigner; it was true that his knowledge of the French language was incomplete and incorrect; but his sense of his own ability urged him forward, and his indefatigable pertinacity kept him at his strange task throughout the whole of his life. He filled volumes, and the contents of those volumes afford probably the most complete illustration in literature of the very trite proverb—*Poeta nascitur, non fit.* The spectacle of that heavy German Muse, with her feet crammed into pointed slippers, executing, with incredible conscientiousness, now the stately measure of a Versailles minuet, and now the spritely steps of a Parisian jig, would be either ludicrous or pathetic—one hardly knows which— were it not so certainly neither the one nor the other, but simply dreary with an unutterable dreariness, from which the eyes of men avert themselves in shuddering dismay.

Frederick himself felt that there was something wrong—
something, but not really very much. All that was wanted
was a little expert advice; and obviously Voltaire was the
man to supply it—Voltaire, the one true heir of the Great
Age, the dramatist who had revived the glories of Racine
(did not Frederick's tears flow almost as copiously over
Mahomet as over *Britannicus?*), the epic poet who had
eclipsed Homer and Virgil (had not Frederick every right
to judge, since he had read the *Iliad* in French prose
and the *Æneid* in French verse?), the lyric master whose
odes and whose epistles occasionally even surpassed (Frederick confessed it with amazement) those of the Marquis
de la Fare. Voltaire, there could be no doubt, would do
just what was needed; he would know how to squeeze in
a little further the waist of the German Calliope, to apply
with his deft fingers precisely the right dab of rouge to her
cheeks, to instil into her movements the last *nuances* of
correct deportment. And, if he did that, of what consequence were the blemishes of his personal character? " On
peut apprendre de bonnes choses d'un scélérat."

And, besides, though Voltaire might be a rogue, Frederick felt quite convinced that he could keep him in order. A
crack or two of the master's whip—a coldness in the royal
demeanour, a hint at a stoppage of the pension—and the
monkey would put an end to his tricks soon enough. It
never seems to have occurred to Frederick that the possession of genius might imply a quality of spirit which was
not that of an ordinary man. This was his great, his fundamental error. It was the ingenuous error of a cynic. He
knew that he was under no delusion as to Voltaire's faults,

and so he supposed that he could be under no delusion as to his merits. He innocently imagined that the capacity for great writing was something that could be as easily separated from the owner of it as a hat or a glove. " C'est bien dommage qu'une âme aussi lâche soit unie à un aussi beau génie." *C'est bien dommage!*—as if there was nothing more extraordinary in such a combination than that of a pretty woman and an ugly dress. And so Frederick held his whip a little tighter, and reminded himself once more that, in spite of that *beau génie,* it was a monkey that he had to deal with. But he was wrong: it was not a monkey; it was a devil, which is a very different thing.

A devil—or perhaps an angel? One cannot be quite sure. For, amid the complexities of that extraordinary spirit, where good and evil were so mysteriously interwoven, where the elements of darkness and the elements of light lay crowded together in such ever-deepening ambiguity, fold within fold, the clearer the vision the greater the bewilderment, the more impartial the judgment the profounder the doubt. But one thing at least is certain; that spirit, whether it was admirable or whether it was odious, was moved by a terrific force. Frederick had failed to realise this; and indeed, though Voltaire was fifty-six when he went to Berlin, and though his whole life had been spent in a blaze of publicity, there was still not one of his contemporaries who understood the true nature of his genius; it was perhaps hidden even from himself. He had reached the threshold of old age, and his life's work was still before him; it was not as a writer of tragedies and epics that he was to take his place in the world. Was he, in the depths of his consciousness, aware

that this was so? Did some obscure instinct urge him forward, at this late hour, to break with the ties of a lifetime,
and rush forth into the unknown?

What his precise motives were in embarking upon the Berlin adventure it is very difficult to say. It is true that he
was disgusted with Paris—he was ill-received at Court, and
he was pestered by endless literary quarrels and jealousies;
it would be very pleasant to show his countrymen that he
had other strings to his bow, that, if they did not appreciate
him, Frederick the Great did. It is true, too, that he
admired Frederick's intellect, and that he was flattered by
his favour. " Il avait de l'esprit," he said afterwards, " des
grâces, et, de plus, il était roi; ce qui fait toujours une
grande séduction, attendu la faiblesse humaine." His vanity
could not resist the prestige of a royal intimacy; and no
doubt he relished to the full even the increased consequence
which came to him with his chamberlain's key and his order
—to say nothing of the addition of £800 to his income.
Yet, on the other hand, he was very well aware that he
was exchanging freedom for servitude, and that he was entering into a bargain with a man who would make quite
sure that he was getting his money's worth; and he knew
in his heart that he had something better to do than to play,
however successfully, the part of a courtier. Nor was he
personally attached to Frederick; he was personally attached
to no one on earth. Certainly he had never been a man
of feeling, and now that he was old and hardened by the
uses of the world he had grown to be completely what in
essence he always was—a fighter, without tenderness, without scruples, and without remorse. No, he went to Berlin

for his own purposes—however dubious those purposes may have been.

And it is curious to observe that in his correspondence with his niece, Madame Denis, whom he had left behind him at the head of his Paris establishment and in whom he confided—in so far as he can be said to have confided in any one—he repeatedly states that there is nothing permanent about his visit to Berlin. At first he declares that he is only making a stay of a few weeks with Frederick, that he is going on to Italy to visit " sa Sainteté " and to inspect " la ville souterraine," that he will be back in Paris in the autumn. The autumn comes, and the roads are too muddy to travel by; he must wait till the winter, when they will be frozen hard. Winter comes, and it is too cold to move; but he will certainly return in the spring. Spring comes, and he is on the point of finishing his *Siècle de Louis XIV.;* he really must wait just a few weeks more. The book is published; but then how can he appear in Paris until he is quite sure of its success? And so he lingers on, delaying and prevaricating, until a whole year has passed, and still he lingers on, still he is on the point of going, and still he does not go. Meanwhile, to all appearances, he was definitely fixed, a salaried official, at Frederick's court; and he was writing to all his other friends, to assure them that he had never been so happy, that he could see no reason why he should ever come away. What were his true intentions? Could he himself have said? Had he perhaps, in some secret corner of his brain, into which even he hardly dared to look, a premonition of the future? At times, in this Berlin adventure, he seems to resemble some great buzzing fly, shooting suddenly into a room through an open window and dashing frantically from side to side; when all at once, as suddenly, he swoops away and out through another window which opens in quite a different direction, towards wide and flowery fields; so that perhaps the reckless creature knew where he was going after all.

In any case, it is evident to the impartial observer that Voltaire's visit could only have ended as it did—in an explosion. The elements of the situation were too combustible for any other conclusion. When two confirmed egotists decide, for purely selfish reasons, to set up house together, every one knows what will happen. For some time their sense of mutual advantage may induce them to tolerate each other, but sooner or later human nature will assert itself, and the *ménage* will break up. And, with Voltaire and Frederick, the difficulties inherent in all such cases were intensified by the fact that the relationship between them was, in effect, that of servant and master; that Voltaire, under a very thin disguise, was a paid menial, while Frederick, condescend as he might, was an autocrat whose will was law. Thus the two famous and perhaps mythical sentences, invariably repeated by historians of the incident, about orange-skins and dirty linen, do in fact sum up the gist of the matter. " When one has sucked the orange, one throws away the skin," somebody told Voltaire that the King had said, on being asked how much longer he would put up with the poet's vagaries. And Frederick, on his side, was informed that Voltaire, when a batch of the royal verses were brought to him for correction, had burst out with " Does the man expect me to go on washing his dirty linen for ever?" Each knew well enough the weak spot in his position, and each was acutely and uncomfortably conscious that the other knew it too. Thus, but a very few weeks after Voltaire's arrival, little clouds of discord become visible on the horizon; electrical discharges of irritability begin to take place, growing more and more frequent and violent as time goes on; and one can overhear the pot and the kettle, in strictest privacy, calling each other black. "The monster," whispers Voltaire to Madame Denis, "he opens all our letters in the post"—Voltaire, whose light-handedness with other people's correspondence was only too notorious. "The monkey," mutters Frederick, "he shows my private letters to his friends"—Frederick, who had thought nothing of betraying Voltaire's letters to the Bishop of Mirepoix. "How happy I should be here," exclaims the callous old poet, "but for one thing—his Majesty is utterly heartless!" And meanwhile Frederick, who had never let a farthing escape from his close fist without some very good reason, was busy concocting an epigram upon the avarice of Voltaire.

It was, indeed, Voltaire's passion for money which brought on the first really serious storm. Three months after his arrival in Berlin, the temptation to increase his already considerable fortune by a stroke of illegal stock-jobbing proved too strong for him; he became involved in a series of shady financial transactions with a Jew; he quarrelled with the Jew; there was an acrimonious lawsuit, with charges and counter-charges of the most discreditable kind; and, though the Jew lost his case on a technical point, the poet certainly did not leave the court without a stain upon his character.

Among other misdemeanours, it is almost certain—the evidence is not quite conclusive—that he committed forgery in order to support a false oath. Frederick was furious, and for a moment was on the brink of dismissing Voltaire from Berlin. He would have been wise if he had done so. But he could not part with his *beau génie* so soon. He cracked his whip, and, setting the monkey to stand in the corner, contented himself with a shrug of the shoulders and the exclamation " C'est l'affaire d'un fripon qui a voulu tromper un filou." A few weeks later the royal favour shone forth once more, and Voltaire, who had been hiding himself in a suburban villa, came out and basked again in those refulgent beams.

And the beams were decidedly refulgent—so much so, in fact, that they almost satisfied even the vanity of Voltaire. Almost, but not quite. For, though his glory was great, though he was the centre of all men's admiration, courted by nobles, flattered by princesses—there is a letter from one of them, a sister of Frederick's, still extant, wherein the trembling votaress ventures to praise the great man's works, which, she says, " vous rendent si célèbre et immortel "—though he had ample leisure for his private activities, though he enjoyed every day the brilliant conversation of the King, though he could often forget for weeks together that he was the paid servant of a jealous despot—yet, in spite of all, there was a crumpled rose-leaf amid the silken sheets, and he lay awake o' nights. He was not the only Frenchman at Frederick's court. That monarch had surrounded himself with a small group of persons—foreigners for the most part—whose business it was to instruct him when he wished to improve his mind, to flatter him when he was out of temper, and to entertain him when he was bored. There was hardly one of them that was not thoroughly second-rate. Algarotti was an elegant dabbler in scientific matters—he had written a book to explain Newton to the ladies; d'Argens was an amiable and erudite writer of a dull free-thinking turn; Chasot was a retired military man with too many debts, and Darget was a good-natured secretary with too many love affairs; La Mettrie was a doctor who had been exiled from France for atheism and bad manners; and Pöllnitz was a decaying baron who, under stress of circumstances, had unfortunately been obliged to change his religion six times.

These were the boon companions among whom Frederick chose to spend his leisure hours. Whenever he had nothing better to do, he would exchange rhymed epigrams with Algarotti, or discuss the Jewish religion with d'Argens, or write long improper poems about Darget, in the style of *La Pucelle*. Or else he would summon La Mettrie, who would forthwith prove the irrefutability of materialism in a series of wild paradoxes, shout with laughter, suddenly shudder and cross himself on upsetting the salt, and eventually pursue his majesty with his buffooneries into a place where even royal persons are wont to be left alone. At other times Frederick would amuse himself by first cutting down the pension of Pöllnitz, who was at the moment a Lutheran, and then writing long and serious letters to him suggesting that if he would only become a Catholic again he might be made a Silesian Abbot. Strangely enough, Frederick was not popular, and one or other of the inmates of his little menagerie was constantly escaping and running away. Darget and Chasot both succeeded in getting through the wires; they obtained leave to visit Paris, and stayed there. Poor d'Argens often tried to follow their example; more than once he set off for France, secretly vowing never to return; but he had no money, Frederick was blandishing, and the wretch was always lured back to captivity. As for La Mettrie, he made his escape in a different manner —by dying after supper one evening of a surfeit of pheasant pie. " Jésus! Marie! " he gasped, as he felt the pains of death upon him. " Ah! " said a priest who had been sent for, " vous voilà enfin retourné à ces noms consolateurs." La Mettrie, with an oath, expired; and Frederick, on hearing of this unorthodox conclusion, remarked, " J'en suis bien aise, pour le repos de son âme."

Among this circle of down-at-heel eccentrics there was a single figure whose distinction and respectability stood out in striking contrast from the rest—that of Maupertuis, who had been, since 1745, the President of the Academy of Sciences at Berlin. Maupertuis has had an unfortunate fate: he was first annihilated by the ridicule of Voltaire, and then re-created by the humour of Carlyle; but he was an ambitious man, very anxious to be famous, and his desire has been gratified in over-flowing measure. During his life he was chiefly known for his voyage to Lapland, and his observations there, by which he was able to substantiate the Newtonian doctrine of the flatness of the earth at the poles. He possessed considerable scientific attainments, he was honest, he was energetic; he appeared to be just the man to revive the waning glories of Prussian science; and when

Frederick succeeded in inducing him to come to Berlin as President of his Academy the choice seemed amply justified. Maupertuis had, moreover, some pretensions to wit; and in his earlier days his biting and elegant sarcasms had more than once overwhelmed his scientific adversaries. Such accomplishments suited Frederick admirably. Maupertuis, he declared, was an *homme d'esprit*, and the happy President became a constant guest at the royal supper-parties. It was the happy—the too happy—President who was the rose-leaf in the bed of Voltaire. The two men had known each other slightly for many years, and had always expressed the highest admiration for each other; but their mutual amiability was now to be put to a severe test. The sagacious Buffon observed the danger from afar: " ces deux hommes," he wrote to a friend, " ne sont pas faits pour demeurer ensemble dans la même chambre." And indeed to the vain and sensitive poet, uncertain of Frederick's cordiality, suspicious of hidden enemies, intensely jealous of possible rivals, the spectacle of Maupertuis at supper, radiant, at his ease, obviously respected, obviously superior to the shady mediocrities who sat around—that sight was gall and wormwood; and he looked closer, with a new malignity; and then those piercing eyes began to make discoveries, and that relentless brain began to do its work.

Maupertuis had very little judgment; so far from attempting to conciliate Voltaire, he was rash enough to provoke hostilities. It was very natural that he should have lost his temper. He had been for five years the dominating figure in the royal circle, and now suddenly he was deprived of his pre-eminence and thrown completely into the shade.

Who could attend to Maupertuis while Voltaire was talking?—Voltaire, who as obviously outshone Maupertuis as
Maupertuis outshone La Mettrie and Darget and the rest.
In his exasperation the President went to the length of
openly giving his protection to a disreputable literary man,
La Beaumelle, who was a declared enemy of Voltaire. This
meant war, and war was not long in coming.

Some years previously Maupertuis had, as he believed,
discovered an important mathematical law—the " principle
of least action." The law was, in fact, important, and has
had a fruitful history in the development of mechanical
theory; but, as Mr. Jourdain has shown in a recent mono-
graph, Maupertuis enunciated it incorrectly, without realis-
ing its true import, and a far more accurate and scientific
statement of it was given, within a few months, by Euler.
Maupertuis, however, was very proud of his discovery,
which, he considered, embodied one of the principal reasons
for believing in the existence of God; and he was therefore
exceedingly angry when, shortly after Voltaire's arrival in
Berlin, a Swiss mathematician, Koenig, published a polite
memoir attacking both its accuracy and its originality, and
quoted in support of his contention an unpublished letter
by Leibnitz, in which the law was more exactly expressed.
Instead of arguing upon the merits of the case, Maupertuis
declared that the letter of Leibnitz was a forgery, and that
therefore Koenig's remarks deserved no further consideration. When Koenig expostulated, Maupertuis decided upon
a more drastic step. He summoned a meeting of the Berlin
Academy of Sciences, of which Koenig was a member, laid
the case before it, and moved that it should solemnly pro-

nounce Koenig a forger, and the letter of Leibnitz supposititious and false. The members of the Academy were frightened; their pensions depended upon the President's good will; and even the illustrious Euler was not ashamed to take part in this absurd and disgraceful condemnation.

Voltaire saw at once that his opportunity had come. Maupertuis had put himself utterly and irretrievably in the wrong. He was wrong in attributing to his discovery a value which it did not possess; he was wrong in denying the authenticity of the Leibnitz letter; above all he was wrong in treating a purely scientific question as the proper subject for the disciplinary jurisdiction of an Academy. If Voltaire struck now, he would have his enemy on the hip. There was only one consideration to give him pause, and that was a grave one: to attack Maupertuis upon this matter was, in effect, to attack the King. Not only was Frederick certainly privy to Maupertuis' action, but he was extremely sensitive of the reputation of his Academy and of its President, and he would certainly consider any interference on the part of Voltaire, who himself drew his wages from the royal purse, as a flagrant act of disloyalty. But Voltaire decided to take the risk. He had now been more than two years in Berlin, and the atmosphere of a Court was beginning to weigh upon his spirit; he was restless, he was reckless, he was spoiling for a fight; he would take on Maupertuis singly or Maupertuis and Frederick combined—he did not much care which, and in any case he flattered himself that he would settle the hash of the President.

As a preparatory measure, he withdrew all his spare cash

from Berlin, and invested it with the Duke of Würtemberg.
"Je mets tout doucement ordre à mes affaires," he told
Madame Denis. Then, on September 18, 1752, there appeared in the papers a short article entitled "Réponse
d'un Académicien de Berlin à un Académicien de Paris."
It was a statement, deadly in its bald simplicity, its studied
coldness, its concentrated force, of Koenig's case against
Maupertuis. The President must have turned pale as he
read it; but the King turned crimson. The terrible indict-
ment could, of course, only have been written by one man,
and that man was receiving a royal pension of £800 a year,
and carrying about a Chamberlain's gold key in his pocket.
Frederick flew to his writing-table, and composed an indig-
nant pamphlet, which he caused to be published with the
Prussian arms on the title-page. It was a feeble work, full
of exaggerated praises of Maupertuis, and of clumsy invec-
tives against Voltaire: the President's reputation was gravely
compared to that of Homer; the author of the "Réponse
d'un Académicien de Berlin" was declared to be a "faiseur
de libelles sans génie," and "imposteur effronté," a "malheureux écrivain"; while the "Réponse" itself was a
"grossièreté plate," whose publication was an "action
malicieuse, lâche, infâme," a "brigandage affreux." The
presence of the royal insignia only intensified the futility
of the outburst. "L'aigle, le sceptre, et la couronne," wrote
Voltaire to Madame Denis, "sont bien étonnés de se trouver
là." But one thing was now certain: the King had joined
the fray. Voltaire's blood was up, and he was not sorry.
A kind of exaltation seized him; from this moment his course
was clear—he would do as much damage as he could, and

then leave Prussia for ever. And it so happened that just then an unexpected opportunity occurred for one of those furious onslaughts so dear to his heart, with that weapon which he knew so well how to wield. "Je n'ai point de sceptre," he ominously shot out to Madame Denis, "mais j'ai une plume."

Meanwhile the life of the Court—which passed for the most part at Potsdam, in the little palace of Sans Souci which Frederick had built for himself—proceeded on its accustomed course. It was a singular life, half military, half monastic, rigid, retired, from which all the ordinary pleasures of society were strictly excluded. "What do you do here?" one of the royal princes was once asked. "We conjugate the verb *s'ennuyer*," was the reply. But, wherever he might be, that was a verb unknown to Voltaire. Shut up all day in the strange little room, still preserved for the eyes of the curious, with its windows opening on the formal garden, and its yellow walls thickly embossed with the brightly coloured shapes of fruits, flowers, and birds, the indefatigable old man worked away at his histories, his tragedies, his *Pucelle*, and his enormous correspondence. He was, of course, ill—very ill; he was probably, in fact, upon the brink of death; but he had grown accustomed to that situation; and the worse he grew the more furiously he worked. He was a victim, he declared, of erysipelas, dysentery, and scurvy; he was constantly attacked by fever, and all his teeth had fallen out. But he continued to work. On one occasion a friend visited him, and found him in bed. "J'ai quatre maladies mortelles," he wailed. "Pourtant," remarked the friend, "vous avez l'œil fort bon." Voltaire leapt up from the pillows: " Ne savez-vous pas," he shouted, " que les scorbutiques meurent l'œil enflammé? " When the evening came it was time to dress, and, in all the pomp of flowing wig and diamond order, to proceed to the little music-room, where his Majesty, after the business of the day, was preparing to relax himself upon the flute. The orchestra was gathered together; the audience was seated; the concerto began. And then the sounds of beauty flowed and trembled, and seemed, for a little space, to triumph over the pains of the living and the hard hearts of men; and the royal master poured out his skill in some long and elaborate cadenza, and the adagio came, the marvellous adagio, and the conqueror of Rossbach drew tears from the author of *Candide*. But a moment later it was supper-time; and the night ended in the oval dining room, amid laughter and champagne, the ejaculations of La Mettrie, the epigrams of Maupertuis, the sarcasms of Frederick, and the devastating coruscations of Voltaire.

Yet, in spite of all the jests and roses, everyone could hear the rumbling of the volcano under the ground. Everyone could hear, but nobody would listen; the little flames leapt up through the surface, but still the gay life went on; and then the irruption came. Voltaire's enemy had written a book. In the intervals of his more serious labours, the President had put together a series of " Letters," in which a number of miscellaneous scientific subjects were treated in a mildly speculative and popular style. The volume was rather dull, and very unimportant; but it happened to appear at this particular moment, and Voltaire pounced upon it with the swift swoop of a hawk on a mouse. The

famous *Diatribe du Docteur Akakia* is still fresh with a
fiendish gaiety after a hundred and fifty years; but to realise
to the full the skill and malice which went to the making
of it, one must at least have glanced at the flat insipid
production which called it forth, and noted with what a diabolical art the latent absurdities in poor Maupertuis' *rêveries*
have been detected, dragged forth into the light of day,
and nailed to the pillory of an immortal ridicule.   The
Diatribe, however, is not all mere laughter; there is a real
criticism in it, too.   For instance, it was not simply a farcical
exaggeration to say that Maupertuis had set out to prove
the existence of God by " A plus B divided by Z "; in
substance, the charge was both important and well founded.
" Lorsque la mètaphysique entre dans la géometrie," Voltaire wrote in a private letter some months afterwards, " c'est
Arimane qui entre dans le royaume d'Oromasde, et qui y
apporte des ténèbres "; and Maupertuis had in fact vitiated
his treatment of the " principle of least action " by his metaphysical pre-occupations.   Indeed, all through Voltaire's
pamphlet, there is an implied appeal to true scientific principles, an underlying assertion of the paramount importance
of the experimental method, a consistent attack upon *a priori*
reasoning, loose statement, and vague conjecture.   But of
course, mixed with all this, and covering it all, there is a
bubbling, sparkling fountain of effervescent raillery—cruel,
personal, insatiable—the raillery of a demon with a grudge.
The manuscript was shown to Frederick, who laughed till
the tears ran down his cheeks.   But, between his gasps, he
forbade Voltaire to publish it on pain of his most terrible
displeasure.   Naturally Voltaire was profuse with promises,

and a few days later, under a royal licence obtained for
another work, the little book appeared in print. Frederick
still managed to keep his wrath within bounds: he collected
all the copies of the edition and had them privately destroyed; he gave a furious wigging to Voltaire; and he flattered himself that he had heard the last of the business.

Ne vous embarrassez de rien, mon cher Maupertuis [he wrote
to the President in his singular orthography]; l'affaire des
libelles est finie. J'ai parlé si vrai à l'hôme, je lui ai lavé si bien
la tête que je ne crois pas qu'il y retourne, et je connais son âme
lache, incapable de sentiments d'honneur. Je l'ai intimidé du
côté de la boursse, ce qui a fait tout l'effet que j'attendais. Je
lui ai déclaré enfin nettement que ma maison devait être un
sanctuaire et non une retraite de brigands ou de célérats qui
distillent des poissons.

Apparently it did not occur to Frederick that this declaration had come a little late in the day. Meanwhile Maupertuis, overcome by illness and by rage, had taken to his bed.
" Un peu trop d'amour-propre," Frederick wrote to Darget,
" l'a rendu trop sensible aux manœuvres d'un singe qu'il
devait mépriser après qu'on l'avait fouetté." But now the
monkey *had* been whipped, and doubtless all would be well.
It seems strange that Frederick should still, after more than
two years of close observation, have had no notion of the
material he was dealing with. He might as well have supposed that he could stop a mountain torrent in spate with
a wave of his hand, as have imagined that he could impose
obedience upon Voltaire in such a crisis by means of a lec-
ture and a threat " du côté de la boursse." Before the month
was out all Germany was swarming with *Akakias;* thousands
of copies were being printed in Holland; and editions were

going off in Paris like hot cakes. It is difficult to withhold one's admiration from the audacious old spirit who thus, on the mere strength of his mother-wits, dared to defy the enraged master of a powerful state. "Votre effronterie m'étonne," fulminated Frederick in a furious note, when he suddenly discovered that all Europe was ringing with the absurdity of the man whom he had chosen to be the President of his favourite Academy, whose cause he had publicly espoused, and whom he had privately assured of his royal protection. "Ah! Mon Dieu, Sire," scribbled Voltaire on the same sheet of paper, " dans l'état où je suis! " He was, of course, once more dying. " Quoi! vous me jugeriez sans entendre! Je demande justice et la mort." Frederick replied by having copies of *Akakia* burnt by the common hangman in the streets of Berlin. Voltaire thereupon returned his Order, his gold key, and his pension. It might have been supposed that the final rupture had now really come at last. But three months elapsed before Frederick could bring himself to realise that all was over, and to agree to the departure of his extraordinary guest. Carlyle's suggestion that this last delay arose from the unwillingness of Voltaire to go, rather than from Frederick's desire to keep him, is plainly controverted by the facts. The King not only insisted on Voltaire's accepting once again the honours which he had surrendered, but actually went so far as to write him a letter of forgiveness and reconciliation. But the poet would not relent; there was a last week of suppers at Potsdam—" soupers de Damoclès " Voltaire called them; and then, on March 26, 1753, the two men parted for ever.

The storm seemed to be over; but the tail of it was still hanging in the wind. Voltaire, on his way to the waters of Plombières, stopped at Leipzig, where he could not resist, in spite of his repeated promises to the contrary, the temptation to bring out a new and enlarged edition of *Akakia*. Upon this Maupertuis utterly lost his head: he wrote to Voltaire, threatening him with personal chastisement. Voltaire issued yet another edition of *Akakia,* appended a somewhat unauthorised version of the President's letter, and added that if the dangerous and cruel man really persisted in his threat he would be received with a vigorous discharge from those instruments of intimate utility which figure so freely in the comedies of Molière. This stroke was the *coup de grâce* of Maupertuis. Shattered in body and mind, he dragged himself from Berlin to die at last in Basle under the ministrations of a couple of Capuchins and a Protestant valet reading aloud the Genevan Bible. In the meantime Frederick had decided on a violent measure. He had suddenly remembered that Voltaire had carried off with him one of the very few privately printed copies of those poetical works upon which he had spent so much devoted labour; it occurred to him that they contained several passages of a highly damaging kind; and he could feel no certainty that those passages would not be given to the world by the malicious Frenchman. Such, at any rate, were his own excuses for the step which he now took; but it seems possible that he was at least partly swayed by feelings of resentment and revenge which had been rendered uncontrollable by the last onslaught upon Maupertuis. Whatever may have been his motives, it is certain that he ordered the Prussian Resident in Frankfort, which was Voltaire's next stopping-place, to hold the poet in arrest until he delivered over the royal volume. A multitude of strange blunders and ludicrous incidents followed, upon which much controversial and patriotic ink has been spilt by a succession of French and German biographers. To an English reader it is clear that in this little comedy of errors none of the parties concerned can escape from blame—that Voltaire was hysterical, undignified, and untruthful, that the Prussian Resident was stupid and domineering, that Frederick was careless in his orders and cynical as to their results. Nor, it is to be hoped, need any Englishman be reminded that the consequences of a system of government in which the arbitrary will of an individual takes the place of the rule of law are apt to be disgraceful and absurd.

After five weeks' detention at Frankfort, Voltaire was free—free in every sense of the word—free from the service of Kings and the clutches of Residents, free in his own mind, free to shape his own destiny. He hesitated for several months, and then settled down by the Lake of Geneva. There the fires, which had lain smouldering so long in the profundities of his spirit, flared up, and flamed over Europe, towering and inextinguishable. In a few years letters began to flow once more to and from Berlin. At first the old grievances still rankled; but in time even the wrongs of Maupertuis and the misadventures of Frankfort were almost forgotten. Twenty years passed, and the King of Prussia was submitting his verses as anxiously as ever to Voltaire, whose compliments and cajoleries were pouring out in their accustomed stream. But their relationship was no longer

that of master and pupil, courtier and King; it was that of
two independent and equal powers.   Even Frederick the
Great was forced to see at last in the Patriarch of Ferney
something more than a monkey with a genius for French
versification.   He actually came to respect the author of
Akakia, and to cherish his memory.   " Je lui fais tous les
matins ma prière," he told d'Alembert, when Voltaire had
been two years in the grave; " je lui dis, Divin Voltaire, *ora
pro nobis.*"

1915.

THE ROUSSEAU AFFAIR

JEAN JACQUES ROUSSEAU

THE ROUSSEAU AFFAIR

No one who has made the slightest expedition into that curious and fascinating country, Eighteenth-Century France, can have come away from it without at least *one* impression strong upon him—that in no other place and at no other time have people ever squabbled so much. France in the eighteenth century, whatever else it may have been—however splendid in genius, in vitality, in noble accomplishment and high endeavour—was certainly not a quiet place to live in. One could never have been certain, when one woke up in the morning, whether, before the day was out, one would not be in the Bastille for something one had said at dinner, or have quarrelled with half one's friends for something one had never said at all.

Of all the disputes and agitations of that agitated age none is more remarkable than the famous quarrel between Rousseau and his friends, which disturbed French society for so many years, and profoundly affected the life and the character of the most strange and perhaps the most potent of the precursors of the Revolution. The affair is constantly cropping up in the literature of the time; it occupies a prominent place in the later books of the *Confessions;* and there is an account of its earlier phases—an account written from the anti-Rousseau point of view—in the *Mémoires* of Madame d'Epinay. The whole story is an exceedingly complex one, and all the details of it have never been satisfactorily explained; but the general verdict of subsequent writers has been decidedly hostile to Rousseau, though it has not subscribed to all the virulent abuse poured upon him by his enemies at the time of the quarrel. This, indeed, is precisely the conclusion which an unprejudiced reader of the *Confessions* would naturally come to. Rousseau's story, even as he himself tells it, does not carry conviction. He would have us believe that he was the victim of a vast and diabolical conspiracy, of which Grimm and Diderot were the moving spirits, which succeeded in alienating from him his dearest friends, and which eventually included all the ablest and most distinguished persons of the age. Not only does such a conspiracy appear, upon the face of it, highly improbable, but the evidence which Rousseau adduces to prove its existence seems totally insufficient; and the reader is left under the impression that the unfortunate Jean Jacques was the victim, not of a plot contrived by rancorous enemies, but of his own perplexed, suspicious, and deluded mind. This conclusion is supported by the account of the affair given by contemporaries, and it is still further strengthened by Rousseau's own writings subsequent to the *Confessions,* where his endless recriminations, his elaborate hypotheses, and his wild inferences bear all the appearance of mania. Here the matter has rested for many years; and it seemed improbable that any fresh reasons would arise for reopening the question. Mrs. F. Macdonald, however, in a recently-published work,[1] has produced some new and important evidence, which throws entirely fresh light upon certain obscure parts of this doubt-

---

[1] *Jean Jacques Rousseau: a New Criticism,* by Frederika Macdonald. In two volumes. Chapman and Hall.

ful history; and is possibly of even greater interest. For it is Mrs. Macdonald's contention that her new discovery completely overturns the orthodox theory, establishes the guilt of Grimm, Diderot, and the rest of the anti-Rousseau party, and proves that the story told in the *Confessions* is simply the truth.

If these conclusions do really follow from Mrs. Macdonald's newly-discovered data, it would be difficult to overestimate the value of her work, for the result of it would be nothing less than a revolution in our judgments upon some of the principal characters of the eighteenth century. To make it certain that Diderot was a cad and a cheat, that d'Alembert was a dupe, and Hume a liar—that, surely, were no small achievement. And, even if these conclusions do not follow from Mrs. Macdonald's data, her work will still be valuable, owing to the data themselves. Her discoveries are important, whatever inferences may be drawn from them; and for this reason her book, " which represents " as she tells us, " twenty years of research," will be welcome to all students of that remarkable age.

Mrs. Macdonald's principal revelations relate to the *Mémoires* of Madame d'Epinay. This work was first printed in 1818, and the concluding quarter of it contains an account of the Rousseau quarrel, the most detailed of all those written from the anti-Rousseau point of view. It has, however, always been doubtful how far the *Mémoires* were to be trusted as accurate records of historical fact. The manuscript disappeared; but it was known that the characters who, in the printed book, appear under the names of real persons, were given pseudonyms in the original document;

and many of the minor statements contradicted known
events. Had Madame d'Epinay merely intended to write a
roman à clef? What seemed, so far as concerned the Rousseau narrative, to put this hypothesis out of court was the
fact that the story of the quarrel as it appears in the
Mémoires is, in its main outlines, substantiated both by
Grimm's references to Rousseau in his *Correspondance Littéraire,* and by a brief memorandum of Rousseau's miscon-
duct, drawn up by Diderot for his private use, and not published until many years after Madame d'Epinay's death.
Accordingly most writers on the subject have taken the accuracy of the *Mémoires* for granted; Sainte-Beuve, for instance, prefers the word of Madame d'Epinay to that of
Rousseau, when there is a direct conflict of testimony;
and Lord Morley, in his well-known biography, uses the
Mémoires as an authority for many of the incidents which he
relates. Mrs. Macdonald's researches, however, have put an
entirely different complexion on the case. She has discovered the manuscript from which the *Mémoires* were printed,
and she has examined the original draft of this manuscript,
which had been unearthed some years ago, but whose full
import had been unaccountably neglected by previous schol-
ars. From these researches, two facts have come to light.
In the first place, the manuscript differs in many respects
from the printed book, and, in particular, contains a conclusion of two hundred sheets, which has never been printed
at all; the alterations were clearly made in order to conceal
the inaccuracies of the manuscript; and the omitted conclusion is frankly and palpably a fiction. And in the second
place, the original draft of the manuscript turns out to be

the work of several hands; it contains, especially in those portions which concern Rousseau, many erasures, corrections,
and notes, while several pages have been altogether cut out;
most of the corrections were made by Madame d'Epinay herself; but in nearly every case these corrections carry out the
instructions in the notes; and the notes themselves are in the
handwriting of Diderot and Grimm. Mrs. Macdonald gives
several facsimiles of pages in the original draft, which amply
support her description of it; but it is to be hoped that before long she will be able to produce a new and complete edition of the *Mémoires,* with all the manuscript alterations
clearly indicated; for until then it will be difficult to realise
the exact condition of the text. However, it is now beyond
dispute both that Madame d'Epinay's narrative cannot be
regarded as historically accurate, and that its agreement with
the statements of Grimm and Diderot is by no means an independent confirmation of its truth, for Grimm and Diderot
themselves had a hand in its compilation.

Thus far we are on firm ground. But what are the conclusions which Mrs. Macdonald builds up from these founda-
tions? The account, she says, of Rousseau's conduct and
character, as it appears in the printed version, is hostile to
him, but it was not the account which Madame d'Epinay
herself originally wrote. The hostile narrative was, in effect,
composed by Grimm and Diderot, who induced Madame
d'Epinay to substitute it for her own story; and thus her own
story could not have agreed with theirs. Madame d'Epinay
knew the truth; she knew that Rousseau's conduct had been
honourable and wise; and so she had described it in her
book; until, falling completely under the influence of Grimm

and Diderot, she had allowed herself to become the instrument for blackening the reputation of her old friend. Mrs. Macdonald paints a lurid picture of the conspirators at work —of Diderot penning his false and malignant instructions, of Madame d'Epinay's half-unwilling hand putting the last touches to the fraud, of Grimm, rushing back to Paris at the time of the Revolution, and risking his life in order to make quite certain that the result of all these efforts should reach posterity. Well! it would be difficult—perhaps it would be impossible—to prove conclusively that none of these things ever took place. The facts upon which Mrs. Macdonald lays so much stress—the mutilations, the additions, the instructing notes, the proved inaccuracy of the story the manuscripts tell—these facts, no doubt, may be explained by Mrs. Macdonald's theories; but there are other facts—no less important, and no less certain—which are in direct contradiction to Mrs. Macdonald's view, and over which she passes as lightly as she can. Putting aside the question of the *Mémoires*, we know nothing of Diderot which would lead us to entertain for a moment the supposition that he was a dishonourable and badhearted man; we do know that his writings bear the imprint of a singularly candid, noble, and fearless mind; we do know that he devoted his life, unflinchingly and unsparingly, to a great cause. We know less of Grimm; but it is at least certain that he was the intimate friend of Diderot, and of many more of the distinguished men of the time. Is all this evidence to be put on one side as of no account? Are we to dismiss it, as Mrs. Macdonald dismisses it, as merely " psychological "? Surely Diderot's reputation as an honest man is as much a fact as his notes in the draft of the *Mémoires*. It is quite true that his reputation *may* have been ill-founded, that d'Alembert, and Turgot, and Hume *may* have been deluded, or *may* have been bribed, into admitting him to their friendship; but is it not clear that we ought not to believe any such hypotheses as these until we have before us such convincing proof of Diderot's guilt that we *must* believe them? Mrs. Macdonald declares that she has produced such proof; and she points triumphantly to her garbled and concocted manuscripts. If there is indeed no explanation of these garblings and concoctions other than that which Mrs. Macdonald puts forward—that they were the outcome of a false and malicious conspiracy to blast the reputation of Rousseau—then we must admit that she is right, and that all our general " psychological " considerations as to Diderot's reputation in the world must be disregarded. But, before we come to this conclusion, how careful must we be to examine every other possible explanation of Mrs. Macdonald's facts, how rigorously must we sift her own explanation of them, how eagerly must we seize upon every loophole of escape!

It is, I believe, possible to explain the condition of the d'Epinay manuscript without having recourse to the iconoclastic theory of Mrs. Macdonald. To explain everything, indeed, would be out of the question, owing to our insufficient data, and the extreme complexity of the events; all that we can hope to do is to suggest an explanation which will account for the most important of the known facts. Not the least interesting of Mrs. Macdonald's discoveries went to show that the *Mémoires*, so far from being historically accurate, were in reality full of unfounded statements, that they concluded with an entirely imaginary narrative, and that, in short, they might be described, almost without exaggeration, in the very words with which Grimm himself actually did describe them in his *Correspondance Littéraire* as " l'ébauche d'un long roman." Mrs. Macdonald eagerly lays emphasis upon this discovery, because she is, of course, anxious to prove that the most damning of all the accounts of Rousseau's conduct is an untrue one. But she has proved too much. The *Mémoires,* she says, are a fiction; therefore the writers of them were liars. The answer is obvious: why should we not suppose that the writers were not liars at all, but simply novelists? Will not this hypothesis fit into the facts just as well as Mrs. Macdonald's? Madame d'Epinay, let us suppose, wrote a narrative, partly imaginary and partly true, based upon her own experiences, but without any strict adherence to the actual course of events, and filled with personages whose actions were, in many cases, fictitious, but whose characters were, on the whole, moulded upon the actual characters of her friends. Let us suppose that when she had finished her work—a work full of subtle observation and delightful writing—she showed it to Grimm and Diderot. They had only one criticism to make: it related to her treatment of the character which had been moulded upon that of Rousseau. " Your Rousseau, chère Madame, is a very poor affair indeed! The most salient points in his character seem to have escaped you. We know what that man really was. We know how he behaved at that time. *C'était un homme à faire peur.* You have missed a great opportunity of drawing a fine picture of a hypocritical rascal." Whereupon they gave her their own impressions of Rousseau's conduct, they showed her the letters that had passed between them, and they jotted down some notes for her guidance. She re-wrote the story in accordance with their notes and their anecdotes; but she rearranged the incidents, she condensed or amplified the letters, as she thought fit—for she was not writing a history, but " l'ébauche d'un long roman." If we suppose that this, or something like this, was what occurred, shall we not have avoided the necessity for a theory so repugnant to common-sense as that which would impute to a man of recognised integrity the meanest of frauds?

To follow Mrs. Macdonald into the inner recesses and elaborations of her argument would be a difficult and tedious task. The circumstances with which she is principally concerned—the suspicions, the accusations, the anonymous letters, the intrigues, the endless problems as to whether Madame d'Epinay was jealous of Madame d'Houdetot, whether Thérèse told fibs, whether, on the 14th of the month, Grimm was grossly impertinent, and whether, on the 15th, Rousseau was outrageously rude, whether Rousseau revealed a secret to Diderot, which Diderot revealed to Saint-Lambert, and whether, if Diderot revealed it, he believed that Rousseau had revealed it before—these circumstances form, as Lord Morley says, " a tale of labyrinthine nightmares," and Mrs. Macdonald has done very little to mitigate either the contortions of the labyrinths or the horror of the dreams. Her book is exceedingly ill-arranged; it is enormously long, filling two large volumes, with an immense apparatus of appendices and notes; it is full of repetitions and of irrelevant matter; and the argument is so indistinctly set forth that even an instructed reader finds great difficulty in following its drift. Without, however, plunging into the abyss of complications which yawns for us in Mrs. Macdonald's pages, it may be worth while to touch upon one point with which she has dealt (perhaps wisely for her own case!) only very slightly—the question of the motives which could have induced Grimm and Diderot to perpetuate a series of malignant lies.

It is, doubtless, conceivable that Grimm, who was Madame d'Epinay's lover, was jealous of Rousseau, who was Madame d'Epinay's friend. We know very little of Grimm's character, but what we do know seems to show that he was a jealous man and an ambitious man; it is possible that a close alliance with Madame d'Epinay may have seemed to him a necessary step in his career; and it is conceivable that he may have determined not to rest until his most serious rival in Madame d'Epinay's affections was utterly cast out. He was probably prejudiced against Rousseau from the beginning, and he may have allowed his prejudices to colour his view of Rousseau's character and acts. The violence of the abuse which Grimm and the rest of the Encyclopædists hurled against the miserable Jean Jacques was certainly quite out of proportion to the real facts of the case. Whenever he is mentioned one is sure of hearing something about *traître* and *mensonge* and *scélératesse*. He is referred to as often as not as if he were some dangerous kind of wild beast. This was Grimm's habitual language with regard to him; and this was the view of his character which Madame d'Epinay finally expressed in her book. The important question is—did Grimm know that Rousseau was in reality an honourable man, and, knowing this, did he deliberately defame him in

order to drive him out of Madame d'Epinay's affections?
The answer, I think, must be in the negative, for the following reason. If Grimm had known that there was something
to be ashamed of in the notes with which he had supplied
Madame d'Epinay, and which led to the alteration of her
Mémoires, he certainly would have destroyed the draft of the
manuscript, which was the only record of those notes having
ever been made. As it happens, we know that he had the
opportunity of destroying the draft, and he did not do so.
He came to Paris at the risk of his life in 1791, and stayed
there for four months, with the object, according to his own
account, of collecting papers belonging to the Empress
Catherine, or, according to Mrs. Macdonald's account, of
having the rough draft of the *Mémoires* copied out by his
secretary. Whatever his object, it is certain that the copy—
that from which ultimately the *Mémoires* were printed—was
made either at that time, or earlier; and that there was nothing on earth to prevent him, during the four months of his
stay in Paris, from destroying the draft. Mrs. Macdonald's
explanation of this difficulty is lamentably weak. Grimm,
she says, must have wished to get away from Paris " without
arousing suspicion by destroying papers." This is indeed an
" exquisite reason," which would have delighted that good
knight Sir Andrew Aguecheek. Grimm had four months at
his disposal; he was undisturbed in his own house; why
should he not have burnt the draft page by page as it was
copied out? There can be only one reply: Why *should* he?

If it is possible to suggest some fairly plausible motives
which might conceivably have induced Grimm to blacken
Rousseau's character, the case of Diderot presents difficulties

which are quite insurmountable. Mrs. Macdonald asserts that Diderot was jealous of Rousseau. Why? Because he was tired of hearing Rousseau described as " the virtuous "; that is all. Surely Mrs. Macdonald should have been the first to recognise that such an argument is a little too " psychological." The truth is that Diderot had nothing to gain by attacking Rousseau. He was not, like Grimm, in love with Madame d'Epinay; he was not a newcomer who had still to win for himself a position in the Parisian world. His acquaintance with Madame d'Epinay was slight; and, if there were any advances, they were from her side, for he was one of the most distinguished men of the day. In fact, the only reason that he could have had for abusing Rousseau was that he believed Rousseau deserved abuse. Whether he was right in believing so is a very different question. Most readers, at the present day, now that the whole noisy controversy has long taken its quiet place in the perspective of Time, would, I think, agree that Diderot and the rest of the Encyclopædists were mistaken. As we see him now, in that long vista, Rousseau was not a wicked man; he was an unfortunate, a distracted, a deeply sensitive, a strangely complex, creature; and, above all else, he possessed one quality which cut him off from his contemporaries, which set an immense gulf betwixt him and them: he was modern. Among those quick, strong, fiery people of the eighteenth century, he belonged to another world—to the new world of self-consciousness, and doubt, and hesitation, of mysterious melancholy and quiet intimate delights, of long reflexions amid the solitudes of Nature, of infinite introspections amid the solitudes of the heart. Who can wonder that he was misunderstood, and buffeted, and driven mad?   Who can wonder that, in his agitations, his perplexities, his writhings, he seemed, to the pupils of Voltaire, little less than a frenzied fiend? "Cet homme est un forcené!" Diderot exclaims. "Je tâche en vain de faire de la poésie, mais cet homme me revient tout à travers mon travail; il me trouble, et je suis comme si j'avais à côté de moi un damné: il est damné, cela est sûr . . . J'avoue que je n'ai jamais éprouvé un trouble d'âme si terrible que celui que j'ai . . . Que je ne revoie plus cet homme-là, il me ferait croire au diable et à l'enfer. Si je suis jamais forcé de retourner chez lui, je suis sûr que je frémirai tout le long du chemin: j'avais la fièvre en revenant . . . On entendait ses cris jusqu'au bout du jardin; et je le voyais! . . . Les poètes ont bien fait de mettre un intervalle immense entre le ciel et les enfers. En vérité, le main me tremble." Every word of that is stamped with sincerity; Diderot was writing from his heart. But he was wrong; the "intervalle immense," across which, so strangely and so horribly, he had caught glimpses of what he had never seen before, was not the abyss between heaven and hell, but between the old world and the new.

1907.

THE POETRY OF BLAKE

THE POETRY OF BLAKE[1]

THE new edition of Blake's poetical works, published by the Clarendon Press, will be welcomed by every lover of English poetry. The volume is worthy of the great university under whose auspices it has been produced, and of the great artist whose words it will help to perpetuate. Blake has been, hitherto, singularly unfortunate in his editors. With a single exception, every edition of his poems up to the present time has contained a multitude of textual errors which, in the case of any other writer of equal eminence, would have been well-nigh inconceivable. The great majority of these errors were not the result of accident: they were the result of deliberate falsification. Blake's text has been emended and corrected and " improved," so largely and so habitually, that there was a very real danger of its becoming permanently corrupted; and this danger was all the more serious, since the work of mutilation was carried on to an accompaniment of fervent admiration of the poet. " It is not a little bewildering," says Mr. Sampson, the present editor, " to find one great poet and critic extolling Blake for the ' glory of

[1] *The Poetical Works of William Blake. A new and verbatim text from the manuscript, engraved, and letter-press originals, with variorum readings and bibliographical notes and prefaces.* By John Sampson, Librarian in the University of Liverpool. Oxford: At the Clarendon Press, 1905.
The Lyrical Poems of William Blake. Text by John Sampson, with an Introduction by Walter Raleigh. Oxford: At the Clarendon Press, 1905.

metre' and 'the sonorous beauty of lyrical work' in the two opening lyrics of the *Songs of Experience,* while he introduces into the five short stanzas quoted no less than seven emendations of his own, involving additions of syllables and important changes of meaning." This is Procrustes admiring the exquisite proportions of his victim. As one observes the countless instances accumulated in Mr. Sampson's notes, of the clippings and filings to which the free and spontaneous expression of Blake's genius has been subjected, one is reminded of a verse in one of his own lyrics, where he speaks of the beautiful garden in which—

> Priests in black gowns were walking their rounds,
> And binding with briers my joys and desires;

and one cannot help hazarding the conjecture, that Blake's prophetic vision recognised, in the lineaments of the " priests in black gowns," most of his future editors. Perhaps, though, if Blake's prescience had extended so far as this, he would have taken a more drastic measure; and we shudder to think of the sort of epigram with which the editorial efforts of his worshippers might have been rewarded. The present edition, however, amply compensates for the past. Mr. Sampson gives us, in the first place, the correct and entire text of the poems, so printed as to afford easy reading to those who desire access to the text and nothing more. At the same time, in a series of notes and prefaces, he has provided an elaborate commentary, containing, besides all the variorum readings, a great mass of bibliographical and critical matter; and, in addition, he has enabled the reader to obtain a clue through the labyrinth of Blake's mythology, by means of ample quotations from those passages in the *Prophetic Books*, which throw light upon the obscurities of the poems. The most important Blake document—the Rossetti MS.—has been freshly collated, with the generous aid of the owner, Mr. W. A. White, to whom the gratitude of the public is due in no common measure; and the long-lost Pickering MS.—the sole authority for some of the most mystical and absorbing of the poems—was, with deserved good fortune, discovered by Mr. Sampson in time for collation in the present edition. Thus there is hardly a line in the volume which has not been reproduced from an original, either written or engraved by the hand of Blake. Mr. Sampson's minute and ungrudging care, his high critical acumen, and the skill with which he has brought his wide knowledge of the subject to bear upon the difficulties of the text, combine to make his edition a noble and splendid monument of English scholarship. It will be long indeed before the poems of Blake cease to afford matter for fresh discussions and commentaries and interpretations; but it is safe to predict that, so far as their form is concerned, they will henceforward remain unchanged. There will be no room for further editing. The work has been done by Mr. Sampson, once and for all.

In the case of Blake, a minute exactitude of text is particularly important, for more than one reason. Many of his effects depend upon subtle differences of punctuation and of spelling, which are too easily lost in reproduction. " Tiger, tiger, burning bright," is the ordinary version of one of his most celebrated lines. But in Blake's original engraving the words appear thus—" Tyger! Tyger! burning bright "; and who can fail to perceive the difference? Even more remarkable is the change which the omission of a single stop has produced in the last line of one of the succeeding stanzas of the same poem.

> And what shoulder, and what art,
> Could twist the sinews of thy heart?
> And when thy heart began to beat,
> What dread hand? and what dread feet?

So Blake engraved the verse; and, as Mr. Sampson points out, " the terrible, compressed force " of the final line vanishes to nothing in the " languid punctuation " of subsequent editions:—" What dread hand and what dread feet? " It is hardly an exaggeration to say, that the re-discovery of this line alone would have justified the appearance of the present edition.

But these considerations of what may be called the mechanics of Blake's poetry are not—important as they are—the only justification for a scrupulous adherence to his autograph text. Blake's use of language was not guided by the ordinarily accepted rules of writing; he allowed himself to be trammelled neither by prosody nor by grammar; he wrote, with an extraordinary audacity, according to the mysterious dictates of his own strange and intimate conception of the beautiful and the just. Thus his compositions, amenable to no other laws than those of his own making, fill a unique place in the poetry of the world. They are the rebels and atheists of literature, or rather, they are the sanctuaries of an Unknown God; and to invoke that deity by means of orthodox incantations is to run the risk of hell fire. Editors may punctuate afresh the text of Shakespeare with impunity, and perhaps even with advantage; but add a

comma to the text of Blake, and you put all Heaven in a
rage. You have laid your hands upon the Ark of the Cove-
nant. Nor is this all. When once, in the case of Blake, the
slightest deviation has been made from the authoritative version, it is hardly possible to stop there. The emendator is on
an inclined plane which leads him inevitably from readjust-
ments of punctuation to corrections of grammar, and from
corrections of grammar to alterations of rhythm; if he is in
for a penny, he is in for a pound. The first poem in the Rossetti MS. may be adduced as one instance—out of the enormous number which fill Mr. Sampson's notes—of the dangers
of editorial laxity.

> I told my love, I told my love,
> I told her all my heart;
> Trembling, cold, in ghastly fears,
> Ah! she doth depart.

This is the first half of the poem; and editors have been contented with an alteration of stops, and the change of " doth "
into " did." But their work was not over; they had, as it
were, tasted blood; and their version of the last four lines
of the poem is as follows:

> Soon after she was gone from me,
> A traveller came by,
> Silently, invisibly:
> He took her with a sigh.

Reference to the MS., however, shows that the last line had
been struck out by Blake, and another substituted in its
place—a line which is now printed for the first time by Mr.
Sampson. So that the true reading of the verse is:

Soon as she was gone from me,
A traveller came by,
Silently, invisibly—
O! was no deny.

After these exertions, it must have seemed natural enough to Rossetti and his successors to print four other expunged lines as part of the poem, and to complete the business by clapping a title to their concoction—*Love's Secret*—a title which there is no reason to suppose had ever entered the poet's mind.

Besides illustrating the shortcomings of his editors, this little poem is an admirable instance of Blake's most persistent quality—his triumphant freedom from conventional restraints. His most characteristic passages are at once so unexpected and so complete in their effect, that the reader is moved by them, spontaneously, to some conjecture of " inspiration." Sir Walter Raleigh, indeed, in his interesting Introduction to a smaller edition of the poems, protests against such attributions of peculiar powers to Blake, or indeed to any other poet. " No man," he says, " destitute of genius, could live for a day." But even if we all agree to be inspired together, we must still admit that there are degrees of inspiration; if Mr. F's aunt was a woman of genius, what are we to say of Hamlet? And Blake, in the hierarchy of the inspired, stands very high indeed. If one could strike an average among poets, it would probably be true to say that, so far as inspiration is concerned, Blake is to the average poet, as the average poet is to the man in the street. All poetry, to be poetry at all, must have the power of making one, now and then, involuntarily ejaculate: " What made him think of that? " With Blake, one is asking the question all the time.

Blake's originality of manner was not, as has sometimes been the case, a cloak for platitude. What he has to say belongs no less distinctly to a mind of astonishing self-dependence than his way of saying it. In English literature, as Sir Walter Raleigh observes, he " stands outside the regular line of succession." All that he had in common with the great leaders of the Romantic Movement was an abhorrence of the conventionality and the rationalism of the eighteenth century; for the eighteenth century itself was hardly more alien to his spirit than that exaltation of Nature—the " Vegetable Universe," as he called it—from which sprang the pantheism of Wordsworth and the paganism of Keats. " Nature is the work of the Devil," he exclaimed one day; " the Devil is in us as far as we are Nature." There was no part of the sensible world which, in his philosophy, was not impregnated with vileness. Even the " ancient heavens " were not, to his uncompromising vision, " fresh and strong "; they were " writ with Curses from Pole to Pole," and destined to vanish into nothingness with the triumph of the Everlasting Gospel.

There are doubtless many to whom Blake is known simply as a charming and splendid lyrist, as the author of *Infant Joy,* and *The Tiger,* and the rest of the *Songs of Innocence and Experience.* These poems show but faint traces of any system of philosophy; but, to a reader of the Rossetti and Pickering MSS., the presence of a hidden and symbolic meaning in Blake's words becomes obvious enough—a meaning which receives its fullest expression in the *Prophetic*

Books. It was only natural that the extraordinary nature of Blake's utterance in these latter works should have given rise to the belief that he was merely an inspired idiot—a madman who happened to be able to write good verses. That belief, made finally impossible by Mr. Swinburne's elaborate Essay, is now, happily, nothing more than a curiosity of literary history; and indeed signs are not wanting that the whirligig of Time, which left Blake for so long in the Paradise of Fools, is now about to place him among the Prophets. Anarchy is the most fashionable of creeds; and Blake's writings, according to Sir Walter Raleigh, contain a complete exposition of its doctrines. The same critic asserts that Blake was " one of the most consistent of English poets and thinkers." This is high praise indeed; but there seems to be some ambiguity in it. It is one thing to give Blake credit for that sort of consistency which lies in the repeated enunciation of the same body of beliefs throughout a large mass of compositions and over a long period of time, and which could never be possessed by a madman or an incoherent charlatan. It is quite another thing to assert that his doctrines form in themselves a consistent whole, in the sense in which that quality would be ordinarily attributed to a system of philosophy. Does Sir Walter mean to assert that Blake is, in this sense too, " consistent "? It is a little difficult to discover. Referring, in his Introduction, to Blake's abusive notes on Bacon's *Essays,* he speaks of—

The sentimental enthusiast, who worships all great men indifferently [and who] finds himself in a distressful position when his gods fall out among themselves. His case [Sir Walter wittily adds] is not much unlike that of Terah, the father of Abraham, who (if the legend be true) was a dealer in idols among the Chaldees, and, coming home to his shop one day, after a brief absence, found that the idols had quarrelled, and the biggest of them had smashed the rest to atoms. Blake is a dangerous idol for any man to keep in his shop.

We wonder very much whether he is kept in Sir Walter Raleigh's.

It seems clear, at any rate, that no claim for a "consistency" which would imply freedom from self-contradiction can be validly made for Blake. His treatment of the problem of evil is enough to show how very far he was from that clarity of thought without which even prophets are liable, when the time comes, to fall into disrepute. "Plato," said Blake, "knew of nothing but the virtues and vices, and good and evil. There is nothing in all that. Everything is good in God's eyes." And this is the perpetual burden of his teaching. "Satan's empire is the empire of nothing"; there is no such thing as evil—it is a mere "negation." And the "moral virtues," which attempt to discriminate between right and wrong, are the idlest of delusions; they are merely "allegories and dissimulations," they "do not exist." Such was one of the most fundamental of Blake's doctrines; but it requires only a superficial acquaintance with his writings to recognise that their whole tenour is an implicit contradiction of this very belief. Every page he wrote contains a moral exhortation; bad thoughts and bad feelings raised in him a fury of rage and indignation which the bitterest of satirists never surpassed. His epigrams on Reynolds are masterpieces of virulent abuse; the punishment which he devised for Klopstock—his impersonation of "flaccid fluency and devout sentiment "—is unprintable; as for those who attempt to enforce moral laws, they shall be " cast out," for they " crucify Christ with the head downwards." The contradiction is indeed glaring. " There is no such thing as wickedness," Blake says in effect, " and you are wicked if you think there is." If it is true that evil does not exist, all Blake's denunciations are so much empty chatter; and, on the other hand, if there is a real distinction between good and bad, if everything, in fact, is *not* good in God's eyes—then why not say so? Really Blake, as politicians say, " cannot have it both ways."

But, of course, his answer to all this is simple enough. To judge him according to the light of reason is to make an appeal to a tribunal whose jurisdiction he had always refused to recognise as binding. In fact, to Blake's mind, the laws of reason were nothing but a horrible phantasm deluding and perplexing mankind, from whose clutches it is the business of every human soul to free itself as speedily as possible. Reason is the " spectre " of Blake's mythology, that spectre, which, he says,

> Around me night and day
> Like a wild beast guards my way.

It is a malignant spirit, for ever struggling with the " Emanation," or imaginative side of man, whose triumph is the supreme end of the universe. Ever since the day when, in his childhood, Blake had seen God's forehead at the window, he had found in imaginative vision the only reality and the only good. He beheld the things of this world " not with, but through, the eye ":

> With my inward Eye, 'tis an old Man grey,
> With my outward, a Thistle across my way.

It was to the imagination, and the imagination alone, that
Blake yielded the allegiance of his spirit. His attitude
towards reason was the attitude of the mystic; and it involved an inevitable dilemma. He never could, in truth,
quite shake himself free of his " spectre "; struggle as he
would, he could not escape altogether from the employment
of the ordinary forms of thought and speech; he is constantly
arguing, as if argument were really a means of approaching
the truth; he was subdued to what he worked in. As in his
own poem, he had, somehow or other, been locked into a
crystal cabinet—the world of the senses and of reason—a
gilded, artificial, gimcrack dwelling, after " the wild " where
he had danced so merrily before.

> I strove to seize the inmost Form
>   With ardour fierce and hands of flame,
> But burst the Crystal Cabinet,
>   And like a Weeping Babe became—
>
> A weeping Babe upon the wild. . . .

To be able to lay hands upon " the inmost form," one must
achieve the impossible; one must be inside and outside the
crystal cabinet at the same time. But Blake was not to be
turned aside by such considerations. He would have it both
ways; and whoever demurred was crucifying Christ with the
head downwards.

Besides its unreasonableness, there is an even more serious
objection to Blake's mysticism—and indeed to all mysticism:
its lack of humanity. The mystic's creed—even when ar-

rayed in the wondrous and ecstatic beauty of Blake's verse
—comes upon the ordinary man, in the rigidity of its uncompromising elevation, with a shock which is terrible, and
almost cruel. The sacrifices which it demands are too vast,
in spite of the divinity of what it has to offer. What shall
it profit a man, one is tempted to exclaim, if he gain his own
soul, and lose the whole world? The mystic ideal is the
highest of all; but it has no breadth. The following lines
express, with a simplicity and an intensity of inspiration
which he never surpassed, Blake's conception of that ideal:

> And throughout all Eternity
> I forgive you, you forgive me.
> As our dear Redeemer said:
> " This the Wine, & this the Bread."

It is easy to imagine the sort of comments to which Voltaire,
for instance, with his " wracking wheel " of sarcasm and
common-sense, would have subjected such lines as these. His
criticism would have been irrelevant, because it would never
have reached the heart of the matter at issue; it would have
been based upon no true understanding of Blake's words.
But that they do admit of a real, an unanswerable criticism,
it is difficult to doubt. Charles Lamb, perhaps, might have
made it; incidentally, indeed, he has. " Sun, and sky, and
breeze, and solitary walks, and summer holidays, and the
greenness of fields, and the delicious juices of meats and
fishes, and society, and the cheerful glass, and candle-light,
and fireside conversations, and innocent vanities, and jests,
and *irony itself* "—do these things form no part of your
Eternity?

The truth is plain: Blake was an intellectual drunkard.

His words come down to us in a rapture of broken fluency
from impossible intoxicated heights. His spirit soared above
the empyrean; and, even as it soared, it stumbled in the gut-
ter of Felpham. His lips brought forth, in the same breath,
in the same inspired utterance, the *Auguries of Innocence*
and the epigrams on Sir Joshua Reynolds. He was in no
condition to chop logic, or to take heed of the existing forms
of things. In the imaginary portrait of himself, prefixed to
Sir Walter Raleigh's volume, we can see him, as he appeared
to his own " inward eye," staggering between the abyss and
the star of Heaven, his limbs cast abroad, his head thrown
back in an ecstasy of intoxication, so that, to the frenzy of
his rolling vision, the whole universe is upside down. We
look, and, as we gaze at the strange image and listen to the
marvellous melody, we are almost tempted to go and do
likewise.

But it is not as a prophet, it is as an artist, that Blake deserves the highest honours and the most enduring fame. In
spite of his hatred of the " vegetable universe," his poems
possess the inexplicable and spontaneous quality of natural
objects; they are more like the works of Heaven than the
works of man. They have, besides, the two most obvious
characteristics of Nature—loveliness and power. In some
of his lyrics there is an exquisite simplicity, which seems, like
a flower or a child, to be unconscious of itself. In his poem
of *The Birds*—to mention, out of many, perhaps a less known
instance—it is not the poet that one hears, it is the birds
themselves.

> O thou summer's harmony,
> I have lived and mourned for thee;

> Each day I mourn along the wood,
> And night hath heard my sorrows loud.

In his other mood—the mood of elemental force—Blake produces effects which are unique in literature. His mastery of the mysterious suggestions which lie concealed in words is complete.

> He who torments the Chafer's Sprite
> Weaves a Bower in endless Night.

What dark and terrible visions the last line calls up! And, with the aid of this control over the secret springs of language, he is able to produce in poetry those vast and vague effects of gloom, of foreboding, and of terror, which seem to be proper to music alone. Sometimes his words are heavy with the doubtful horror of an approaching thunderstorm:

> The Guests are scattered thro' the land,
> For the Eye altering alters all;
> The Senses roll themselves in fear,
> And the flat Earth becomes a Ball;
>
> The Stars, Sun, Moon, all shrink away,
> A desart vast without a bound,
> And nothing left to eat or drink,
> And a dark desart all around.

And sometimes Blake invests his verses with a sense of nameless and infinite ruin, such as one feels when the drum and the violin mysteriously come together, in one of Beethoven's Symphonies, to predict the annihilation of worlds:

> On the shadows of the Moon,
> Climbing through Night's highest noon:
> In Time's Ocean falling, drowned:
> In Aged Ignorance profound,

Holy and cold, I clipp'd the Wings
Of all Sublunary Things . . .
But when once I did descry
The Immortal Man that cannot Die,
Thro' evening shades I haste away
To close the Labours of my Day.
The Door of Death I open found,
And the Worm Weaving in the Ground;
Thou'rt my Mother, from the Womb;
Wife, Sister, Daughter, to the Tomb:
Weaving to Dreams the Sexual strife,
And weeping over the Web of Life.

Such music is not to be lightly mouthed by mortals; for us, in our weakness, a few strains of it, now and then, amid the murmur of ordinary converse, are enough. For Blake's words will always be strangers on this earth; they could only fall with familiarity from the lips of his own Gods:

above Time's troubled fountains,
On the great Atlantic Mountains,
In my Golden House on high.

They belong to the language of Los and Rahab and Enitharmon; and their mystery is revealed for ever in the land of the Sunflower's desire.

1906.

THE LAST ELIZABETHAN

THE LAST ELIZABETHAN

THE shrine of Poetry is a secret one; and it is fortunate that this should be the case; for it gives a sense of security. The cult is too mysterious and intimate to figure upon census papers; there are no turnstiles at the temple gates; and so, as all inquiries must be fruitless, the obvious plan is to take for granted a good attendance of worshippers, and to pass on. Yet, if Apollo were to come down (after the manner of deities) and put questions—must we suppose to the Laureate?—as to the number of the elect, would we be quite sure of escaping wrath and destruction? Let us hope for the best; and perhaps, if we were bent upon finding out the truth, the simplest way would be to watch the sales of the new edition of the poems of Beddoes, which Messrs. Routledge have lately added to the "Muses' Library." How many among Apollo's pew-renters, one wonders, have ever read Beddoes, or, indeed, have ever heard of him? For some reason or another, this extraordinary poet has not only never received the recognition which is his due, but has failed almost entirely to receive any recognition whatever. If his name is known at all, it is known in virtue of the one or two of his lyrics which have crept into some of the current anthologies. But Beddoes' highest claim to distinction does not rest upon his lyrical achievements, consummate as those achievements are; it rests upon his extraordinary eminence as a master of dramatic blank verse. Perhaps his greatest

endowed with high and varied intellectual capacities and a
rare independence of character. His scientific attainments
were recognised by the University of Oxford, where he held
the post of Lecturer in Chemistry, until the time of the
French Revolution, when he was obliged to resign it, owing
to the scandal caused by the unconcealed intensity of his liberal opinions. He then settled at Clifton as a physician, established a flourishing practice, and devoted his leisure to
politics and scientific research. Sir Humphry Davy, who
was his pupil, and whose merit he was the first to bring to
light, declared that " he had talents which would have exalted him to the pinnacle of philosophical eminence, if they
had been applied with discretion." The words are curiously
suggestive of the history of his son; and indeed the poet
affords a striking instance of the hereditary transmission of
mental qualities. Not only did Beddoes inherit his father's
talents and his father's inability to make the best use of
them; he possessed in a no less remarkable degree his father's
independence of mind. In both cases, this quality was coupled with a corresponding eccentricity of conduct, which occasionally, to puzzled onlookers, wore the appearance of
something very near insanity. Many stories are related of
the queer behaviour of Dr. Beddoes. One day he astonished
the ladies of Clifton by appearing at a tea-party with a
packet of sugar in his hand; he explained that it was East
Indian sugar, and that nothing would induce him to eat the
usual kind, which came from Jamaica and was made by
slaves. More extraordinary were his medical prescriptions;
for he was in the habit of ordering cows to be conveyed into
his patients' bedrooms, in order, as he said, that they might

" inhale the animals' breath." It is easy to imagine the delight which the singular spectacle of a cow climbing upstairs
into an invalid's bedroom must have given to the future author of *Harpagus* and *The Oviparous Tailor*. But " little
Tom," as Miss Edgeworth calls him, was not destined to enjoy for long the benefit of parental example; for Dr. Beddoes
died in the prime of life, when the child was not yet six
years old.

The genius at school is usually a disappointing figure, for,
as a rule, one must be commonplace to be a successful boy.
In that preposterous world, to be remarkable is to be over-
looked; and nothing less vivid than the white-hot blaze of a
Shelley will bring with it even a distinguished martyrdom.
But Beddoes was an exception, though he was not a martyr.
On the contrary, he dominated his fellows as absolutely as
if he had been a dullard and a dunce. He was at Charter-
house; and an entertaining account of his existence there has
been preserved to us in a paper of school reminiscences, written by Mr. C. D. Bevan, who had been his fag. Though his
place in the school was high, Beddoes' interests were devoted
not so much to classical scholarship as to the literature of his
own tongue. Cowley, he afterwards told a friend, had been
the first poet he had understood; but no doubt he had begun
to understand poetry many years before he went to Charter-
house; and, while he was there, the reading which he chiefly
delighted in was the Elizabethan drama. " He liked act-
ing," says Mr. Bevan, " and was a good judge of it, and used
to give apt though burlesque imitations of the popular actors,
particularly Kean and Macready. Though his voice was
harsh and his enunciation offensively conceited, he read with

them into life; and indeed, here and there, the breath has
come, the warm, the true, the vital breath of Apollo. No one,
surely, whose lips had not tasted of the waters of Helicon,
could have uttered such words as these:

> Here's the blue violet, like Pandora's eye,
> When first it darkened with immortal life;

or a line of such intense imaginative force as this:

> I've huddled her into the wormy earth;

or this splendid description of a stormy sunrise:

> The day is in its shroud while yet an infant;
> And Night with giant strides stalks o'er the world,
> Like a swart Cyclops, on its hideous front
> One round, red, thunder-swollen eye ablaze.

The play was written on the Elizabethan model, and, as a
play, it is disfigured by Beddoes' most characteristic faults:
the construction is weak, the interest fluctuates from character to character, and the motives and actions of the characters themselves are for the most part curiously remote from
the realities of life. Yet, though the merit of the tragedy depends almost entirely upon the verse, there are signs in it
that, while Beddoes lacked the gift of construction, he nevertheless possessed one important dramatic faculty—the power
of creating detached scenes of interest and beauty. The
scene in which the half-crazed Lenora imagines to herself,
beside the couch on which her dead daughter lies, that the
child is really living after all, is dramatic in the highest sense
of the word; the situation, with all its capabilities of pathetic

irony, is conceived and developed with consummate art and absolute restraint. Lenora's speech ends thus:

> . . . Speak, I pray thee, Floribel,
> Speak to thy mother; do but whisper " aye ";
> Well, well, I will not press her; I am sure
> She has the welcome news of some good fortune,
> And hoards the telling till her father comes;
> . . . Ah! She half laughed. I've guessed it then;
> Come tell me, I'll be secret. Nay, if you mock me,
> I must be very angry till you speak.
> Now this is silly; some of these young boys
> Have dressed the cushions with her clothes in sport.
> 'Tis very like her. I could make this image
> Act all her greetings; she shall bow her head:
> " Good-morrow, mother "; and her smiling face
> Falls on my neck.—Oh, heaven, 'tis she indeed!
> I know it all—don't tell me.

The last seven words are a summary of anguish, horror, and despair, such as Webster himself might have been proud to write.

The Bride's Tragedy was well received by critics; and a laudatory notice of Beddoes in the *Edinburgh*, written by Bryan Waller Procter—better known then than now under his pseudonym of Barry Cornwall—led to a lasting friendship between the two poets. The connection had an important result, for it was through Procter that Beddoes became acquainted with the most intimate of all his friends—Thomas Forbes Kelsall, then a young lawyer at Southampton. In the summer of 1823 Beddoes stayed at Southampton for several months, and, while ostensibly studying for his Oxford degree, gave up most of his time to conversations with Kelsall and to dramatic composition. It was a culminating point in his life: one of those moments which come, even to the most fortunate, once and once only—when youth, and hope, and the high exuberance of genius combine with circumstance and opportunity to crown the marvellous hour. The spadework of *The Bride's Tragedy* had been accomplished; the seed had been sown; and now the harvest was beginning. Beddoes, " with the delicious sense," as Kelsall wrote long afterwards, " of the laurel freshly twined around his head," poured out, in these Southampton evenings, an eager stream of song. " His poetic composition," says his friend, " was then exceedingly facile: more than once or twice has he taken home with him at night some unfinished act of a drama, in which the editor (Kelsall) had found much to admire, and, at the next meeting, has produced a new one, similar in design, but filled with other thoughts and fancies, which his teeming imagination had projected, in its sheer abundance, and not from any feeling, right or fastidious, of unworthiness in its predecessor. Of several of these very striking fragments, large and grand in their aspect as they each started into form,

Like the red outline of beginning Adam,

. . . the only trace remaining is literally the impression thus deeply cut into their one observer's mind. The fine verse just quoted is the sole remnant, indelibly stamped on the editor's memory, of one of these extinct creations." Fragments survive of at least four dramas, projected, and brought to various stages of completion, at about this time. Beddoes was impatient of the common restraints; he was dashing forward in the spirit of his own advice to another poet:

> Creep not nor climb,
> As they who place their topmost of sublime
> On some peak of this planet, pitifully.
> Dart eaglewise with open wings, and fly
> Until you meet the gods!

Eighteen months after his Southampton visit, Beddoes took his degree at Oxford, and, almost immediately, made up his mind to a course of action which had the profoundest effect upon his future life. He determined to take up the study of medicine; and with that end in view established himself, in 1825, at the University of Göttingen. It is very clear, however, that he had no intention of giving up his poetical work. He took with him to Germany the beginnings of a new play—" a very Gothic-styled tragedy," he calls it, " for which I have a jewel of a name—DEATH'S JEST-BOOK; of course," he adds, " no one will ever read it "; and during his four years at Göttingen he devoted most of his leisure to the completion of this work. He was young; he was rich; he was interested in medical science; and no doubt it seemed to him that he could well afford to amuse himself for half-a-dozen years, before he settled down to the poetical work which was to be the serious occupation of his life. But, as time passed, he became more and more engrossed in the study of medicine, for which he gradually discovered he had not only a taste but a gift; so that at last he came to doubt whether it might not be his true vocation to be a physician, and not a poet after all. Engulfed among the students of Göttingen, England and English ways of life, and even English poetry, became dim to him; " dir, dem Anbeter der seligen Gottheiten der Musen, u.s.w.," he wrote to Kelsall, " was Unterheltendes kann der Liebhaber von Knochen, der fleissige Botaniker und Phisiolog mittheilen? " In 1830 he was still hesitating between the two alternatives. " I sometimes wish," he told the same friend, " to devote myself exclusively to the study of anatomy and physiology in science, of languages, and dramatic poetry "; his pen had run away with him; and his " exclusive " devotion turned out to be a double one, directed towards widely different ends. While he was still in this state of mind, a new interest took possession of him—an interest which worked havoc with his dreams of dramatic authorship and scientific research: he became involved in the revolutionary movement which was at that time beginning to agitate Europe. The details of his adventures are unhappily lost to us, for we know nothing more of them than can be learnt from a few scanty references in his rare letters to English friends; but it is certain that the part he played was an active, and even a dangerous one. He was turned out of Würzburg by " that ingenious Jackanapes," the King of Bavaria; he was an intimate friend of Hegetschweiler, one of the leaders of liberalism in Switzerland; and he was present in Zurich when a body of six thousand peasants, " half-unarmed, and the other half armed with scythes, dungforks and poles, entered the town and overturned the liberal government." In the tumult Hegetschweiler was killed, and Beddoes was soon afterwards forced to fly the canton. During the following years we catch glimpses of him, flitting mysteriously over Germany and Switzerland, at Berlin, at Baden, at Giessen, a strange solitary figure, with tangled hair and meerschaum pipe, scribbling lampoons upon the King of Prussia, translating

Grainger's *Spinal Cord* into German, and Schoenlien's *Diseases of Europeans* into English, exploring Pilatus and the Titlis, evolving now and then some ghostly lyric or some rabelaisian tale, or brooding over the scenes of his " Gothic-styled tragedy," wondering if it were worthless or inspired, and giving it—as had been his wont for the last twenty years —just one more touch before he sent it to the press. He appeared in England once or twice, and in 1846 made a stay of several months, visiting the Procters in London, and going down to Southampton to be with Kelsall once again. Eccentricity had grown on him; he would shut himself for days in his bedroom, smoking furiously; he would fall into fits of long and deep depression. He shocked some of his relatives by arriving at their country house astride a donkey; and he amazed the Procters by starting out one evening to set fire to Drury Lane Theatre with a lighted five-pound note. After this last visit to England, his history becomes even more obscure than before. It is known that in 1847 he was in Frankfort, where he lived for six months in close companionship with a young baker called Degen—" a nice-looking young man, nineteen years of age," we are told, " dressed in a blue blouse, fine in expression, and of a natural dignity of manner "; and that, in the spring of the following year, the two friends went off to Zurich, where Beddoes hired the theatre for a night in order that Degen might appear on the stage in the part of Hotspur. At Basel, however, for some unexplained reason, the friends parted, and Beddoes fell immediately into the profoundest gloom. " Il a été misérable," said the waiter at the Cigogne Hotel, where he was staying, " il a voulu se tuer." It was true. He inflicted a deep wound

in his leg with a razor, in the hope, apparently, of bleeding
to death. He was taken to the hospital, where he constantly
tore off the bandages, until at last it was necessary to ampu-
tate the leg below the knee. The operation was successful,
Beddoes began to recover, and, in the autumn, Degen came
back to Basel. It seemed as if all were going well; for the
poet, with his books around him, and the blue-bloused Degen
by his bedside, talked happily of politics and literature, and
of an Italian journey in the spring. He walked out twice;
was he still happy? Who can tell? Was it happiness, or
misery, or what strange impulse, that drove him, on his third
walk, to go to a chemist's shop in the town, and to obtain
there a phial of deadly poison? On the evening of that day
—the 26th of January, 1849—Dr. Ecklin, his physician, was
hastily summoned, to find Beddoes lying insensible upon the
bed. He never recovered consciousness, and died that night.
Upon his breast was found a pencil note, addressed to one of
his English friends. " My dear Philips," it began, " I am
food for what I am good for—worms." A few testamentary
wishes followed. Kelsall was to have the manuscripts; and
—" W. Beddoes must have a case (50 bottles) of Champagne Moet, 1847 growth, to drink my death in . . . I
ought to have been, among other things," the gruesome document concluded, " a good poet. Life was too great a bore
on one peg, and that a bad one. Buy for Dr. Ecklin one of
Reade's best stomach-pumps." It was the last of his additions to *Death's Jest Book,* and the most *macabre* of all.

Kelsall discharged his duties as literary executor with ex-
emplary care. The manuscripts were fragmentary and confused. There were three distinct drafts of *Death's Jest Book,*

each with variations of its own; and from these Kelsall compiled his first edition of the drama, which appeared in 1850. In the following year he brought out the two volumes of poetical works, which remained for forty years the only record of the full scope and power of Beddoes' genius. They contain reprints of *The Bride's Tragedy* and *Death's Jest Book,* together with two unfinished tragedies, and a great number of dramatic fragments and lyrics; and the poems are preceded by Kelsall's memoir of his friend. Of these rare and valuable volumes the Muses' Library edition is an almost exact reprint, except that it omits the memoir and revives the *Improvisatore*. Only one other edition of Beddoes exists —the limited one brought out by Mr. Gosse in 1890, and based upon a fresh examination of the manuscripts. Mr. Gosse was able to add ten lyrics and one dramatic fragment to those already published by Kelsall; he made public for the first time the true story of Beddoes' suicide, which Kelsall had concealed; and, in 1893, he followed up his edition of the poems by a volume of Beddoes' letters. It is clear, therefore, that there is no one living to whom lovers of Beddoes owe so much as to Mr. Gosse. He has supplied most important materials for the elucidation of the poet's history; and, among the lyrics which he has printed for the first time, are to be found one of the most perfect specimens of Beddoes' command of unearthly pathos—*The Old Ghost*— and one of the most singular examples of his vein of grotesque and ominous humour—*The Oviparous Tailor*. Yet it may be doubted whether even Mr. Gosse's edition is the final one. There are traces in Beddoes' letters of unpublished compositions which may still come to light. What has

happened, one would like to know, to *The Ivory Gate,* that
" volume of prosaic poetry and poetical prose," which Beddoes talked of publishing in 1837? Only a few fine stanzas
from it have ever appeared. And, as Mr. Gosse himself tells
us, the variations in *Death's Jest Book* alone would warrant
the publication of a variorum edition of that work—" if,"
he wisely adds, for the proviso contains the gist of the matter—" if the interest in Beddoes should continue to grow."

" Say what you will, I am convinced the man who is to
awaken the drama must be a bold, trampling fellow—no
creeper into worm-holes—no reviver even—however good.
These reanimations are vampire-cold." The words occur in
one of Beddoes' letters, and they are usually quoted by
critics, on the rare occasions on which his poetry is discussed,
as an instance of the curious incapacity of artists to practise
what they preach. But the truth is that Beddoes was not a
" creeper into worm-holes," he was not even a " reviver ";
he was a reincarnation. Everything that we know of him
goes to show that the laborious and elaborate effort of literary reconstruction was quite alien to his spirit. We have
Kelsall's evidence as to the ease and abundance of his composition; we have the character of the man, as it shines forth
in his letters and in the history of his life—records of a
" bold, trampling fellow," if ever there was one; and we have
the evidence of his poetry itself. For the impress of a fresh
and vital intelligence is stamped unmistakably upon all that
is best in his work. His mature blank verse is perfect. It is
not an artificial concoction galvanized into the semblance of
life; it simply lives. And, with Beddoes, maturity was pre-
cocious, for he obtained complete mastery over the most diffi-

cult and dangerous of metres at a wonderfully early age.
Blank verse is like the Djin in the *Arabian Nights;* it is
either the most terrible of masters, or the most powerful of
slaves. If you have not the magic secret, it will take your
best thoughts, your bravest imaginations, and change them
into toads and fishes; but, if the spell be yours, it will turn
into a flying carpet and lift your simplest utterance into the
highest heaven. Beddoes had mastered the " open sesame "
at an age when most poets are still mouthing ineffectual
wheats and barleys. In his twenty-second year, his thoughts
filled and moved and animated his blank verse as easily and
familiarly as a hand in a glove. He wishes to compare, for
instance, the human mind, with its knowledge of the past, to
a single eye receiving the light of the stars; and the object of
the comparison is to lay stress upon the concentration on one
point of a vast multiplicity of objects. There could be no
better exercise for a young verse-writer than to attempt his
own expression of this idea, and then to examine these lines
by Beddoes—lines where simplicity and splendour have been
woven together with the ease of accomplished art.

> How glorious to live! Even in one thought
> The wisdom of past times to fit together,
> And from the luminous minds of many men
> Catch a reflected truth; as, in one eye,
> Light, from unnumbered worlds and farthest planets
> Of the star-crowded universe, is gathered
> Into one ray.

The effect is, of course, partly produced by the diction; but
the diction, fine as it is, would be useless without the phras-
ing—that art by which the two forces of the metre and the

> Strike, you myrtle-crownèd boys,
> Ivied maidens, strike together! . . .

and Marcello is left alone:

>   I went forth
> Joyfully, as the soul of one who closes
> His pillowed eyes beside an unseen murderer,
> And like its horrible return was mine,
> To find the heart, wherein I breathed and beat,
> Cold, gashed, and dead. Let me forget to love,
> And take a heart of venom: let me make
> A staircase of the frightened breasts of men,
> And climb into a lonely happiness!
> And thou, who only art alone as I,
> Great solitary god of that one sun,
> I charge thee, by the likeness of our state,
> Undo these human veins that tie me close
> To other men, and let your servant griefs
> Unmilk me of my mother, and pour in
> Salt scorn and steaming hate!

A moment later he learns that the duke has suddenly died, and that the dukedom is his. The rest of the play affords an instance of Beddoes' inability to trace out a story, clearly and forcibly, to an appointed end. The succeeding acts are crowded with beautiful passages, with vivid situations, with surprising developments, but the central plot vanishes away into nothing, like a great river dissipating itself among a thousand streams. It is, indeed, clear enough that Beddoes was embarrassed with his riches, that his fertile mind conceived too easily, and that he could never resist the temptation of giving life to his imaginations, even at the cost of killing his play. His conception of Orazio, for instance, began by being that of a young Bacchus, as he appears in the opening scene. But Beddoes could not leave him there; he must have a romantic wife, whom he has deserted; and the wife, once brought into being, must have an interview with her husband. The interview is an exquisitely beautiful one, but it shatters Orazio's character, for, in the course of it, he falls desperately in love with his wife; and meanwhile the wife herself has become so important and interesting a figure that she must be given a father, who in his turn becomes the central character in more than one exciting scene. But, by this time, what has happened to the second brother? It is easy to believe that Beddoes was always ready to begin a new play rather than finish an old one. But it is not so certain that his method was quite as inexcusable as his critics assert. To the reader, doubtless, his faulty construction is glaring enough; but Beddoes wrote his plays to be acted, as a passage in one of his letters very clearly shows. " You are, I think," he writes to Kelsall, " disinclined to the stage: now I confess that I think this is the highest aim of the dramatist, and should be very desirous to get on it. To look down on it is a piece of impertinence, as long as one chooses to write in the form of a play, and is generally the result of one's own inability to produce anything striking and affecting in that way." And it is precisely upon the stage that such faults of construction as those which disfigure Beddoes' tragedies matter least. An audience, whose attention is held and delighted by a succession of striking incidents clothed in splendid speech, neither cares nor knows whether the effect of the whole, as a whole, is worthy of the separate parts. It would be foolish, in the present melancholy condition of the art of dramatic declamation, to wish for the public performance of

rate, Beddoes is among the roses: it is in his expression
that his greatness lies. His verse is an instrument of many
modulations, of exquisite delicacy, of strange suggestiveness, of amazing power. Playing on it, he can give utterance to the subtlest visions, such as this:

> Just now a beam of joy hung on his eyelash;
> But, as I looked, it sunk into his eye,
> Like a bruised worm writhing its form of rings
> Into a darkening hole.

Or to the most marvellous of vague and vast conceptions,
such as this:

> I begin to hear
> Strange but sweet sounds, and the loud rocky dashing
> Of waves, where time into Eternity
> Falls over ruined worlds.

Or he can evoke sensations of pure loveliness, such as these:

> So fair a creature! of such charms compact
> As nature stints elsewhere: which you may find
> Under the tender eyelid of a serpent,
> Or in the gurge of a kiss-coloured rose,
> By drops and sparks: but when she moves, you see,
> Like water from a crystal overfilled,
> Fresh beauty tremble out of her and lave
> Her fair sides to the ground.

Or he can put into a single line all the long memories of
adoration:

> My love was much;
> My life but an inhabitant of his.

Or he can pass in a moment from tiny sweetness to colossal
turmoil:

> I should not say
> How thou art like the daisy in Noah's meadow,
> On which the foremost drop of rain fell warm
> And soft at evening: so the little flower
> Wrapped up its leaves, and shut the treacherous water
> Close to the golden welcome of its breast,
> Delighting in the touch of that which led
> The shower of oceans, in whose billowy drops
> Tritons and lions of the sea were warring,
> And sometimes ships on fire sunk in the blood
> Of their own inmates; others were of ice,
> And some had islands rooted in their waves,
> Beasts on their rocks, and forest-powdering winds,
> And showers tumbling on their tumbling self,
> And every sea of every ruined star
> Was but a drop in the world-melting flood.

He can express alike the beautiful tenderness of love, and the hectic, dizzy, and appalling frenzy of extreme rage:—

> . . . What shall I do? I speak all wrong,
> And lose a soul-full of delicious thought
> By talking. Hush! Let's drink each other up
> By silent eyes. Who lives, but thou and I,
> My heavenly wife? . . .
> I'll watch thee thus, till I can tell a second
> By thy cheek's change.

In that, one can almost feel the kisses; and, in this, one can almost hear the gnashing of the teeth. "Never!" exclaims the duke to his son Torrismond:

> There lies no grain of sand between
> My loved and my detested! Wing thee hence,
> Or thou dost stand to-morrow on a cobweb
> Spun o'er the well of clotted Acheron,
> Whose hydrophobic entrails stream with fire!

> And may this intervening earth be snow,
> And my step burn like the mid coal of Ætna,
> Plunging me, through it all, into the core,
> Where in their graves the dead are shut like seeds,
> If I do not—O, but he is my son!

Is not that tremendous? But, to find Beddoes in his most characteristic mood, one must watch him weaving his mysterious imagination upon the woof of mortality. One must wander with him through the pages of *Death's Jest Book*, one must grow accustomed to the dissolution of reality, and the opening of the nettled lips of graves; one must learn that " the dead are most and merriest," one must ask— " Are the ghosts eavesdropping? "—one must realise that " murder is full of holes." Among the ruins of his Gothic cathedral, on whose cloister walls the Dance of Death is painted, one may speculate at ease over the fragility of existence, and, within sound of that dark ocean,

> Whose tumultuous waves
> Are heaped, contending ghosts,

one may understand how it is that

> Death is mightier, stronger, and more faithful
> To man than Life.

Lingering there, one may watch the Deaths come down from their cloister, and dance and sing amid the moonlight; one may laugh over the grotesque contortions of skeletons; one may crack jokes upon corruption; one may sit down with phantoms, and drink to the health of Death.

In private intercourse Beddoes was the least morbid of human beings. His mind was like one of those Gothic cathedrals of which he was so fond—mysterious within, and filled with a light at once richer and less real than the light of day; on the outside, firm, and towering, and immediately impressive; and embellished, both inside and out, with grinning gargoyles. His conversation, Kelsall tells us, was full of humour and vitality, and untouched by any trace of egoism or affectation. He loved discussion, plunging into it with fire, and carrying it onward with high dexterity and good-humoured force. His letters are excellent; simple, spirited, spicy, and as original as his verse; flavoured with that vein of rattling open-air humour which had produced his school-boy novel in the style of Fielding. He was a man whom it would have been a rare delight to know. His character, so eminently English, compact of courage, of originality, of imagination, and with something coarse in it as well, puts one in mind of Hamlet: not the melodramatic sentimentalist of the stage; but the real Hamlet, Horatio's Hamlet, who called his father's ghost old truepenny, who forged his uncle's signature, who fought Laertes, and ranted in a grave, and lugged the guts into the neighbour room. His tragedy, like Hamlet's, was the tragedy of an over-powerful will—a will so strong as to recoil upon itself, and fall into indecision. It is easy for a weak man to be decided —there is so much to make him so; but a strong man, who can do anything, sometimes leaves everything undone. Fortunately Beddoes, though he did far less than he might have done, possessed so rich a genius that what he did, though small in quantity, is in quality beyond price. " I might have been, among other things, a good poet," were his last words. " Among other things! " aye, there's the

rub. But, in spite of his own "might have been," a good
poet he was. Perhaps for him, after all, there was very
little to regret; his life was full of high nobility; and what
other way of death would have befitted the poet of death?
There is a thought constantly recurring throughout his writings—in his childish as in his most mature work—the
thought of the beauty and the supernal happiness of soft
and quiet death. He had visions of "rosily dying," of
"turning to daisies gently in the grave," of a "pink reclin-
ing death," of death coming like a summer cloud over the
soul. "Let her deathly life pass into death," says one of
his earliest characters, "like music on the night wind."
And, in *Death's Jest Book*, Sibylla has the same thoughts:

> O Death! I am thy friend,
> I struggle not with thee, I love thy state:
> Thou canst be sweet and gentle, be so now;
> And let me pass praying away into thee,
> As twilight still does into starry night.

Did his mind, obsessed and overwhelmed by images of death,
crave at last for the one thing stranger than all these—
the experience of it? It is easy to believe so, and that, ill,
wretched, and abandoned by Degen at the miserable Cigogne
Hotel, he should seek relief in the gradual dissolution which
attends upon loss of blood. And then, when he had recovered, when he was almost happy once again, the old thoughts,
perhaps, came crowding back upon him—thoughts of the
futility of life, and the supremacy of death and the mystical
whirlpool of the unknown, and the long quietude of the
grave. In the end, Death had grown to be something more

than Death to him—it was, mysteriously and transcenden-
tally, Love as well.

> Death's darts are sometimes Love's. So Nature tells,
> When laughing waters close o'er drowning man;
> When in flowers' honied corners poison dwells;
> When Beauty dies: and the unwearied ken
> Of those who seek a cure for long despair
> Will learn . . .

What learning was it that rewarded him? What ghostly
knowledge of eternal love?

> If there are ghosts to raise,
>   What shall I call,
> Out of hell's murky haze,
>   Heaven's blue pall?
> —Raise my loved long-lost boy
> To lead me to his joy.—
>   There are no ghosts to raise;
>   Out of death lead no ways;
>   Vain is the call.
>
> —Know'st thou not ghosts to sue?
>   No love thou hast.
> Else lie, as I will do,
>   And breathe thy last.
> So out of Life's fresh crown
> Fall like a rose-leaf down.
>   Thus are the ghosts to woo;
>   Thus are all dreams made true,
>   Ever to last!

1907.

HENRI BEYLE

HENRI BEYLE

HENRI BEYLE

In the whole of French literature it would be difficult to point to a figure at once so important, so remarkable, and so little known to English readers as Henri Beyle. Most of us are, no doubt, fairly familiar with his pseudonym of " Stendhal "; some of us have read *Le Rouge et Le Noir* and *La Chartreuse de Parme;* but how many of us have any further knowledge of a man whose works are at the present moment appearing in Paris in all the pomp of an elaborate and complete edition, every scrap of whose manuscripts is being collected and deciphered with enthusiastic care, and in honour of whose genius the literary periodicals of the hour are filling entire numbers with exegesis and appreciation? The eminent critic, M. André Gide, when asked lately to name the novel which stands in his opinion first among the novels of France, declared that since, without a doubt, the place belongs to one or other of the novels of Stendhal, his only difficulty was in making his choice among these; and he finally decided upon *La Chartreuse de Parme.* According to this high authority, Henri Beyle was indisputably the creator of the greatest work of fiction in the French language, yet on this side of the Channel we have hardly more than heard of him! Nor is it merely as a writer that Beyle is admired in France. As a man, he seems to have come in, sixty or seventy years after his death, for a singular devotion. There are " Beylistes," or " Stend-

haliens," who dwell with rapture upon every detail of the
master's private life, who extend with pious care the long
catalogue of his amorous adventures, who discuss the shades
of his character with the warmth of personal friendship,
and register his opinions with a zeal which is hardly less
than sectarian. But indeed it is precisely in these extremes
of his French devotees that we shall find a clue to the explanation of our own indifference. Beyle's mind contained,
in a highly exaggerated form, most of the peculiarly distinctive elements of the French character. This does not
mean that he was a typical Frenchman; far from it. He
did not, like Voltaire or Hugo, strike a note to which the
whole national genius vibrated in response. He has never
been, it is unlikely that he ever will be, a popular writer.
His literary reputation in France has been confined, until
perhaps quite lately, to a small distinguished circle. " On
me lira," he was fond of saying, " vers 1880 "; and the
" Beylistes " point to the remark in triumph as one further
proof of the almost divine prescience of the great man. But
in truth Beyle was always read by the *élite* of French critics
and writers—" the happy few," as he used to call them;
and among these he has never been without enthusiastic
admirers. During his lifetime Balzac, in an enormous
eulogy of *La Chartreuse de Parme*, paid him one of the
most magnificent compliments ever received by a man of
letters from a fellow craftsman. In the next generation
Taine declared himself his disciple; a little later—" vers
1880," in fact—we find Zola describing him as " notre père
à tous," and M. Bourget followed with elaborate incense.
To-day we have writers of such different tendencies as

M. Barrès and M. Gide acclaiming him as a supreme master, and the fashionable idolatry of the " Beylistes." Yet, at the same time, running parallel to this stream of homage, it is easy to trace a line of opinion of a totally different kind. It is the opinion of the more solid, the more middle-class elements of French life. Thus Sainte-Beuve, in two characteristic " Lundis," poured a great deal of very tepid water upon Balzac's flaming panegyric. Then Flaubert—" vers 1880," too—confessed that he could see very little in Stendhal. And, only a few years ago, M. Chuquet, of the Institute, took the trouble to compose a thick book in which he has collected with scrupulous detail all the known facts concerning the life and writings of a man whom he forthwith proceeds to damn through five hundred pages of faint praise. These discrepancies are curious: how can we account for such odd differences of taste? How are we to reconcile the admiration of Balzac with the dislike of Flaubert, the raptures of M. Bourget and M. Barrès with the sniffs of Sainte-Beuve and M. Chuquet of the Institute? The explanation seems to be that Beyle occupies a position in France analogous to that of Shelley in England. Shelley is not a national hero, not because he lacked the distinctive qualities of an Englishman, but for the opposite reason— because he possessed so many of them in an extreme degree. The idealism, the daring, the imagination, and the unconventionality which give Shakespeare, Nelson, and Dr. Johnson their place in our pantheon—all these were Shelley's, but they were his in too undiluted and intense a form, with the result that, while he will never fail of worshippers among us, there will also always be Englishmen unable to appreciate him at all. Such, *mutatis mutandis*—and in this case the proviso is a very large one—is the position of Beyle in France. After all, when Bunthorne asked for a not-too-French French bean he showed more commonsense than he intended. Beyle is a too-French French writer—too French even for the bulk of his own compatriots; and so for us it is only natural that he should be a little difficult. Yet this very fact is in itself no bad reason for giving him some attention. An understanding of this very Gallic individual might give us a new insight into the whole strange race. And besides, the curious creature is worth looking at for his own sake too.

But, when one tries to catch him and pin him down on the dissecting-table, he turns out to be exasperatingly elusive. Even his most fervent admirers cannot agree among themselves as to the true nature of his achievements. Balzac thought of him as an artist, Taine was captivated by his conception of history, M. Bourget adores him as a psychologist, M. Barrès lays stress upon his " sentiment d'honneur," and the " Beylistes " see in him the embodiment of modernity. Certainly very few writers have had the good fortune to appeal at once so constantly and in so varied a manner to succeeding generations as Henri Beyle. The circumstances of his life no doubt in part account for the complexity of his genius. He was born in 1783, when the *ancien régime* was still in full swing; his early manhood was spent in the turmoil of the Napoleonic wars; he lived to see the Bourbon reaction, the Romantic revival, the revolution of 1830, and the establishment of Louis Philippe; and when he died, at the age of sixty, the nineteenth century was nearly half-way through. Thus his life exactly spans the interval between the old world and the new. His family, which belonged to the magistracy of Grenoble, preserved the living tradition of the eighteenth century. His grandfather was a polite, amiable, periwigged sceptic after the manner of Fontenelle, who always spoke of " M. de Voltaire " with a smile " mélangé de respect et d'affection "; and when the Terror came, two representatives of the people were sent down to Grenoble, with the result that Beyle's father was pronounced (with a hundred and fifty others) " notoirement suspect " of disaffection to the Republic, and confined to his house. At the age of sixteen Beyle arrived in Paris, just after the *coup d'état* of the 18th Brumaire had made Bonaparte First Consul, and he immediately came under the influence of his cousin Daru, that extraordinary man to whose terrific energies was due the organisation of Napoleon's greatest armies, and whose leisure moments—for apparently he had leisure moments—were devoted to the composition of idylls in the style of Tibullus and to an enormous correspondence on literary topics with the poetasters of the day. It was as a subordinate to this remarkable personage that Beyle spent nearly the whole of the next fifteen years of his life—in Paris, in Italy, in Germany, in Russia—wherever the whirling tempest of the Napoleonic policy might happen to carry him. His actual military experience was considerably slighter than what, in after years, he liked to give his friends to understand it had been. For hardly more than a year, during the Italian campaign, he was in the army as a lieutenant of dragoons: the rest of his public service was spent in the commissariat department.

The descriptions which he afterwards delighted to give of his adventures at Marengo, at Jéna, at Wagram, or at the crossing of the Niémen have been shown by M. Chuquet's unkind researches to have been imaginary. Beyle was present at only one great battle—Bautzen. " Nous voyons fort bien," he wrote in his journal on the following day, " de midi à trois heures, tout ce qu'on peut voir d'une bataille, c'est à dire rien." He was, however, at Moscow in 1812, and he accompanied the army through the horrors of the retreat. When the conflagration had broken out in the city he had abstracted from one of the deserted palaces a finely bound copy of the *Facéties* of Voltaire; the book helped to divert his mind as he lay crouched by the camp-fire through the terrible nights that followed; but, as his companions showed their disapproval of any one who could smile over Akakia and Pompignan in such a situation, one day he left the red-morocco volume behind him in the snow.

The fall of Napoleon threw Beyle out of employment, and the period of his literary activity began. His books were not successful; his fortune gradually dwindled; and he drifted in Paris and Italy, and even in England, more and more disconsolately, with thoughts of suicide sometimes in his head. But in 1830 the tide of his fortunes turned. The revolution of July, by putting his friends· into power, brought him a competence in the shape of an Italian consulate; and in the same year he gained for the first time some celebrity by the publication of *Le Rouge et Le Noir*. The rest of his life was spent in the easy discharge of his official duties at Civita Vecchia, alternating with periods of leave—one of them lasted for three years—spent in Paris among his friends, of whom the most distinguished was Prosper Mérimée. In 1839 appeared his last published work—*La Chartreuse de Parme;* and three years later he died suddenly in Paris. His epitaph, composed by himself with the utmost care, was as follows:

QUI GIACE

ARRIGO BEYLE MILANESE

VISSE, SCRISSE, AMO.

The words, read rightly, indicate many things—his adoration of Italy and Milan, his eccentricity, his scorn of the conventions of society and the limits of nationality, his adventurous life, his devotion to literature, and, lastly, the fact that, through all the varieties of his experience—in the earliest years of his childhood, in his agitated manhood, in his calm old age—there had never been a moment when he was not in love.

Beyle's work falls into two distinct groups—the first consisting of his novels, and the second of his miscellaneous writings, which include several biographies, a dissertation on Love, some books of criticism and travel, his letters and various autobiographical fragments. The bulk of the latter group is large; much of it has only lately seen the light; and more of it, at present in MS. at the Library of Grenoble, is promised us by the indefatigable editors of the new complete edition which is now appearing in Paris. The interest of this portion of Beyle's writings is almost entirely personal: that of his novels is mainly artistic. It was as a novelist that Beyle first gained his celebrity, and it is still as a novelist—or rather as the author of *Le Rouge et Le Noir* and *La Chartreuse de Parme* (for an earlier work, *Armance,* some short stories, and some later posthumous fragments may be left out of account) that he is most widely known to-day. These two remarkable works lose none of their significance if we consider the time at which they were composed. It was in the full flood of the Romantic revival, that marvellous hour in the history of French literature when the tyranny of two centuries was shattered for ever, and a boundless wealth of inspirations, possibilities, and beauties before undreamt-of suddenly burst upon the view. It was the hour of Hugo, Vigny, Musset, Gautier, Balzac, with their new sonorities and golden cadences, their new lyric passion and dramatic stress, their new virtuosities, their new impulse towards the strange and the magnificent, their new desire for diversity and the manifold comprehension of life. But, if we turn to the contemporaneous pages of Stendhal, what do we find? We find a succession of colourless, unemphatic sentences; we find cold reasoning and exact narrative; we find polite irony and dry wit. The spirit of the eighteenth century is everywhere; and if the old gentleman with the perruque and the " M. de Voltaire " could have taken a glance at his grandson's novels, he would have rapped his snuff-box and approved. It is true that Beyle joined the ranks of the Romantics for a moment with a *brochure* attacking Racine at the expense of Shakespeare; but this was merely one of those contradictory changes of front which were inherent in his nature; and in reality the whole Romantic movement meant nothing to him. There is a story of a meeting in the house of a common friend between him and Hugo, in which the two men faced each other like a couple of cats with their backs up and their whiskers bristling. No wonder! But Beyle's true attitude towards his great contemporaries was hardly even one of hostility: he simply could not open their books. As for Chateaubriand, the god of their idolatry, he loathed him like poison. He used to describe how, in his youth, he had been on the point of fighting a duel with an officer who had ventured to maintain that a phrase in *Atala*— " la cime indéterminée des forêts "—was not intolerable. Probably he was romancing (M. Chuquet says so); but at any rate the story sums up symbolically Beyle's attitude towards his art. To him the whole apparatus of " fine writing "—the emphatic phrase, the picturesque epithet, the rounded rhythm—was anathema. The charm that such ornaments might bring was in reality only a cloak for loose thinking and feeble observation. Even the style of the eighteenth century was not quite his ideal; it was too elegant; there was an artificial neatness about the form which imposed itself upon the substance, and degraded it. No, there was only one example of the perfect style, and that was the *Code Napoléon;* for there alone everything was subordinated to the exact and complete expression of what was to be said. A statement of law can have no place for irrelevant beauties, or the vagueness of personal feeling; by its very nature, it must resemble a sheet of plate glass through which every object may be seen with absolute distinctness, in its true shape. Beyle declared that he was in the habit of reading several paragraphs of the Code every morning after breakfast " pour prendre le ton." This again was for long supposed to be one of his little jokes; but quite lately the searchers among the MSS. at Grenoble have discovered page after page copied out from the Code in Beyle's handwriting. No doubt, for that wayward lover of paradoxes, the real joke lay in everybody taking for a joke what *he* took quite seriously.

This attempt to reach the exactitude and the detachment of an official document was not limited to Beyle's style; it runs through the whole tissue of his work. He wished to present life dispassionately and intellectually, and if he could have reduced his novels to a series of mathematical symbols, he would have been charmed. The contrast between his method and that of Balzac is remarkable. That wonderful art of materialisation, of the sensuous evocation of the forms, the qualities, the very stuff and substance of things, which was perhaps Balzac's greatest discovery, Beyle neither possessed nor wished to possess. Such matters were to him of the most subordinate importance, which it was no small part of the novelist's duty to keep very severely in their place. In the earlier chapters of *Le Rouge et Le Noir*, for instance, he is concerned with almost the same subject as Balzac in the opening of *Les Illusions Perdues*—the position of a young man in a provincial town, brought suddenly from the humblest surroundings into the midst of the leading society of the place through his intimate relations with a woman of refinement. But while in Balzac's pages what emerges is the concrete vision of provincial life down to the last pimple on the nose of the lowest footman, Beyle concentrates his whole attention on the personal problem, hints in a few rapid strokes at what Balzac has spent all his genius in describing, and reveals to us instead, with the precision of a surgeon at an operation, the inmost fibres of his hero's mind. In fact, Beyle's method is the classical method—the method of selection, of omission, of unification, with the object of creating a central impression of supreme reality. Zola criticises him for disregarding " le milieu."

Il y a [he says] un épisode célèbre dans *Le Rouge et Le Noir,* la scéne où Julien, assis un soir à côté de Mme. de Rénal, sous les branches noires d'un arbre, se fait un devoir de lui prendre la main, pendant qu'elle cause avec Mme. Derville. C'est un petit drame muet d'une grande puissance, et Stendhal y a analysé merveilleusement les états d'âme de ses deux personnages. Or, le milieu n'apparaît pas une seule fois. Nous pourrions être n'importe où dans n'importe quelles conditions, la scène resterait la même pourvu qu'il fit noir. . . . Donnez l'épisode à un écrivain pour qui les milieux existent, et dans la défaite de cette femme, il fera entrer la nuit, avec ses odeurs, avec ses voix, avec ses voluptés molles. Et cet écrivain sera dans le vérité, son tableau sera plus complet.

More complete, perhaps; but would it be more convincing? Zola, with his statistical conception of art, could not understand that you could tell a story properly unless you described in detail every contingent fact. He could not see that Beyle was able, by simply using the symbol " nuit," to suggest the " milieu " at once to the reader's imagination. Everybody knows all about the night's accessories—" ses odeurs, ses voix, ses voluptés molles "; and what a relief it is to be spared, for once in a way, an elaborate expatiation upon them! And Beyle is perpetually evoking the gratitude of his readers in this way. " Comme il insiste peu! " as M. Gide exclaims. Perhaps the best test of a man's intelligence is his capacity for making a summary. Beyle knew this, and his novels are full of passages which read like nothing so much as extraordinarily able summaries of some enormous original narrative which has been lost.

It was not that he was lacking in observation, that he had no eye for detail, or no power of expressing it; on the contrary, his vision was of the sharpest, and his pen could call up pictorial images of startling vividness, when he wished. But he very rarely did wish: it was apt to involve a tiresome insistence. In his narratives he is like a brilliant talker in a sympathetic circle, skimming swiftly from point to point, taking for granted the intelligence of his audience, not afraid here and there to throw out a vague " etc." when the rest of the sentence is too obvious to state; always plain of speech, never self-assertive, and taking care above all things never to force the note. His famous description of the Battle of Waterloo in *La Chartreuse de Parme* is certainly the finest example of this side of his art. Here he produces an indelible impression by a series of light touches applied with unerring skill. Unlike Zola, unlike Tolstoi, he shows us neither the loathsomeness nor the devastation of a battlefield, but its insignificance, its irrelevant detail, its unmeaning grotesquenesses and indignities, its incoherence, and its empty weariness. Remembering his own experience at Bautzen, he has made his hero—a young Italian impelled by Napoleonic enthusiasm to join the French army as a volunteer on the eve of the battle—go through the great day in such a state of vague perplexity that in the end he can never feel quite certain that he really *was* at Waterloo. He experiences a succession of trivial and unpleasant inci-

dents, culminating in his being hoisted off his horse by two
of his comrades, in order that a general, who has had his
own shot from under him, might be supplied with a mount;
for the rest, he crosses and recrosses some fields, comes upon
a dead body in a ditch, drinks brandy with a *vivandière,*
gallops over a field covered with dying men, has an indefinite
skirmish in a wood—and it is over. At one moment, having
joined the escort of some generals, the young man allows
his horse to splash into a stream, thereby covering one of
the generals with muddy water from head to foot. The
passage that follows is a good specimen of Beyle's narrative
style:

En arrivant sur l'autre rive, Fabrice y avait trouvé les
généraux tout seuls; le bruit du canon lui sembla redoubler; ce
fut à peine s'il entendit le général, par lui si bien mouillé, qui
criait à son oreille:
Où as-tù pris ce cheval?
Fabrice était tellement troublé, qu'il répondit en Italien: *l'ho
comprato poco fa.* (Je viens de l'acheter à l'instant).
Que dis-tu? lui cria le général.
Mais le tapage devint tellement fort en ce moment, que
Fabrice ne put lui répondre. Nous avouerons que notre héros
était fort peu héros en ce moment. Toutefois, la peur ne venait
chez lui qu'en seconde ligne; il était surtout scandalisé de ce
bruit qui lui faisait mal aux oreilles. L'escorte prit le galop; on
traversait une grande pièce de terre labourée, située au delà du
canal, et ce champ était jonché de cadavres.

How unemphatic it all is! What a paucity of epithet,
what a reticence in explanation! How a Romantic would
have lingered over the facial expression of the general, and
how a Naturalist would have analysed that " tapage "! And
yet, with all their efforts, would they have succeeded in

conveying that singular impression of disturbance, of cross-purposes, of hurry, and of ill-defined fear, which Beyle with his quiet terseness has produced?

It is, however, in his psychological studies that the de-tached and intellectual nature of Beyle's method is most clearly seen. When he is describing, for instance, the de-velopment of Julien Sorel's mind in *Le Rouge et Le Noir*, when he shows us the soul of the young peasant with its ignorance, its ambition, its pride, going step by step into the whirling vortex of life—then we seem to be witnessing not so much the presentment of a fiction as the unfolding of some scientific fact. The procedure is almost mathematical: a proposition is established, the inference is drawn, the next proposition follows, and so on until the demonstration is complete. Here the influence of the eighteenth century is very strongly marked. Beyle had drunk deeply of that fountain of syllogism and analysis that flows through the now forgotten pages of Helvétius and Condillac; he was an ardent votary of logic in its austerest form—" la lo-gique " he used to call it, dividing the syllables in a kind of awe-inspired emphasis; and he considered the ratiocinative style of Montesquieu almost as good as that of the *Code Civil*.

If this had been all, if we could sum him up simply as an acute and brilliant writer who displays the scientific and prosaic sides of the French genius in an extreme degree, Beyle's position in literature would present very little diffi-culty. He would take his place at once as a late—an abnor-mally late—product of the eighteenth century. But he was not that. In his blood there was a virus which had never tingled in the veins of Voltaire. It was the virus of modern

life—that new sensibility, that new passionateness, which
Rousseau had first made known to the world, and which
had won its way over Europe behind the thunder of Napoleon's artillery. Beyle had passed his youth within earshot
of that mighty roar, and his inmost spirit could never lose
the echo of it. It was in vain that he studied Condillac
and modelled his style on the Code; in vain that he sang
the praises of *la Lo-gique*, shrugged his shoulders at the
Romantics, and turned the cold eye of a scientific investi-
gator upon the phenomena of life; he remained essentially
a man of feeling. His unending series of *grandes passions*
was one unmistakeable sign of this; another was his intense
devotion to the Fine Arts. Though his taste in music and
painting was the taste of his time—the literary and sentimental taste of the age of Rossini and Canova—he nevertheless brought to the appreciation of works of art a kind
of intimate gusto which reveals the genuineness of his emotion. The " jouissances d'ange," with which at his first
entrance into Italy he heard at Novara the *Matrimonio
Segreto* of Cimarosa, marked an epoch in his life. He adored
Mozart: " I can imagine nothing more distasteful to me,"
he said, " than a thirty-mile walk through the mud; but
I would take one at this moment if I knew that I should
hear a good performance of *Don Giovanni* at the end of
it." The virgins of Guido Reni sent him into ecstasies and
the Goddesses of Correggio into raptures. In short, as he
himself admitted, he never could resist " le Beau " in whatever form he found it. *Le Beau!* The phrase is characteristic of the peculiar species of ingenuous sensibility which
so oddly agitated this sceptical man of the world. His whole

vision of life was coloured by it. His sense of values was impregnated with what he called his " espagnolisme "—his immense admiration for the noble and the high-resounding in speech or act or character—an admiration which landed him often enough in hysterics and absurdity. Yet this was the soil in which a temperament of caustic reasonableness had somehow implanted itself. The contrast is surprising, because it is so extreme. Other men have been by turns sensible and enthusiastic: but who before or since has combined the emotionalism of a schoolgirl with the cold penetration of a judge on the bench? Beyle, for instance, was capable of writing, in one of those queer epitaphs of himself which he was constantly composing, the high-falutin' words " Il respecta un seul homme: Napoleon "; and yet, as he wrote them, he must have remembered well enough that when he met Napoleon face to face his unabashed scrutiny had detected swiftly that the man was a play-actor, and a vulgar one at that. Such were the contradictions of his double nature, in which the elements, instead of being mixed, came together, as it were, in layers, like superimposed strata of chalk and flint.

In his novels this cohabitation of opposites is responsible both for what is best and what is worst. When the two forces work in unison the result is sometimes of extraordinary value—a product of a kind which it would be difficult to parallel in any other author. An eye of icy gaze is turned upon the tumultuous secrets of passion, and the pangs of love are recorded in the language of Euclid. The image of the surgeon inevitably suggests itself—the hand with the iron nerve and the swift knife laying bare the trembling mysteries within. It is the intensity of Beyle's observation, joined with such an exactitude of exposition, that makes his dry pages sometimes more thrilling than the wildest tale of adventure or all the marvels of high romance. The passage in *La Chartreuse de Parme* describing Count Mosca's jealousy has this quality, which appears even more clearly in the chapters of *Le Rouge et Le Noir* concerning Julien Sorel and Mathilde de la Mole. Here Beyle has a subject after his own heart. The loves of the peasant youth and the aristocratic girl, traversed and agitated by their overweening pride, and triumphing at last rather over themselves than over each other—these things make up a gladiatorial combat of " espagnolismes," which is displayed to the reader with a supreme incisiveness. The climax is reached when Mathilde at last gives way to her passion, and throws herself into the arms of Julien, who forces himself to make no response:

Ses bras se roidirent, tant l'effort imposé par la politique était pénible. Je ne dois pas même me permettre de presser contre mon cœur ce corps souple et charmant; ou elle me méprise, ou elle me maltraite. Quel affreux caractère!

Et en maudissant le caractère de Mathilde, il l'en aimait cent fois plus; il lui semblait avoir dans ses bras une reine.

L'impassible froideur de Julien redoubla le malheur de Mademoiselle de la Mole. Elle était loin d'avoir le sang-froid nécessaire pour chercher à deviner dans ses yeux ce qu'il sentait pour elle en cet instant. Elle ne put se résoudre à le regarder; elle tremblait de rencontrer l'expression du mépris.

Assise sur le divan de la bibliothèque, immobile et la tête tournée du côté opposé à Julien, elle était en proie aux plus vives douleurs que l'orgueil et l'amour puissent faire éprouver à une âme humaine. Dans quelle atroce démarche elle venait de tomber!

Il m'était réservé, malheureuse que je suis! de voir repoussées

" noble " rhetoric of the French Classical Drama; they find the tirades of Napoleon, which animated the armies of France to victory, pieces of nauseous clap-trap. And just now it is this side—to us the obviously weak side—of Beyle's genius that seems to be most in favour with French critics. To judge from M. Barrès, writing dithyrambically of Beyle's " sentiment d'honneur," that is his true claim to greatness. The sentiment of honour is all very well, one is inclined to mutter on this side of the Channel; but oh, for a little sentiment of humour too!

The view of Beyle's personality which his novels give us may be seen with far greater detail in his miscellaneous writings. It is to these that his most modern admirers devote their main attention—particularly to his letters and his autobiographies; but they are all of them highly characteristic of their author, and—whatever the subject may be, from a guide to Rome to a life of Napoleon—one gathers in them, scattered up and down through their pages, a curious, dimly-adumbrated philosophy—an ill-defined and yet intensely personal point of view—*le Beylisme*. It is in fact almost entirely in this secondary quality that their interest lies; their ostensible subject-matter is unimportant. An apparent exception is the book in which Beyle has embodied his reflections upon Love. The volume, with its meticulous apparatus of analysis, definition, and classification, which gives it the air of being a parody of " L'Esprit des Lois," is yet full of originality, of lively anecdote and keen observation. Nobody but Beyle could have written it; nobody but Beyle could have managed to be at once so stimulating and so jejune, so clear-sighted and so exasperating. But here

again, in reality, it is not the question at issue that is interesting—one learns more of the true nature of Love in one
or two of La Bruyère's short sentences than in all Beyle's
three hundred pages of disquisition; but what is absorbing
is the sense that comes to one, as one reads it, of the presence, running through it all, of a restless and problematical
spirit. " Le Beylisme " is certainly not susceptible of any
exact definition; its author was too capricious, too unmethod-
ical, in spite of his *lo-gique,* ever to have framed a coherent
philosophy; it is essentially a thing of shreds and patches,
of hints, suggestions, and quick visions of flying thoughts.
M. Barrès says that what lies at the bottom of it is a " passion de collectionner les belles énergies."   But there are
many kinds of " belles énergies," and some of them
certainly do not fit into the framework of " le Beylisme."
" Quand je suis arrêté par des voleurs, ou qu'on me tire des
coups de fusil, je me sens une grande colère contre le gouv-
ernement et le curé de l'endroit. Quand au voleur, il me
plaît, s'il est énergique, car il m'amuse." It was the energy
of self-assertiveness that pleased Beyle; that of self-restraint
did not interest him. The immorality of the point of view
is patent and at times it appears to be simply based upon
the common selfishness of an egotist. But in reality it was
something more significant than that. The " chasse au bon-
heur " which Beyle was always advocating was no respectable epicureanism; it had about it a touch of the fanatical.
There was anarchy in it—a hatred of authority, an impa-
tience with custom, above all a scorn for the commonplace
dictates of ordinary morality. Writing his memoirs at the
age of fifty-two, Beyle looked back with pride on the joy

LADY HESTER STANHOPE

LADY HESTER STANHOPE

LADY HESTER STANHOPE

The Pitt nose has a curious history. One can watch its transmigrations through three lives. The tremendous hook of old Lord Chatham, under whose curve Empires came to birth, was succeeded by the bleak upward-pointing nose of William Pitt the younger—the rigid symbol of an indomitable *hauteur*. With Lady Hester Stanhope came the final stage. The nose, still with an upward tilt in it, had lost its masculinity; the hard bones of the uncle and the grandfather had disappeared. Lady Hester's was a nose of wild ambitions, of pride grown fantastical, a nose that scorned the earth, shooting off, one fancies, towards some eternally eccentric heaven. It was a nose, in fact, altogether in the air.

Noses, of course, are aristocratic things; and Lady Hester was the child of a great aristocracy. But, in her case, the aristocratic impulse, which had carried her predecessors to glory, had less fortunate results. There has always been a strong strain of extravagance in the governing families of England; from time to time they throw off some peculiarly ill-balanced member, who performs a strange meteoric course. A century earlier, Lady Mary Wortley Montagu was an illustrious example of this tendency: that splendid comet, after filling half the heavens, vanished suddenly into desolation and darkness. Lady Hester Stanhope's spirit was still more uncommon; and she met with a most uncommon fate.

She was born in 1776, the eldest daughter of that extraordinary Earl Stanhope, Jacobin and inventor, who made the first steamboat and the first calculating machine, who defended the French Revolution in the House of Lords and erased the armorial bearings—" damned aristocratical nonsense "—from his carriages and his plate. Her mother, Chatham's daughter and the favourite sister of Pitt, died when she was four years old. The second Lady Stanhope, a frigid woman of fashion, left her stepdaughters to the care of futile governesses, while " Citizen Stanhope " ruled the household from his laboratory with the violence of a tyrant. It was not until Lady Hester was twenty-four that she escaped from the slavery of her father's house, by going to live with her grandmother, Lady Chatham. On Lady Chatham's death, three years later, Pitt offered her his protection, and she remained with him until his death in 1806.

Her three years with Pitt, passed in the very centre of splendid power, were brilliant and exciting. She flung herself impetuously into the movement and the passion of that vigorous society; she ruled her uncle's household with high vivacity; she was liked and courted; if not beautiful, she was fascinating—very tall, with a very fair and clear complexion, and dark-blue eyes, and a countenance of wonderful expressiveness. Her talk, full of the trenchant nonchalance of those days, was both amusing and alarming: " My dear Hester, what are you saying? " Pitt would call out to her from across the room. She was devoted to her uncle, who warmly returned her affection. She was devoted, too—but in a more dangerous fashion—to the intoxicating Antinous, Lord Granville Leveson Gower. The reckless manner in which she carried on this love-affair was the first indication of something overstrained, something wild and unaccountable, in her temperament. Lord Granville, after flirting with her outrageously, declared that he could never marry her, and went off on an embassy to St. Petersburg. Her distraction was extreme: she hinted that she would follow him to Russia; she threatened, and perhaps attempted, suicide; she went about telling everybody that he had jilted her. She was taken ill, and then there were rumours of an accouchement, which, it was said, she took care to *afficher*, by appearing without rouge and fainting on the slightest provocation. In the midst of these excursions and alarums there was a terrible and unexpected catastrophe. Pitt died. And Lady Hester suddenly found herself a dethroned princess, living in a small house in Montagu Square on a pension of £1,200 a year.

She did not abandon society, however, and the tongue of gossip continued to wag. Her immediate marriage with a former lover, Mr. Hill, was announced: " il est bien bon," said Lady Bessborough. Then it was whispered that Canning was " le regnant "—that he was with her " not only all day, but almost all night." She quarrelled with Canning and became attached to Sir John Moore. Whether she was actually engaged to marry him—as she seems to have asserted many years later—is doubtful; his letters to her, full as they are of respectful tenderness, hardly warrant the conclusion; but it is certain that he died with her name on his lips. Her favourite brother, Charles, was killed beside him; and it was natural that under this double blow she should have retired from London. She buried herself in Wales; but not for long. In 1810 she set sail for Gibraltar with her brother James, who was rejoining his regiment in the Peninsula. She never returned to England.

There can be no doubt that at the time of her departure the thought of a lifelong exile was far from her mind. It was only gradually, as she moved further and further eastward, that the prospect of life in England—at last even in Europe—grew distasteful to her; as late as 1816 she was talking of a visit to Provence. Accompanied by two or three English fellow travellers, her English maid, Mrs. Fry, her private physician, Dr. Meryon, and a host of servants, she progressed, slowly and in a great state, through Malta and Athens, to Constantinople. She was conveyed in battleships, and lodged with governors and ambassadors. After spending many months in Constantinople, Lady Hester discovered that she was " dying to see Napoleon with her own eyes," and attempted accordingly to obtain passports to France. The project was stopped by Stratford Canning, the English Minister, upon which she decided to visit Egypt, and, chartering a Greek vessel, sailed for Alexandria in the winter of 1811. Off the island of Rhodes a violent storm sprang up; the whole party were forced to abandon the ship, and to take refuge upon a bare rock, where they remained without food or shelter for thirty hours. Eventually, after many severe privations, Alexandria was reached in safety; but this disastrous voyage was a turning-point in Lady Hester's career. At Rhodes she was forced to exchange her torn and dripping raiment for the attire of a Turkish gentleman—a dress which she never afterwards abandoned. It was the first step in her orientalization.

She passed the next two years in a triumphal progress. Her appearance in Cairo caused the greatest sensation, and she was received in state by the Pasha, Mehemet Ali. Her costume on this occasion was gorgeous: she wore a turban of cashmere, a brocaded waistcoat, a priceless pelisse, and a vast pair of purple velvet pantaloons embroidered all over in gold. She was ushered by chamberlains with silver wands through the inner courts of the palace to a pavilion in the harem, where the Pasha, rising to receive her, conversed with her for an hour. From Cairo she turned northwards, visiting Jaffa, Jerusalem, Acre, and Damascus. Her travelling dress was of scarlet cloth trimmed with gold, and, when on horseback, she wore over the whole a white-hooded and tasselled burnous. Her maid, too, was forced, protesting, into trousers, though she absolutely refused to ride astride. Poor Mrs. Fry had gone through various and dreadful sufferings—shipwreck and starvation, rats and blackbeetles unspeakable—but she retained her equanimity. Whatever her Ladyship might think fit to be, *she* was an Englishwoman to the last, and Philippaki was Philip Parker and Mustapha Mr. Farr.

Outside Damascus, Lady Hester was warned that the town was the most fanatical in Turkey, and that the scandal of a woman entering it in man's clothes, unveiled, would be so great as to be dangerous. She was begged to veil herself, and to make her entry under cover of darkness. " I must take the bull by the horns," she replied, and rode into the city unveiled at midday. The population were thunderstruck; but at last their amazement gave way to enthusiasm, and the incredible lady was hailed everywhere as Queen, crowds followed her, coffee was poured out before her, and the whole bazaar rose as she passed. Yet she was not satisfied with her triumphs; she would do something still more glorious and astonishing; she would plunge into the desert and visit the ruins of Palmyra, which only half-a-dozen of the boldest travellers had ever seen. The Pasha of Damascus offered her a military escort, but she preferred to throw herself upon the hospitality of the Bedouin Arabs, who, overcome by her horsemanship, her powers of sight, and her courage, enrolled her a member of their tribe. After a week's journey in their company, she reached Palmyra, where the inhabitants met her with wild enthusiasm, and under the Corinthian columns of Zenobia's temple crowned her head with flowers. This happened in March, 1813; it was the apogee of Lady Hester's life. Henceforward her fortunes gradually but steadily declined.

The rumour of her exploits had spread through Syria, and from the year 1813 onwards, her reputation was enormous. She was received everywhere as a royal, almost as a supernatural, personage: she progressed from town to town amid official prostrations and popular rejoicings. But she herself was in a state of hesitation and discontent. Her future was uncertain; she had grown scornful of the West —must she return to it? The East alone was sympathetic, the East alone was tolerable—but could she cut herself off for ever from the past? At Laodicea she was suddenly struck down by the plague, and, after months of illness, it was

borne in upon her that all was vanity. She rented an empty
monastery on the slopes of Mount Lebanon, not far from
Sayda (the ancient Sidon), and took up her abode there.
Then her mind took a new surprising turn; she dashed to
Ascalon, and, with the permission of the Sultan, began ex-
cavations in a ruined temple with the object of discovering
a hidden treasure of three million pieces of gold. Having
unearthed nothing but an antique statue, which, in order
to prove her disinterestedness, she ordered her appalled
doctor to break into little bits, she returned to her monastery. Finally, in 1816, she moved to another house, further up Mount Lebanon, and near the village of Djoun; and
at Djoun she remained until her death, more than twenty
years later.

Thus, almost accidentally as it seems, she came to the
end of her wanderings, and the last, long, strange, mythical
period of her existence began. Certainly the situation that
she had chosen was sublime. Her house, on the top of a
high bare hill among great mountains, was a one-storied
group of buildings, with many ramifying courts and out-
houses, and a garden of several acres surrounded by a
rampart wall. The garden, which she herself had planted
and tended with the utmost care, commanded a glorious
prospect. On every side but one the vast mountains tow-
ered, but to the west there was an opening, through which,
in the far distance, the deep blue Mediterranean was revealed. From this romantic hermitage, her singular renown
spread over the world. European travellers who had been
admitted to her presence brought back stories full of Eastern
mystery; they told of a peculiar grandeur, a marvellous

prestige, an imperial power. The precise nature of Lady
Hester's empire was, indeed, dubious; she was in fact merely
the tenant of her Djoun establishment, for which she paid
a rent of £20 a year. But her dominion was not subject
to such limitations. She ruled imaginatively, transcenden-
tally; the solid glory of Chatham had been transmuted into
the phantasy of an Arabian Night. No doubt she herself
believed that she was something more than a chimerical
Empress. When a French traveller was murdered in the
desert, she issued orders for the punishment of the offenders;
punished they were, and Lady Hester actually received the
solemn thanks of the French Chamber. It seems probable,
however, that it was the Sultan's orders rather than Lady
Hester's which produced the desired effect. In her feud
with her terrible neighbour, the Emir Beshyr, she main-
tained an undaunted front. She kept the tyrant at bay;
but perhaps the Emir, who, so far as physical force was
concerned, held her in the hollow of his hand, might have
proceeded to extremities if he had not received a severe
admonishment from Stratford Canning at Constantinople.
What is certain is that the ignorant and superstitious popu-
lations around her feared and loved her, and that she, react-
ing to her own mysterious prestige, became at last even as
they. She plunged into astrology and divination; she awaited
the moment when, in accordance with prophecy, she should
enter Jerusalem side by side with the Mahdi, the Messiah;
she kept two sacred horses, destined, by sure signs, to carry
her and him to their last triumph. The Orient had mastered
her utterly. She was no longer an Englishwoman, she declared; she lothed England; she would never go there again;

if she went anywhere it would be to Arabia, to "her own people."

Her expenses were immense—not only for herself but for others, for she poured out her hospitality with a noble hand. She ran into debt, and was swindled by the moneylenders; her steward cheated her, her servants pilfered her; her distress was at last acute. She fell into fits of terrible depression, bursting into dreadful tears and savage cries. Her habits grew more and more eccentric. She lay in bed all day, and sat up all night, talking unceasingly for hour upon hour to Dr. Meryon, who alone of her English attendants remained with her, Mrs. Fry having withdrawn to more congenial scenes long since. The doctor was a poor-spirited and muddle-headed man, but he was a good listener; and there he sat while that extraordinary talk flowed on—talk that scaled the heavens and ransacked the earth, talk in which memories of an abolished past—stories of Mr. Pitt and of George III., vituperations against Mr. Canning, mimicries of the Duchess of Devonshire—mingled phantasmagorically with doctrines of Fate and planetary influence, and speculations on the Arabian origin of the Scottish clans, and lamentations over the wickedness of servants; till the unaccountable figure, with its robes and its long pipe, loomed through the tobacco-smoke like some vision of a Sibyl in a dream. She might be robbed and ruined, her house might crumble over her head; but she talked on. She grew ill and desperate; yet still she talked. Did she feel that the time was coming when she should talk no more?

Her melancholy deepened into a settled gloom when the news came of her brother James's death. She had quar-

relled with all her English friends, except Lord Hardwicke
—with her eldest brother, with her sister, whose kind letters
she left unanswered; she was at daggers drawn with the
English consul at Alexandria, who worried her about her
debts.   Ill and harassed, she hardly moved from her bedroom, while her servants rifled her belongings and reduced
the house to a condition of indescribable disorder and filth.
Three dozen hungry cats ranged through the rooms, filling
the courts with frightful noises.   Dr. Meryon, in the midst
of it all, knew not whether to cry or laugh.   At moments
the great lady regained her ancient fire; her bells pealed
tumultuously for hours together; or she leapt up, and ar-
raigned the whole trembling household before her, with her
Arab war-mace in her hand.   Her finances grew more and
more involved—grew at length irremediable.   It was in
vain that the faithful Lord Hardwicke pressed her to return
to England to settle her affairs.   Return to England, indeed!
To England, that ungrateful, miserable country, where, so
far as she could see, they had forgotten the very name of
Mr. Pitt!   The final blow fell when a letter came from the
English authorities threatening to cut off her pension for the
payment of her debts.   Upon that, after dispatching a series
of furious missives to Lord Palmerston, to Queen Victoria,
to the Duke of Wellington, she renounced the world.   She
commanded Dr. Meryon to return to Europe, and he—how
could he have done it?—obeyed her.   Her health was broken,
she was over sixty, and, save for her vile servants, absolutely
alone.   She lived for nearly a year after he left her—we
know no more.   She had vowed never again to pass through
the gate of her house; but did she sometimes totter to her

garden—that beautiful garden which she had created, with its roses and its fountains, its alleys and its bowers—and look westward at the sea? The end came in June, 1839. Her servants immediately possessed themselves of every moveable object in the house. But Lady Hester cared no longer: she was lying back in her bed—inexplicable, grand, preposterous, with her nose in the air.

1919.

MR. CREEVEY

MR. CREEVEY

CLIO is one of the most glorious of the Muses; but, as every one knows, she (like her sister Melpomene) suffers from a sad defect: she is apt to be pompous. With her buskins, her robes, and her airs of importance she is at times, indeed, almost intolerable. But fortunately the Fates have provided a corrective. They have decreed that in her stately advances she should be accompanied by certain apish, impish creatures, who run round her tittering, pulling long noses, threatening to trip the good lady up, and even sometimes whisking to one side the corner of her drapery, and revealing her undergarments in a most indecorous manner. They are the diarists and letter-writers, the gossips and journalists of the past, the Pepyses and Horace Walpoles and Saint-Simons, whose function it is to reveal to us the littleness underlying great events and to remind us that history itself was once real life. Among them is Mr. Creevey. The Fates decided that Mr. Creevey should accompany Clio, with appropriate gestures, during that part of her progress which is measured by the thirty years preceding the accession of Victoria; and the little wretch did his job very well.

It might almost be said that Thomas Creevey was " born about three of the clock in the afternoon, with a white head and something a round belly." At any rate, we know nothing of his youth, save that he was educated at Cambridge, and he presents himself to us in the early years of the

nineteenth century as a middle-aged man, with a character
and a habit of mind already fixed and an established position
in the world. In 1803 we find him what he was to be for
the rest of his life—a member of Parliament, a familiar
figure in high society, an insatiable gossip with a rattling
tongue. That he should have reached and held the place
he did is a proof of his talents, for he was a very poor man;
for the greater part of his life his income was less than
£200 a year. But those were the days of patrons and jobs,
pocket-boroughs and sinecures; they were the days, too, of
vigorous, bold living, torrential talk, and splendid hospitality; and it was only natural that Mr. Creevey, penniless
and immensely entertaining, should have been put into Parliament by a Duke, and welcomed in every great Whig
House in the country with open arms. It was also only
natural that, spending his whole political life as an advanced
Whig, bent upon the destruction of abuses, he should have
begun that life as a member for a pocket-borough and ended
it as the holder of a sinecure. For a time his poverty was
relieved by his marriage with a widow who had means of
her own; but Mrs. Creevey died, her money went to her
daughters by her previous husband, and Mr. Creevey re-
verted to a possessionless existence—without a house, without servants, without property of any sort—wandering from
country mansion to country mansion, from dinner-party to
dinner-party, until at last in his old age, on the triumph of
the Whigs, he was rewarded with a pleasant little post which
brought him in about £600 a year. Apart from these small
ups and downs of fortune, Mr. Creevey's life was static—
static spiritually, that is to say; for physically he was always

on the move. His adventures were those of an observer, not of an actor; but he was an observer so very near the centre of things that he was by no means dispassionate; the rush of great events would whirl him round into the vortex, like a leaf in an eddy of wind; he would rave, he would gesticulate, with the fury of a complete partisan; and then, when the wind dropped, he would be found, like the leaf, very much where he was before. Luckily, too, he was not merely an agitated observer, but an observer who delighted in passing on his agitations, first with his tongue, and then—for so the Fates had decided—with his pen. He wrote easily, spicily, and persistently; he had a favourite step-daughter, with whom he corresponded for years; and so it happens that we have preserved to us, side by side with the majestic march of Clio (who, of course, paid not the slightest attention to him), Mr. Creevey's exhilarating *pas de chat*.

Certainly he was not over-given to the praise of famous men. There are no great names in his vocabulary—only nicknames: George III. is " Old Nobs," the Regent " Prinney," Wellington " the Beau," Lord John Russell " Pie and Thimble," Brougham, with whom he was on very friendly terms, is sometimes " Bruffam," sometimes " Beelzebub," and sometimes " Old Wickedshifts "; and Lord Durham, who once remarked that one could " jog along on £40,000 a year," is " King Jog." The latter was one of the great Whig potentates, and it was characteristic of Creevey that his scurrility should have been poured out with a special gusto over his own leaders. The Tories were villains of course— Canning was all perfidy and " infinite meanness," Huskisson a mass of " intellectual confusion and mental dirt," Castle-

reagh . . . But all that was obvious and hardly worth
mentioning; what was really too exacerbating to be borne
was the folly and vileness of the Whigs. "King Jog," the
"Bogey," "Mother Cole," and the rest of them—they were
either knaves or imbeciles. Lord Grey was an exception;
but then Lord Grey, besides passing the Reform Bill, presented Mr. Creevey with the Treasurership of the Ordnance,
and in fact was altogether a most worthy man.

Another exception was the Duke of Wellington, whom,
somehow or other, it was impossible not to admire. Creevey,
throughout his life, had a trick of being "in at the death"
on every important occasion; in the House, at Brooks's, at
the Pavilion, he invariably popped up at the critical moment; and so one is not surprised to find him at Brussels
during Waterloo. More than that, he was the first English
civilian to see the Duke after the battle, and his report of
the conversation is admirable; one can almost hear the "It
has been a damned serious business. Blücher and I have
lost 30,000 men. It has been a damned nice thing—the
nearest run thing you ever saw in your life," and the "By
God! I don't think it would have done if I had not been
there." On this occasion the Beau spoke, as was fitting,
"with the greatest gravity all the time, and without the least
approach to anything like triumph or joy." But at other
times he was jocular, especially when "Prinney" was the
subject. "By God! you never saw such a figure in your life
as he is. Then he speaks and swears so like old Falstaff,
that damn me if I was not ashamed to walk into the room
with him."

When, a few years later, the trial of Queen Caroline came

on, it was inevitable that Creevey should be there. He had
an excellent seat in the front row, and his descriptions of
" Mrs. P.," as he preferred to call her Majesty, are characteristic:

Two folding doors within a few feet of me were suddenly
thrown open, and in entered her Majesty. To describe to you
her appearance and manner is far beyond my powers. I had
been taught to believe she was as much improved in looks as
in dignity of manners; it is therefore with much pain I am
obliged to observe that the nearest resemblance I can recollect
to this much injured Princess is a toy which you used to call
Fanny Royds (a Dutch doll). There is another toy of a rabbit
or a cat, whose tail you squeeze under its body, and then out
it jumps in half a minute off the ground into the air. The first
of these toys you must suppose to represent the person of the
Queen; the latter the manner by which she popped all at once
into the House, made a *duck* at the throne, another to the Peers,
and a concluding jump into the chair which was placed for her.
Her dress was black figured gauze, with a good deal of trim-
ming, lace, &c., her sleeves white, and perfectly episcopal; a
handsome white veil, so thick as to make it very difficult to me,
who was as near to her as anyone, to see her face; such a back
for variety and in equality of ground as you never beheld;
with a few straggling ringlets on her neck, which I flatter
myself from their appearance were not her Majesty's own
property.

Mr. Creevey, it is obvious, was not the man to be abashed
by the presence of Royalty.

But such public episodes were necessarily rare, and the
main stream of his life flowed rapidly, gaily, and unobtru-
sively through the fat pastures of high society. Everywhere
and always he enjoyed himself extremely, but his spirits and
his happiness were at their highest during his long summer

sojourns at those splendid country houses whose hospitality he chronicles with indefatigable *verve*. "This house," he says at Raby, "is itself *by far* the most magnificent and unique in several ways that I have ever seen. . . . As long as I have heard of anything, I have heard of being driven into the hall of this house in one's carriage, and being set down by the fire. You can have no idea of the magnificent perfection with which this is accomplished." At Knowsley "the new dining room is opened; it is 53 feet by 37, and such a height that it destroys the effect of all the other apartments. . . . There are two fireplaces; and the day we dined there, there were 36 wax candles over the table, 14 on it, and ten great lamps on tall pedestals about the room." At Thorp Perrow "all the living rooms are on the ground floor, one a very handsome one about 50 feet long, with a great bow furnished with rose-coloured satin, and the whole furniture of which cost £4,000." At Goodwood the rooms were done up in "brightest yellow satin," and at Holkham the walls were covered with Genoa velvet, and there was gilding worth a fortune on "the roofs of all the rooms and the doors." The fare was as sumptuous as the furniture. Life passed amid a succession of juicy chops, gigantic sirloins, plump fowls, pheasants stuffed with pâté de foie gras, gorgeous Madeiras, ancient Ports. Wine had a double advantage: it made you drunk; it also made you sober: it was its own cure. On one occasion, when Sheridan, after days of riotous living, showed signs of exhaustion, Mr. and Mrs. Creevey pressed upon him "five or six glasses of light French wine" with excellent effect. Then, at midnight, when the talk began to flag and the spirits grew a little weary, what could be more rejuvenating than to ring the bell for a broiled bone? And one never rang in vain—except, to be sure, at King Jog's. There, while the host was guzzling, the guests starved. This was too much for Mr. Creevey, who, finding he could get nothing for breakfast, while King Jog was " eating his own fish as comfortably as could be," fairly lost his temper.

My blood beginning to boil, I said: " Lambton, I wish you could tell me what quarter I am to apply to for some fish." To which he replied in the most impertinent manner: " The servant, I suppose." I turned to Mills and said pretty loud: " Now, if it was not for the fuss and jaw of the thing, I would leave the room and the house this instant "; and dwelt on the damned outrage. Mills said: " He hears every word you say ": to which I said: " I hope he does." It was a regular scene.

A few days later, however, Mr. Creevey was consoled by finding himself in a very different establishment, where " everything is of a piece—excellent and plentiful dinners, a fat service of plate, a fat butler, a table with a barrel of oysters and a hot pheasant, &c., wheeled into the drawing-room every night at half-past ten."

It is difficult to remember that this was the England of the Six Acts, of Peterloo, and of the Industrial Revolution. Mr. Creevey, indeed, could hardly be expected to remember it, for he was utterly unconscious of the existence—of the possibility—of any mode of living other than his own. For him, dining-rooms 50 feet long, bottles of Madeira, broiled bones, and the brightest yellow satin were as necessary and obvious a part of the constitution of the universe as the light of the sun and the law of gravity. Only once in his life was he seriously ruffled; only once did a public question present itself to him as something alarming, something portentous, something more than a personal affair. The occasion is significant. On March 16, 1825, he writes:

I have come to the conclusion that our Ferguson is *insane*. He quite foamed at the mouth with rage in our Railway Committee in support of this infernal nuisance—the loco-motive Monster, carrying *eighty tons* of goods, and navigated by a tail of smoke and sulphur, coming thro' every man's grounds between Manchester and Liverpool.

His perturbation grew. He attended the committee assiduously, but in spite of his efforts it seemed that the railway Bill would pass. The loco-motive was more than a joke. He sat every day from 12 to 4; he led the opposition with long speeches. " This railway," he exclaims on May 31, " is the devil's own." Next day, he is in triumph: he had killed the Monster.

Well—this devil of a railway is strangled at last. . . . To-day we had a clear majority in committee in our favour, and the promoters of the Bill withdrew it, and took their leave of us.

With a sigh of relief he whisked off to Ascot, for the festivities of which he was delighted to note that " Prinney " had prepared " by having 12 oz. of blood taken from him by cupping."

Old age hardly troubled Mr. Creevey. He grew a trifle deaf, and he discovered that it was possible to wear woollen stockings under his silk ones; but his activity, his high spirits, his popularity, only seemed to increase. At the end of a party ladies would crowd round him. " Oh, Mr. Creevey,

how agreeable you have been! " " Oh, thank you, Mr.
Creevey! how useful you have been! " " Dear Mr.
Creevey, I laughed out loud last night in bed at one of your
stories." One would like to add (rather late in the day, perhaps) one's own praises. One feels almost affectionate; a
certain sincerity, a certain immediacy in his response to
stimuli, are endearing qualities; one quite understands that
it was natural, on the pretext of changing house, to send him
a dozen of wine. Above all, one wants him to go on. Why
should he stop? Why should he not continue indefinitely
telling us about " Old Salisbury " and " Old Madagascar "?
But it could not be.

> Le temps s'en va, le temps s'en va, Madame;
> Las! Le temps non, mais nous, nous, en allons.

It was fitting that, after fulfilling his seventy years, he
should catch a glimpse of " little Vic " as Queen of England,
laughing, eating, and showing her gums too much at the
Pavilion. But that was enough: the piece was over; the
curtain had gone down; and on the new stage that was preparing for very different characters, and with a very different style of decoration, there would be no place for Mr.
Creevey.

1919.

INDEX